Advance Praise for *Ghosts of Revolution*

"*Ghosts of Revolution* gives us a great lesson in humanism at a time in
history when we insist on the outer signs of international conflicts and
lose sight of the inner struggles and sufferings of the people, each taken
individually, who are the unbreakable core of what really matters. Shahla
Talebi is a survivor with no hatred in her heart. We are all implicated in
what she has to say."

—Etel Adnan, author of *Master of the Eclipse* and *Sitt Marie Rose*

"With a courageous act of painful but empowering recollection, Shahla
Talebi restores dignity to an entire generation of political prisoners
and rescues the art and craft of memoir. Westerners, who have too
often been assured that in Iran young women are reading *Lolita* while
waiting to be liberated by the US Marines, will come away with entirely
different picture of the country and of a caring, defiant, courageous, and
determined woman. *Ghosts of Revolution* is the forbidden and forgotten
social history of Iran, the moral vindication of a people written from the
vantage point of a political prisoner, from the bared life of a liberating
conscience. Judiciously poetic, pulling no punches, but above all showing
an abiding love for the people of a homeland that is now blessed to have
her as its storyteller, Shahla Talebi reassures the world that the right and
the beautiful are still triumphant."

—Hamid Dabashi, Columbia University

"*Ghosts of Revolution* is both a powerful testimony and an important
political act from an author sharing her singular experience of eight years
behind prison bars. Remarkable in Talebi's memoir is her profound sense
of dignity and resilience in the face of absolute despair and brutality.
With a philosophical edge, her book helps us all to face our humanity
and vulnerability and, most of all, to grasp that fine barrier between life
and death, hope and submission. With clarity, honesty, and a lack of
sentimentality, *Ghosts of Revolution* speaks to the resilient nature of the
human spirit in the face of adversity and the abyss."

—Shirin Neshat

"This searing memoir of women's visceral pain, principled resilience, and redemptive imagination in Iran's brutal political prisons will leave you shaken, forever. Talebi's voice is remarkable for its generous empathy, its poetry in evoking the tortured humanity of the women with whom she shared her prison experience, and its brilliance in analyzing the dark horrors inflicted on the men and women condemned to these death-spaces that were, in the 1970s and 1980s, and are even today, so strangely tied to the exercise of power in Iran."

—Lila Abu-Lughod, Columbia University,
author of *Writing Women's Worlds*

"Shaʻhla Talebi's observations about language, writing, death, modes of consciousness, the depravity of the state and its prisons, and the experience of love and solidarity in the most abject circumstances in which she found herself speak for themselves. Her portraits of fellow prisoners are unforgettable. By far the most moving, sensitive, and profound book about torture I have read."

—Vincent Crapanzano, The CUNY Graduate Center

"Not memoir nor autobiography, but an extraordinary beading of visions beyond the person, and even the specific history of Iran, this book casts new eyes on the deathly zones of the post-revolutionary years without ever emptying the Revolution of its spiritual-political hope. In parsimony of words the author's voice is woven in conversation with the dead, as a gesture of love. It bears witness to death, madness, and betrayal for the sake of the living, and of community, mindful at all moments that the risk of destruction and madness is as much the product of historical processes as it is nested in the human soul. Act of witnessing and work of literature, *Ghosts of Revolution* makes an important impact for the transformation of cultural memory. It is a work of art in the fullest sense: a creation at the limits of life."

—Stefania Pandolfo, University of California, Berkeley,
author of *Impasse of the Angels: Scenes from a Moroccan Space of Memory*

Ghosts of Revolution

Ghosts of Revolution

REKINDLED MEMORIES OF
IMPRISONMENT IN IRAN

Shahla Talebi

Drawings by Soudabeh Ardavan

STANFORD UNIVERSITY PRESS

STANFORD, CALIFORNIA

Stanford University Press
Stanford, California

Printed in the United States of America on acid-free, archival-quality paper

Library of Congress Cataloging-in-Publication Data

Talebi, Shahla, 1957–
  Ghosts of revolution : rekindled memories of imprisonment in Iran / Shahla Talebi ; drawings by Soudabeh Ardavan.
    p. cm.
  Includes bibliographical references.
  ISBN 978-0-8047-7201-3 (cloth : alk. paper)
  1. Talebi, Shahla, 1957–. 2. Women political prisoners—Iran—Biography. 3. Political persecution—Iran—History. 4. Iran—Politics and government—1979–1997. I. Ardavan, Sudabah. II. Title.
  DS318.84. T35 2011
  365'.45092—dc22
  [B]

                        2010026520

Designed by Bruce Lundquist
Typeset at Stanford University Press in 9.5/15 Palatino

People like to say: Revolution is beautiful, it is only the terror arising from it which is evil. But this is not true. The evil is already present in the beautiful, hell is already contained in the dream of paradise.

—Milan Kundera, interview with Philip Roth, *New York Times*, November 30, 1980

Contents

Ghosts of Revolution

Emerging from Prison

Opening the enormous metal gate, the guard suddenly took away my blindfold and asked me, tauntingly, if I would recognize my parents. With my eyes hurting from the strange light and anger in my voice, I assured him that I would. Suddenly, I was pushed through the gate and the door was slammed behind me. After more than eight years, here I was, finally, out of jail, in this other world, and there they were, my parents, older and smaller yet still familiar. Holding me in their arms, they were simultaneously crying and laughing while I was still frozen, in shock. The pleasant summer breeze was gently penetrating the chador covering me, drying the sweat of prison on my body. "Let's get out of this hellish place," my mother said. No car was allowed to drive into the street on which the prison was located except for those of the prison employees. We walked toward the main street where we could take a cab. My father was almost running, but my feet felt so heavy, as if I were walking in mud or some invisible threads were pulling me back.

I did not get the chance to say good-bye to my cellmate or leave my money for her. I had none of my clothes or other belongings, many of which were my beloved lost friends' last possessions. "Darling, don't even think about what you've left there. Nothing in that hell is worth thinking about. You're out and that's what matters; put everything else behind you," my mother advised. But I was preoccupied with the reality inside the prison cell. My heart was torn between contradictory feelings: guilt for putting my family through so much fear, hardship, and humiliation, and anger for feeling betrayed because my father had negotiated my temporary release against my will. My thoughts were interrupted by my parents' voices, telling me that everyone was waiting for me at home.

"I will not go home before I go to the cemetery," I responded, and continued the rest of the sentence in my mind, "to visit Hamid, my husband, and my other friends' graves as I have promised them." The deep fear in my parents' eyes became more transparent as they feigned calmness and content. I felt angrier and guiltier at the same time. I had seen and lived all this years before, in 1978, the first time out of prison, when my parents did everything humanly possible to make sure that nothing would upset me, terrified that prison had already pushed me to the edge and if pushed further, I could easily go mad. This fear had resurfaced now even more intensely than the first time, though more subtly. There were of course uncanny similarities between my first and second arrests and releases. Both times, my arrest occurred after the harshest crackdown on opponents under each regime, yet at the beginning of changes in prison conditions.

My arrest in 1977 took place at the end of the most severe phase of political suppression by Mohammad Reza Shah Pahlavi's regime, which followed the first armed struggle of a leftist guerrilla group, Sazman-e Cherikha-ye Fadayee-e Khalgh-e Iran (Iranian People's Self-Sacrificing Guerrilla Organization) in 1970, and was intensified between 1974 and 1976 when the leftist-leaning Islamic organization, Sazman-e Mojahedin-e Khalgh-e Iran (Iranian People's Warriors' Organization) also joined in militant activities against the regime. During this period, arrests and executions reached a new pinnacle and incredibly horrific means of torture were utilized to force the detainees to confess even to the most trivial "accusations" or "crimes."

For instance, Goli, the woman I met in jail then had been severely tortured and sentenced to ten years for having owned, read, and passed along a book of fiction, *Cheshmhayash* (Her Eyes), written by the leftist-leaning author Bozorg Alavi. Her story was, however, by no means an exception. Within prisons and the country, which had itself turned into a larger prison, the ambiance felt deadly suffocating. The regime appeared stronger than ever; the facade of stability erected under an iron fist made the country the most appealing place in the region for foreign investments and the geopolitical interests of the United States. It was due, however, to this very illusive sense of stability and the consequences of the brutal treatment of opponents that by the end of 1976 the regime found itself under pressure from the outside world, particularly from Jimmy Carter, at the time president of the United States, the regime's closest ally.

My arrest coincided with the end of this period of extreme brutality and the beginning of a new phase when physical torture was less commonly employed during interrogations. Obviously, this did not prevent the regime from subjecting prisoners to this so-called white, or soft, torture. It did not stop the regime, for example, from forcing prisoners to stand on their feet for days and nights, violently waking them up every time they seemed to have fallen sleep or when moving one leg up to give it a rest. I still remember a woman who had been subjected to these techniques. She was brought to my cell, only for about half an hour, in the early weeks of my imprisonment in 1977. I never found out whether my encounter with her resulted from a simple mistake by a guard or if it was an intentional act to intimidate me by making me witness the gruesome consequences of this "white" torture. Either way, my heart ached, and still aches, at the sight and the memory of her horrifyingly swollen legs, which no longer fit in her pants. I could not assess the extent of the impact those sleepless days and nights of standing on her feet had had on her mental being and her body. Yet her confused stare, disoriented demeanor, and robotic gestures, along with her inability to verbally communicate her ordeal to me, were indicative of the suffering she had to endure as long as she lived, if she were to live.

As I tried to gently massage her dark blue feet and legs, which looked more like two deformed tree trunks, the skin began to tear, and I felt the blood about to gush out. I asked her whether she was the woman I had been seeing since the day of my arrest every time I was taken out of my cell for the toilet or interrogation. She moved her eyelashes up and down as a way of offering a positive response to my question, but suddenly her eyes took flight, perhaps to the dream world. For a few minutes, her stare remained frozen on the wall. Did she fall asleep with her eyes open? Was she able to sleep with open eyes during all those days and nights while standing in the hallway?

But while in the hallway, her face was covered with a jacket, a piece of prison uniform. This meant that her eyes were not exposed to the guards and that she could not see her surroundings even with her eyes open. In order to sleep without the guards noticing her, she had to remain alert to every movement. She must have learned to sleep while awake, and remain awake while asleep. I did not have the chance to ask her, nor was she able to communicate to me, whether she had in fact acquired this skill. Later, during my second imprisonment (1983–1992), under the Islamic Republic, I would meet several prisoners who had mastered this "skill-trick" of sleeping while awake and being awake while asleep. Pori, who had spent ten months during 1983–1984 in the so-called *tabootha* (graves) or *dastgahha* (machines), the extreme punishment ward in Ghezel Hesar Prison, was one of those prisoners who had challenged the boundaries of sleep and waking states, stretching their threshold.

I was unable to discover the consequences of the torment or the future of the woman I met in 1977. However, deeply submerged in my memory, her frozen stare returned to haunt me; I became acutely aware of it especially in the aftermath of September 11, 2001. This was particularly in response to the fact that, time and again, I came to hear debates about the practice of enhanced interrogation techniques exercised on detainees arrested in relation to the U.S. "War on Terror." Rather than a discussion of ethics, these debates basically revolved around such questions as whether or not these measures could be considered torture and if they were effective. Politicians concerned with such techniques mainly asked, for example, whether or not performing waterboarding on a detainee more than eighty times produced the kind of result that was worth damaging the image of the United States in the world. Those who discussed and wrote about these techniques in so much detail did so perhaps without having ever been haunted by the frozen stare of a woman or a man subjected to these methods of torture.

By the time of my arrest in early 1977, when I met the woman whose name I never learned, the old-style, hard-core torture was giving way to the white, nonphysical interrogation techniques. The regime could now claim that prisoners were no longer tortured. As long as one's legs were torn apart not by the heavy strikes of cables on the soles of the feet but rather by forced standing on them, no torture had occurred. In today's world in which machines, technologies, and devices seem to be doing all the work, where hands have nearly become the extensions of technology rather than the other way around, any production without devices and machines may easily be construed as nonwork, nonproduction. By the same token, in the apparent absence of devices, the exerted pain is claimed as nontorture. But when I was arrested, I knew nothing of these changes. The atmosphere in the society out of which I was taken to jail felt heavier than ever. My knowledge of prison and torture amounted to no more than a few banned books and pamphlets I had read; some horrific stories I had heard on the underground radio broadcasts from outside Iran; and plenty of rumors circulating within Iran, which were substantiated during family gatherings by whispers about distant young male relatives who had emerged from jail but remained mute and lost, with deformed feet and their toenails having fallen off.

No wonder therefore that when I found myself in the Komiteh-ye Moshtarak-e Zedd-e Kharabkari (United Anti-sabotage Committee), a notorious detention center built under the Shah's regime on the site of the former central prison, my then young heart vacillated between pausing for breath and pounding heavily. I still vividly remember that as I read the carved writings of legendary dissidents on the walls of the cell into which I was thrown after my interrogation, I simultaneously felt proud, burdened by the responsibility of living up to the level of their resistance, and somewhat out of place. But the timing of my arrest would save me from witnessing or being subjected to some of the most horrific devices of torture that had severely scarred many women arrested earlier whom I would meet in jail in the next two years. For since early 1978, having agreed that political prisons could be inspected by the Red Cross, the Shah's regime could no longer use its old torture devices to inflict overt torture or enduring pain on detainees.

It did not take long for this place to once again fully function as a torture chamber, now by the Islamic Republic and under a new title, Komiteh-ye Touhid (Unity Committee). If under the Shah the function of this torture chamber was to use the regime's penal system against its political dissidents, whom they tortured or eliminated under the guise of fighting *kharabkari* (sabotage), under the Islamic Republic the interrogators crushed their opponents under the pretext of extracting Satan from their souls. Through torture or killing, they brought the lost souls of dissidents into unity with God, or so the name Unity Committee implied.

A Haunting Detour

I did not experience interrogation under the Unity Committee, for my arrest in early 1983 was not made by the Revolutionary Guards of the Islamic Republic, who ran the infamous Unity Committee and oversaw all its interrogations and torture. Rather, I was hunted down by the Revolutionary Public Persecution of Tehran, which ruled over the notorious Evin Prison. In 1983, on the way to Evin, I was driven through the *piche toubeh* (repentance curve), the name the agents who arrested me used to refer to the last curve of the road before reaching the prison. In Evin also, as *piche toubeh* suggested, prisoners were to either be killed or become repentant. Although I never repented nor was I killed in prison, at least not in the conventional sense of these terms, I trembled with a range of mixed emotions when after eight years, in 2004, during my return to Iran to conduct my field research, I visited the Unity Committee.

By 2004, the Iranian sociopolitical landscape had changed. A reformist, Mohammad Khatami, was president. The Unity Committee was now opened to the public as Moozeh-ye Ettela'at (Museum of Information). I visited this site of death and torture, which until recently had been in use by this very regime. From the ominous clouds that were rapidly gathering over the Iranian political scene, one could easily anticipate the rising of new waves of state violence. With an eerie feeling, I thus read my name on the wall of this once horrific dungeon, along with the names of many others who had inhabited this place under the Shah's regime. To visit this museum, I had to make a reservation in person—I had to write down my name and the time and date of my visit. Hesitantly, I signed my name, fearful that the guard might check the records and realize that I had been a prisoner of both regimes. In this place only a few years earlier the interrogators of this very government had ushered many of their opponents into "unity with God." These detainees were either eradicated or were forced to live a "bare life," as walking dead. It was partially a result of this brutal suppression of dissidents in the first ten years following the revolution that, in the early 2000s, the Islamic Republic felt confident enough to make a spectacle of the Shah's torture chamber while remaining entirely silent about the death, suffering, and destruction that occurred there by its own hands.

In this journey through the labyrinth of the Museum of Information I was accompanied by a woman friend, Ferdous, who was also a former political prisoner but interrogated and tortured in the Unity Committee. The bitter taste in my mouth from witnessing the nearly absolute erasure of the history of the leftists' resistance and suffering under the United Anti-sabotage Committee and an exaggerated predominance of religious clergy presented in this museum became unbearable when Ferdous recalled the different spots where she had been interrogated and beaten.

We strolled back and forth between our own realities and memories and those we saw portrayed in front of us in this bluntly selective depiction of a particular history, when a large group of junior high school boys swarmed in. They had obviously been brought here on a school field trip to learn about the atrocities of the former regime. Yet soon, only the tour guide's voice disturbed our thoughts while the boys began to play hide and seek in the mazes that not long ago were the site of a bloodbath for so many men and women not much older than these boys. They ran around, laughed loudly, and screamed almost hysterically and playfully as we shivered to our bones at the horrific sight of the human-size statues that too closely represented victims of torture and their torturers. The boys' mockery reminded me of a more bitter parody, that of a dream that was once expressed by some of us during those elated moments of the victory of the Revolution of 1979 of the possibility of a day when all the Shah's prisons would be turned into museums.

Now here we were, walking around this prison-museum, whose opening to the public felt like a slap in the face, considering that both Ferdous and I had lived through the torture chambers of this regime. I was dumbfounded by the cynical depiction in this prison-museum, not merely in its blunt silencing of some experiences while highlighting others but also by the way it continued to exercise violence in other prisons when turning this one into a museum. Through transforming this jail into a museum while maintaining and even expanding others, the regime at once ignored and reenacted the beheading of all those dreams of a brief moment in the "spring of freedom," following the 1979 revolution, when the idea of closing prisons and opening them to the public as museums was envisioned. Soon, however, I would realize that compared to what was to come after 2004, this period, though itself cynical, was, relatively speaking, a semi-spring of freedom.

For the Sake of the Friend

At the time of visiting this museum, nevertheless, while wary of the dark clouds, I was still unaware of the scale of violence that was to reemerge. Preoccupied by the sufferings and resistances of the past, I vaguely heard the whispers of the ghosts of the future whose cries have just recently shaken the entire world. The new wave of horror was near, waiting just around the next corner, perhaps to claim even these playful boys, who seemed so oblivious to the shrieks of the ghosts that haunted this place, demanding to be seen, to be heard, and to be remembered. Suddenly, I felt as if I had gone deaf to all that was going on around me.

All I could hear was the howling of my many tortured friends amid the cacophony of laughter and threats of interrogators of both regimes. I do not know if it was caused by these voices in my head, the disgust I felt at the regime's ruthlessly selective narration of the past, even the boys' obliviousness to this, or all these combined, but I suddenly felt nauseous. I looked at Ferdous, her now utterly bloodless face, her rapidly moving eyelids, and her forehead covered with sweat. I whispered, "Let's go." We almost ran out of this hellish place where each of us had been an inhabitant, I under the Shah's regime and she under the Islamic Republic of Iran.

As we left the Museum of Information, I thought of the double connotation of the term *ettela'at*, which means both "information obtained, upheld, and revealed by the secret police," and "information as knowledge whose purpose is to raise consciousness." We passed the Museum of Coins nearby. A strange sense of abhorrence toward these two museums of money and violence overtook me. Sitting close to one another, their interconnectedness and similarity were further emphasized. I thought of the contaminating power of violence and money, of the way they both often spoil whoever or whatever comes their way. Had I survived the contamination by violence? Had my soul survived its tarnishing effect? I would remain wary and, I hope, sensitive to these questions, perhaps as long as I live. I hence write today for the sake of all those friends—whom I either knew personally or my soul knew of their spirit of resistance and desire for justice—whose refusal to submit to the power of money and violence cost their lives. It is in the spirit and for the sake of these always present friends—ghosts of justice and freedom—that I live.

In the Footsteps of the Giants

When I was arrested in 1977, I knew very little of the changes on the horizon that were soon to transform not only the Iranian sociopolitical landscape but its penal system, and hence my own experiences of imprisonment. I was a girl from a modest family background. We had moved to Tehran only about three and a half years earlier, carrying along the experiences and memories of a life in provincial towns and remote countryside, with most summers spent in a village. I had just graduated from high school and entered university as a freshman when I found myself in jail. Yet, from my first day of school in Tehran, in my tenth-grade year, when, shockingly, I heard my classmates making a mockery of the national anthem by twisting its words "May our king live forever" to "The donkey has tail and hoof" to that late evening of my arrest by three SAVAK agents, the world had drastically changed around and in me.

Here I was, now, in the United Anti-sabotage Committee, perhaps the most notorious detention center for political prisoners in Iran at the time, faced with the interrogators whose names I had heard on the underground radio, who had acquired their fame through demonstrations of the utmost brutality against many legendary dissidents. I tried to imagine their heroic resistance and felt so incredibly small in comparison. Even with my insufficient knowledge of the SAVAK and its jails, I was well aware of the fact that one did not need to be a serious threat to the regime to be severely tortured. My pursuit of banned books and dissident views was enough to subject me to torture and imprisonment. Nonetheless, the fact that I had no connection to the guerrilla movement would have to be a factor in easing my interrogation process, at least in that particular historical moment.

When I was delivered to the interrogator, Rahmani, a man who appeared to be in his late thirties or early forties, he received me with the exclamation, "Oh finally, there she is!" and with a joyous tone as if a serious threat had been just eliminated from the face of the earth. His reaction overwhelmed me with a simultaneous sense of surprise, intimidation, and pride. As his voyeuristic gaze violently examined my entire body, nearly undressing me with his lustful eyes—in my mind, even with his widely grinning teeth—and as he moved from advising "this young, pretty, and smart girl to save herself" from the torment of torture to slapping, hitting with his fists, and kicking, I awaited and imagined myself under the "real torture" with which he was threatening me. But he continued offering me more obscene curses spiced by his dirty, sexual, penetrating stare.

This episode was prolonged and turned into a violent orgy of penetrating stares and verbal sexual assaults with the addition of two other interrogators, Riyahi and Rasouli. The metaphorical marriage of sex and violence found a real face when Hosseini, the most infamous torturer in the United Anti-sabotage Committee, sat quietly as an emblem of sheer animalistic violence, while others put on a show of competition of the most penetrating gaze on my body and the dirtiest assaults on my character. I clenched inside as they apparently enjoyed this visual feast, with remarks like, "She looks as sweet as her first name," alluding to the name Shirin, which means "sweet," which the friend who had reported me to SAVAK used to call me; or "She is as edible as her last name," referring to my last name, Talebi, which means "melon." Rasouli kept repeating the words *Talebi-e Shirin*, or "sweet melon," while blinking with a dirty look in his eyes. Even now, after so many years, once in a while I still wake up in the middle of the night, feeling a sense of choking as if interrogator Riyahi's bottom is covering my mouth, as it did then. About six feet tall, he stood in the narrow space between my chair and Rahmani's table, pretending to talk to him, while bending in a way that his bottom pushed toward and covered my mouth and entire face.

I, however, tried to concentrate on what I assumed to be awaiting me, the real torture. I pushed my nails into my skin as hard and as long as I could to test my tolerance level, angry at myself for not knowing the limits of my endurance. Would I be able to withstand the severe torture that I conjured to be imminent? I wondered. I kept telling myself, again and again, that I needed to remember the poverty, discrimination, and all the injustices I had witnessed around me so the pain could not break me. That my devotion to justice should help me to stay firm, for no matter how excruciating my pain, it could never be as everlasting as that of the dispossessed people who live with constant humiliation and die gradually, I assured myself. Was I going to be able to prove my love and commitment to the people and to my ideal of justice? I anxiously pondered these questions as the interrogators poured their insulting words over me, violated me with their gazes, and belittled my entire existence. As fearful as I was of the menace of torture with which they were threatening me, I felt even more terrified of feeling so belittled. I therefore kept telling myself that, if put under real torture, I had to show them that I was more than a "little pretty girl," as they kept calling me.

I was, nevertheless, sent to solitary confinement, without being subjected to that real torture. For the next four days, I waited, restlessly, for a call to interrogation and torture, nearly disappointed that I was not and horrified that I would be. What if I could not prove my loyalty to my ideals and the strength of my love for the people? The possibility petrified me. I read and touched the writings on the walls of my cell, one of them written by the poet whose poetry I loved, as if hoping that through my touch their magical power would penetrate my body and soul, and I would become immune to the desires and weaknesses of my own flesh. I felt inspired and burdened by breathing in the same space that had once been occupied by the men and women about whom I had read or heard.

But only a few days later the guards took me to the upper floor and put me in a room with five other inmates. It was here that I began to see the rapid changes in that jail. They painted the rooms, cleaned the hallways, fixed the toilets and bathrooms, gave us spoons for eating, and treated prisoners less harshly. But once again, neither I nor the others in jail knew yet of the transforming power dynamics that were forcing the regime to change its penal policies.

Thus, when only six days after my arrest, Azodi, one of the highest-ranking SAVAK officials, came into the room and I remained sitting while other inmates stood up as an indication of their respect for him, as was the unwritten rule, I expected to be sent directly to the torture room. I was literally terrified at the sight of him. I recalled the story I had heard on the underground radio a couple of years earlier of a man who had refused to stand up during one of Azodi's visits to his cell and was subjected to severe torture. I hence sat there, looking at the rage that emanated from Azodi and his men's eyes, while my heart beat as rapidly as that of a bird. Although threatened, I was not beaten. Even when on the day of my trial, I resisted the government-assigned lawyer's advice to "beg forgiveness from the Shah and the judge," I believed his threat about the possibility of being sentenced to death. But I received a two-year sentence, which made me feel somewhat embarrassed, for I knew that the stance I took in the court could have easily resulted in a much harsher sentence had I been arrested a few months earlier. Little did I know that even before my two-year sentence was completed, I would be among those prisoners the Shah was forced to free under the pressure of the revolutionary movement. It would be awhile before I could understand the extent of these political transformations imposed on the regime and its new trajectory.

These metamorphoses were part of much larger sociopolitical and economic changes in Iran and in its relationship to the outside world. The increase in the price of oil in the early 1970s, which had brought about a high economic growth rate in the country, widened the already huge gap between the haves and have-nots in society. More important, the euphoria arising from this rapid growth evaporated along with a strong sense of disillusionment when the price dropped. On the other hand, the Shah seemed to have begun playing a risky game between the United States and the former Soviet Union, initiating deals and purchasing heavy military weaponry from both sides. Some politicians among his Western allies began to see his new policies as a threat to the balance of power in the region and to their own dominance. SAVAK's infamy had become too widespread to be ignored by the Western countries without undermining their already questionable sincerity in positing themselves as defenders of human rights in the world. The Iranian students studying abroad were gaining the support of their cohorts in their host countries.

Thus, when Jimmy Carter became president of the United States, he put pressure on the Shah to alleviate political suppression, reduce censorship, and improve prison conditions. These changes reconfigured the landscape of Iranian society, as well as its detention centers and prisons. Initially, the regime pressed prisoners to sign letters of pardon to the Shah requesting their release. Those who did so were freed in November 1977. Many others refused to ask for a pardon and remained jailed. But by November 1978, people had turned into roaring rivers, demonstrating on the street and chanting for the freedom of political prisoners and making other demands. These increasingly growing mass demonstrations compelled the Shah to order the unconditional release of the majority of prisoners. About four months before my sentence was over, my name appeared along with 999 other prisoners for release.

Even though the period of my stay in jail was less than two years, the outside world had radically changed between the time of my arrest and release. The government hoped that by freeing these prisoners, it could prevent the movement from becoming more radicalized. But resentment against the regime had already reached the boiling point. People who awaited us in front of the jails were moving to the next stage, demanding not only the freedom of all political prisoners but also the collapse of the entire regime.

The Lonely Shoulders

Unlike my release in 1978, my departure from jail in 1991 under the Islamic Republic was not instigated by the power of a revolutionary movement. There were no people waiting outside the jail this time to carry prisoners on their shoulders or take them to the demonstration. In 1978, I had to change my prison uniform to the only other piece of clothing I had, a worn-out tunic, to avoid being raised on people's shoulders, for I did not see my "trivial" imprisonment worthy of such attention. Although my release in late 1991 was also an attempt by the regime to resolve the problem of political prisoners, the plan to free prisoners in the 1990s was dependent on accepting the regime's condition of release, which required signing a printed form known as *enzejar nameh*, a letter of repugnance or repudiation, or at least a mild version of it, which indicated the person denounced all dissident organizations and promised to avoid having any relationship with any kind of dissidence. Those of us who did not accept this condition were set free only on a temporary basis, even though we were not asked to return to jail when the period of our temporary release was up. Our sentence was, however, pending in case the government decided to enforce it.

The fact that the release of prisoners in the1990s was not initiated by a revolutionary movement did not mean that there was no pressure both within and outside Iran to urge the government toward this decision. Rather, it implied that, as in 1977, in the early 1990s the state was confident enough to negotiate its power over prisoners and press them to accept the condition of release. Those who remained fierce in refusing to submit were not freed, at least not officially. Yet my release in 1978, which seemed such a radical freedom, was abruptly ended by my arrest and return to jail under the new regime. This time, however, I would be married to Hamid, whom I would lose to execution. My ten-day release under the Islamic Republic would last much longer, though mostly outside Iran.

Ironically, the temporary nature of this freedom would allow me, and others in similar circumstances, to leave the country more easily, for since we had not been legally released, our names were not in the computer system as people who were prohibited from traveling abroad, at least, so the interrogators told my father after my departure from Iran in late 1993. But those prisoners who had given in to the condition of release and had signed papers had to report to the regime on a regular, first weekly, then biweekly, and finally monthly, basis. They were not allowed to leave the country; strangely, therefore, those of us who had not been officially released were able to leave the country legally, while many of those who had been legally freed had to take the risk of being smuggled out.

Yet our unofficial release remained precarious, for we could easily be forced to serve the remainder of our sentence if we were ever arrested again; this does not mean that others could not be rearrested but that our freedom felt even more fragile. This anxiety about the fragility of my release was reflected in my father's persistence, against his desire to keep me close, to urge me to leave the country not too long after my release. His fear of the possibility of my rearrest and imprisonment was so grave for him that he preferred for us to live apart so I could be free and safe. My freedom felt so shaky that when I was deciding to visit Iran in 2002, for the first time since having left in late 1993, I not only had to deal with my friends' opposition to the idea—in fact, one of my dissertation advisers believed that I was returning to Iran because of my urge for a "heroic act"—but to hide it from my parents until I knew I was able to leave the airport rather than be arrested on the spot. To protect my parents from worrying about the possibility of my arrest, and the heartache in case I was arrested, I had told only one of my sisters about the date of my arrival and asked her not to tell anyone until I had safely exited the airport gate.

The temporary basis of this release also made it hard to feel a real sense of freedom. My body relived prison experiences whenever I felt that an authoritative force was challenging the limits of my will. I dreamed of torture when I felt pressured even by the deadlines I set for myself while writing my doctoral dissertation, which led to my unconscious resistance to meeting them. I remained highly sensitive to issues that had to do with prisoners' sufferings, wherever or whoever they were. My heart ached for my nephew's little bird in the cage even before it was caught in the fire in our apartment and died. The image of this suffocating little bird conflated with the images of my fellow inmates and became a recurring theme of my nightmares for years.

But in 1978, our freedom involved no conditions or formalities; we were not asked to sign any papers but were simply told to get ready and leave. We, however, took hours to digest the news and decide what to do. There were those among us who could not believe that the news could be real. They argued that the regime might be trying to trick us into leaving so they could shoot us on the pretext that we were trying to escape—this they claimed had been done in Chile to a group of prisoners. Others insisted that we should refuse to leave until the regime accepted the release of all political prisoners—a small number of prisoners were not freed because they were considered more serious threats to the regime. Still others believed that we should immediately leave prison and join the fight for our friends' freedom along with other revolutionary demands.

That entire evening, we continued discussing our options among ourselves—should we immediately leave, refuse to leave until everyone is set free, or choose another option—while the officials came in and out, baffled as to why we were not running out now that the regime was letting us leave without any conditions for release of the sort that kept so many prisoners jailed, sometimes for years after their time was over. The officials did not understand why, even though we were free to leave, we spent the entire evening debating—they obviously must have had no clue what we were discussing. Late in the evening, we finally came to a collective decision: we would not leave in the dark of night but wait until the next morning. The guards' and the prison officials' constant pleas did not change our minds. They finally left us alone to spend the night bidding farewell to our friends, laughing, crying, and exchanging addresses. A couple of other inmates and I were assigned to remember and communicate to the people outside, upon our release, the names of those prisoners who were still jailed.

We passed a sleepless night, and soon we would learn, so did our families outside. We were still laughing, crying, and saying our good-byes when the guards came in and told us to leave. We were led toward the gate behind the ward, through the meeting hall, through the gate from which the families used to come in to the meeting hall to visit us. It was barely past nine in the morning when the gate was opened and about a hundred women prisoners were ushered through the gate to the outside, to the bosom of a crowd of strangers who acted like members of a single family. It was a beautiful, sunny fall day in Tehran. I looked for my family, and it took me more than half an hour to find my parents. Even though I was not in prison uniform, I am not sure if it was my worn-out tunic or the simultaneous excitement and confusion in my eyes that exposed my status as a former political prisoner. But in the half an hour that I searched for my family in the dense crowd that had gathered in front of Ghasr, or Palace, Prison, I was hugged and greeted by numerous strangers, and finally a group of them asked me to ride with them to a demonstration at Tehran University. At the very moment that I agreed, I saw my parents' panicked eyes suddenly catching my own, to which they reacted with a sigh of relief and with tears that poured down their smiling faces.

IN NOVEMBER 1978, the victory of the revolutionary movement was, though not yet clearly in sight, looming on the horizon. Although the risk of violent death in a demonstration was looming over any participant's head, torture and long-term imprisonment were becoming issues of the past. Since 1977, under pressure from President Jimmy Carter, the regime had allowed the Red Cross to inspect its political prisons. In response to the rapidly growing protests, the regime had been forced to free the majority of its political prisoners. The release of these prisoners was a defining moment in signaling the regime's defeat and the subsequent giving in to people's demands—a failed attempt in curtailing the protests.

This was the time when not taking part in protests was itself an anomaly. It should not thus come as a surprise that upon my release and right after finding my parents, I would leave them behind to join the ongoing protests. I did not consider it unusual to leave their tearful eyes behind and ride with a group of strangers directly from jail to my first demonstration against the regime. This was not a gesture of apathy or due to a lack of my love for my parents. In retrospect, this seemingly normal behavior must have caused great pain and disappointment for my parents. I can only imagine their perplexity in having to return that long way home, on foot and bus, alone, while I had begun to befriend a group of strangers and to feel at home with a newly encountered, but long-awaited, revolutionary movement.

How acute my parents' sorrow must have been, considering that I, a young woman, was the first member of my family arrested under the Shah. My imprisonment had doubly terrified them because of the rumors about the commonality of rape, especially of young women, by the interrogators—a rumor that was circulated by the populace as much as by the regime. Spreading exaggerated rumors about their own brutality has been a technique deployed by most totalitarian regimes to induce greater fear and thus silence their opponents. During the nearly two years that I was in prison, my parents hid my arrest even from the closest members of the family, especially those on my father's side. They were worried that, considering the religio-cultural and class background of these relatives, the stigma of my possible rape—which did not happen—would be too overwhelming for my family to bear.

For about two years, they thus essentially withdrew from their families, endured the pain of separation and their relentless fear, and cried silently in seclusion. They, however, did anything and everything humanly possible to get me out of jail—bore humiliation, withstood beatings, and finally eagerly joined the fight against the regime to release its political prisoners. I was now out, ready to join the revolutionary ocean, only to leave them alone with their embrace still thirsty to hug and protect me. So eager was I to be part of the movement that I did not even have time to acknowledge their exhaustion from having spent an entire sleepless night, during which they did not know if we would ever emerge from jail—for we, the women prisoners, whose names were in newspapers as those to be released, had refused to leave that very night. This refusal was meant to at once emphasize our demand for the release of all inmates and deny the regime a chance to send us out in the darkness of night—its tactic to prevent families from another gathering since every gathering was a chance for people to cry out their demand for the freedom of all political prisoners. These remaining prisoners were freed in the next few months, the last ones by the people on the day of victory of the 1979 revolution. In short, at the time of my release in November 1978, the horizon appeared much brighter than at the time of my second release in November 1991.

IN 1978, while I was riding to the university rally, a six-year-old boy spoke to me as though he had known me forever. Only a couple of minutes after sitting in the car, he asked me if I would like to hear a joke and immediately posed another question, which was a way of initiating the joke. "Do you know how many syllables are in 'marg bar Shah' [down with the Shah]?" Learning to count and sound the syllables of words were two of the first things children were taught in first grade. I asked him what grade he was in, and he said he was in the first grade. In November, he was thus in the second month of the school year and had begun learning about syllables. I remembered that when I was in first grade, one of the first words with which I learned to sound syllables was my own name, Shahla—it has two syllables, *shah* and *la*, with the accent on the second *h*. Now this six-year-old was sounding out this dangerous phrase for me. He held three fingers of his left hand up and loudly sounded each word, "marg bar Shah," while demonstrating the numbers of the syllables by moving his right hand up and down three times and announcing verbally that "marg bar Shah" has three syllables, as though taking delight in its repetition. "Marg bar Shah," he shouted again in a tone that made me tremble. Nothing could perhaps be more illustrative of the distinctive moods of my two releases in 1978 and 1991 than the difference between the atmosphere of this ride and the ride in my brother's car in 1991 on our visit to the cemetery when the imported Persian music from Los Angeles playing on the radio made me feel nauseous.

On that day of my release in 1978, I did not even wait long enough to find my siblings among the jammed crowd in front of the jail. Rather, I ran into two of my sisters while marching at Tehran University. I still vividly remember the shiver of my eldest sister's body as she squeezed me in her arms. She had come to find me in the demonstration, after not seeing me in front of the jail. As I felt her shaky knees, my own knees shook, too, though perhaps no less from the excitement, joy, and shock of the chants of protesters and hearing my own voice shouting with them, for the first time, "Down with this fascistic regime." It was precisely in this elated moment that I saw my sister, first anxiously running along with the marchers, evidently looking for me, and then suddenly screaming as her eyes caught sight of me. Crying and laughing at the same time, she threw herself into my arms, her delicate skinny body nearly tumbling over. She was the first one of my siblings whom I saw and held once again upon my release in 1991, though this time not in a revolutionary march but on the way to visit a cemetery of executed dissidents where my husband and many of my friends lay. Little did I know in 1978 how short lived my seemingly permanent freedom would be and how soon those very prisons would be holding ten times as many people.

At my second arrest, I was no longer single; hence all my worries were at least doubled to also include my husband, Hamid, and his family. This time hard-core torture would not be a mere threat but a reality that I would have to endure both on my own body and as witness to others' subjection to it, including my own Hamid. Not to just two years, but to fifteen years would I be sentenced, and even that sentence I would owe, once again, to the end of a particularly harsh era and the beginning of a relatively less aggressive set of penal policies. This time I would spend more than eight years in jail and meet and live not with about a hundred women but with more than a thousand.

When I was released in 1978, I could hardly even imagine the rapid wave of political suppression that would sweep so many lives away under a new regime that had risen to power on our own shoulders—I, and in fact many others, did anticipate it, but no one could have imagined its scale and severity. In 1991, when I was asked to sign a paper for a ten-day temporary release, which I refused to do and was nevertheless thrown out of jail, no serious popular movement against the regime appeared in sight. Even if the students' uprising of 1999 was only around the next corner, I could barely envisage it at the time. Unlike in 1978, the release of nearly all political prisoners by 1992 was to signal the Islamic Republic regime's confidence in having crushed its opponents and silenced the people. Yet, if the Shah's desperate hope in appearing lenient did not save his regime from collapsing, the stability of the Islamic Republic was much more precarious than it appeared.

BECAUSE THE NEW REGIME came to power by way of a revolutionary movement, as in most such states, new arrests began immediately after the victory of the 1979 revolution. Aside from the selective execution of the Shah's officials that took place only days after the revolution, from 1981 until 1988, massive arrests and summary executions became familiar features of the new regime.

The massacre of political prisoners in the summer of 1988 marked a turning point in the history of political suppression in Iran: about five thousand prisoners were executed in the course of two months, and a majority of these prisoners had already been sentenced to jail time or were about to be released. The massacre occurred immediately after the announcement of the cease-fire in the Iran-Iraq War. Mojahedin, an Iranian militant organization then based in and supported by Iraq, acted upon this as an opportunity to attack and briefly occupy some villages and towns along the western border of Iran. The Iranian state, in turn, used the attack as an opportunity to resolve its age-old problem of political prisoners by summarily killing thousands of individuals, none of whom were responsible for the attack. In fact, many of those killed were either leftists or had other political inclinations with no connection to Mojahedin. The "Era of Reconstruction" was announced by President Ali Akbar Hashemi Rafsanjani, whose great hope to attract foreign investments faced the obstacle of the Iranian regime's human rights abuses, at the center of which was the question of political prisoners. Now with the massacre of most jailed dissidents, the regime considered the potential threat to its future stability eliminated, at least for the most part. The release of the rest of the prisoners became the regime's mission, which it undertook to accomplish with a spirit of confidence and necessity.

The regime's confidence hinged upon the assumption that, by killing so many dissidents and pushing the remainder of them into a state of despair through torture, the movement was beheaded. It seemed to have forgotten the old Persian proverb *mar dar āstin parvaradan*, "breeding the snake in one's own sleeve": that is, the new dissidence was already growing in and from its very midst. The signs of this reality were already too evident to be ignored. That Ayatollah Khomeini, the Supreme Religious Leader, was forced to expel Ayatollah Montazeri, who was assigned to be his successor, was an exemplary indication of what was to come. The flip side of this confidence was the pressure and an urgent need to create a new sociopolitical environment in the aftermath of the Iran-Iraq War. To implement Hashemi Rafsanjani's sociopolitical and economic plans toward reconstructing the country after the war, it seemed imperative to attract foreign investments, hence to initiate a new relationship with the outside world, especially with the West. This required taking steps to assuage concerns about Iran's human rights violations. Releasing prisoners was one of the most important steps that the regime had to take, albeit in an excruciatingly complex and violent process that was to avoid the fate of the Shah's regime. Within the larger society, Rafsanjani attempted to ease the rigid regulations of veiling and lifted restrictions concerning variety of color in dress codes, even allocating particular areas as "free zones" wherein economic rules of the free market demanded much looser Islamic rules of social conduct.

The release of prisoners thus became the goal that the state pursued at nearly all costs, except that it was to appear not as an act of a defeated regime, like that of the Shah, but as a gesture of strength and stability by a state that no longer felt threatened by its opponents. In fact, the regime preferred the more colorful story in which its prisons had turned all its opponents to its supporters. As the Shah did in 1977, the Islamic Republic regime began by forcing prisoners to submit to the condition of their release, which required their renunciation of their past and any political and ideological inclinations and affiliations that diverged from those of the official discourse of the state. The denouncing of their past and the recanting of beliefs had been the condition for prisoners' release since the early 1980s. An uneven battle, which had been going on between the prison officials and prisoners from the very early days of the Islamic Republic, was intensified, not in the quality of the recantation or renunciation but in its concentrated reinforcement of acquiring prisoners' submission and therefore their release.

From the early 1980s to 1990s, the state-mandated denunciation of their past as the condition for prisoners' release saw many changes, but the basic demand for renunciation remained until nearly the end, when the regime had to give in and free prisoners, though officially on a temporary basis. In the early 1980s, for example, the denunciation entailed a much more elaborate recantation and expression of repudiation of dissident organizations. This recantation-confession had to be made publicly—if not televised and broadcast on national television or on closed-circuit prison television, then at least carried out among a large crowd of prisoners in the huge prison halls, *husseiniyeh*. But from 1985 on, after the severe crackdown on the main dissident organizations of the early 1980s and prisoners' resistance, the condition of release became less daunting—signing a letter of repugnance.

FOLLOWING THE MASSACRE of the summer of 1988, the regime undertook the project of releasing prisoners by two means: pressure and negotiation. Those of us who refused to sign the renunciation paper were pressed to request a *morakhasi*, a temporary release. *Morakhasi* was a tactic used by the regime to achieve two goals at once. First, the regime was aware that for many resistant prisoners, requesting a temporary release was meant to legitimize their imprisonment based on their dissident views, which the officials considered illegitimate. The regime thus attempted and hoped to press as many of them as possible to request their temporary release. Second, it counted on the fact that, while out, under the pressure of their families and friends and their own desire for freedom, they might sign the paper to be freed permanently. Aside from all the pressure, what was unbearable for these prisoners was the fact that upon their refusal to sign the form, it was the responsibility of their families to deliver them to prison. The stories of the suffering of these prisoners and their families in this often long process leading to prisoners' release are abundant. Soosan's experience offers only one example.

In 1990, the guards brought Soosan to my cell from the hospital where her mother lay in critical condition following a heart attack, apparently induced by anxiety because Soosan's one-week temporary release had ended but she refused to sign the paper and was to return to jail. Soosan was one of the prisoners who had remained imprisoned beyond their sentence terms; in fact, her one-year sentence had ended in 1982, but because she refused to submit to the condition of her release, she was still in jail. Her mother had begged, cried, and finally fought with her to accept the condition. Soosan had tried to explain to her why she could and would not do so. She had left her mother crying and telling her that if she died, Soosan would be the one who killed her. Only two hours after Soosan returned to her cell, the guards informed her that her mother had passed away. She did not have to hear the harsh words of the guards about how she was a murderer and killed her own mother to feel guilty. Her guilt was already too overwhelming. The prison officials did not allow her to attend the funeral. Instead, in response to her request to attend the funeral, they bombarded her with more blame, accusing her of being selfish and the cause of her mother's death.

In regard to those prisoners who rejected requesting temporary release, the regime turned to their families to convince them to press their children to comply. Terrified of losing their loved ones in light of the massacre of 1988, and understandably in favor of their loved ones' release, even if temporary, most of these families, of course out of love, became the source of pressure on their loved ones to give in to the regime's demand. A few of these families were so eager to see their children released that they even seemed not to mind their subjection to torture if it forced them to submit to the regime's condition. While it pained them to see their loved ones subjected to torture, for some of these families the desire for the release and the saving of their loved ones was a higher priority. Sima was one of these women whom the regime brought to a face-to-face visit with her parents after she had been severely tortured. Instead of hiding her scars, the regime claimed that in fact her family had themselves wanted her to be beaten until she agreed to sign the letter of repugnance. This experience proved too painful for Sima. She could not take the torture of the interrogators and the pressure from her family. This particular encounter was too emotionally disturbing. She finally signed the paper and was released.

By 1990, a large number of prisoners had signed the papers and were freed. For those of us who did not budge and resisted requesting our temporary release, the regime accepted our families' request on our behalf. I had told my parents not to do so, but obviously my father was convinced that his request did not jeopardize my integrity and my stance against the regime. Thus, when that morning in November 1991, the guard opened the door of my cell and called my name "for the hospital," so she claimed, I left the cell unaware that this was to be my day to leave prison. In general, we anticipated our temporary release, for we knew that the wave of releases was growing larger every day. We had been taken to solitary confinement after most of our friends had gone through many rounds of being in and out of prison. At some point during these processes, one by one, most of them had accepted the condition and were released; those who had not, despite all the pressure, finally won. The regime let them remain outside without an official release. Now the parents of these comrades were visiting ours, convincing them that they, too, should not listen to us but should simply go ahead and request our temporary release since the regime had made the condition even easier to comply with than before.

Our numbers were shrinking. While at first we were in solitary confinement, later two of us shared a cell; we felt lonelier with every friend who was released. In the cells, our conditions worsened. The guards made every effort to render our daily life in jail as unbearable as possible. Their constant verbal assaults, random beatings, canceling of our shower time, and so on were part of our daily routine. Yet none of this was new to us. What made these experiences so hard to take was the empty space left in jail, first by the massacre of 1988 and now by the release of our friends, which obviously should have brought us joy. It did make us happy to some extent, but the circumstances under which this all happened shadowed our happiness. The night before, my cellmate and I had discussed the possibility of who would be the next to leave, and she, being from a provincial town with a family of much more modest means than even mine, argued that it could not be her. I told her that my father would never go against my wishes to request my release and that even if he decided to do so, he did not have the means to provide the regime with the huge bail that was required for my release. The bail had to be posted whether the release was temporary or permanent. It had to be valuable real estate, such as a house, land, or a supermarket.

But now I was out, again before my sentence was completed and supposedly only for ten days. But my first destination was a cemetery to which my family, for whom I had become a near stranger, was to take me. After both releases, my heart remained with the small group who were still jailed. But at this point, the issue about the release of prisoners, at least the leftists, was mainly the question of who could afford to bail them out. My cellmate came out about a year later, for her family could not afford to bail her out. In my case, a relative had agreed to offer his house.

Restless Dogs and Drunken Ants

Now I was out, and even before seeing my siblings, I was insisting on visiting the graves of my loved ones, including the mass graves somewhere within which my husband must have been buried. As we walked away from prison, my father's fast pace and my mother's words about forgetting all that I had left behind were indicative of their attempt to bring me back to the outside world. In choosing the dissident cemetery as the point of my entry to this world, I was at once attesting to my attachment to my dead comrades and those still in prison, and promising to bear witness to their untimely deaths and unjust sufferings. This could only terrify my parents. Unwilling to disagree with me, they nervously told me that we had to go to my oldest sister's house, where we could wait for my youngest brother to come and drive us to the cemetery, which they explained was too far away for us to go on our own. I had no choice but to comply. I reluctantly sat in the cab that drove us to my sister's house.

The water pressure in the shower in my sister's second-floor apartment was so slight that I could not completely wash off the sweat from prison. Although frustrated, deep down I felt more comfortable, for I could go to the cemetery still feeling more like an inhabitant of jail than of this other world. Regardless, in my sister's house, I was already becoming acquainted with a world in which kids had been born and raised in my absence. Life had been going on. I did not want to feel a strong connection to this world, not until I could "see" Hamid and my other loved ones from whom I had been so violently separated. I felt the urge to talk to them and have them hear me through all the soil that covered them, as though wanting to do so before my voice and soul were tarnished by the pollution of the outside world. Fresh from jail, I had to promise them that I was not going to let them die in silence, that I would never forget them. How naïve I was then!

Everyone expected me to seem strange, but I was trying my best to appear normal. After all, hadn't I longed for this freedom and for being with my family again? I played with my one-year-old niece, whom I had not met before. In no time, she was smiling and following me around with her eyes as if she had known me forever. Around noon, my youngest brother arrived, having borrowed a friend's car to drive us to the cemetery and then to my parents' home. In shock, we looked at one another. This man who was standing in front of me was my little brother, whom I had left behind when he was only fifteen years old, whose brilliance and outspoken attitude I so adored. I had not seen him in about nine years, and here he was, in his early twenties, his hair already grayed around his forehead. He was among those lost generations of young Iranians who were born and raised in particularly disjointed times.

Although my brother was brilliant, the opportunity for attending the university was denied to him when the regime rejected his admission, despite having passed the competitive national entrance exam, merely because his siblings were considered dissidents of the government. He thus had to register as a conscript for two and a half years of military service, which coincided with one of the worst periods of the Iran-Iraq War, from 1985 to 1988—the conscription service had been increased from two to two and a half years during the war. Ironically therefore, while I was living the nightmarish days and nights of that hellish summer in 1988, he was caught between two sides of a war, between the Iranian regime and the Mojahedin who had attacked Iran. A pacifist at heart, he had lived the entire war, first between Iran and Iraq and now between Iran and an Iranian militant organization, under an impossible situation, trying not to kill and not to be killed. This was how he once related the story of those impossible times, during the Mojahedin's attack on the Iranian western border in 1988.

> It had already been so hard to be in the military and make sure you did not kill anyone but not let the commanders or others on your side notice this. It was nearly the end of my conscription term. I had begun to tell myself, okay, you did it. I thought I had survived this war without killing, without becoming a murderer. But then came this crazy thing. Mojahedin attacked. We were literally caught in the middle. A few of my friends and I who had nothing to do with this war found ourselves under the fire and the eyes of both sides. Ahead of us were Mojahedin whom we were trying to avoid killing, while at the same time we were trying to avoid being killed by them. Behind us were, however, our own troops watching us, and if we did not shoot at Mojahedin, they would shoot us. Then we got lost. For three days, we were lost in the mountainous areas of the western border, with no food, nothing to drink, and no sense of direction. For three days all we ate was ice. At the end of the third day, when we finally found our way back, the attack had already been defeated. When I finally took a shower and looked at myself in the mirror while shaving, I suddenly noticed the gray hair on both sides of my forehead. The three longest days and nights of nightmare I had ever lived had really made me grow old. I had become a twenty-year-old, old man.

I watched this now grayed brother of mine, whom I used to take care of as if my own child, as he stared at my drastically changed appearance. It was as if we each were looking for the traces of significant moments of Iranian recent history, revolution, war, and political violence on the other's face and body, imagining their carvings on each other's soul. It was already late afternoon when, after a long drive through the crowded streets and highways of Tehran, all the way from the northwestern part to the southeast, finally my brother branched off the main road and drove the short distance of a dirt alley before stopping in front of the metal gate of the cemetery.

I took a few steps into this strange-looking graveyard, but my feet and heart felt too heavy to allow me to go on walking. I also felt lost. I had no sense of direction. There was no sign indicating the whereabouts of my Hamid and other loved ones' graves. There was no one in the cemetery except us. In my heart, I called Hamid and my other dead loved ones and tried to hear them, but all I could hear was silence. I stopped and looked around. Right across the entrance, beyond the wall that enclosed the cemetery, a small window in a church tower stood tall with a view of almost the entirety of this otherwise godforsaken landscape. The church was located within the Christian cemetery, segregating the Christian dead, as the dead of other non-Muslims were, from the mainstream Muslim cemetery.

The window was staring at me. I tried to imagine the crimes it must have witnessed. Only later I learned that it was through this very window that the secret of the political massacre of 1988 was revealed to the German journalists who were visiting Iran that summer. It was during this summer that my Hamid and about five thousand other prisoners were executed. The journalists did not perhaps stay long enough to see how night after night during those two months, meat trucks carried the bodies of hundreds of political prisoners and hastily dumped them into the ditches that were clumsily dug in the dark of night. They would have nevertheless noticed the freshness of the soil and the restless dogs. The families learned about those horrifying nights, only in fragments, from some immigrant Afghani men who worked and lived in the area and whispered to them what they witnessed night after night, while scared that revealing these ugly secrets of the government might jeopardize their own lives.

These men also told the families about the restless dogs who barked through all those nights as the graves were dug and the bodies were secretly dumped into them. Drunk with flesh and blood, the dogs dragged these hastily buried bodies out. There were families who came to visit the grave of one child only to encounter the exposed arm or legs of another son. Some mothers uncovered these mass graves with their bare hands to find some solace in learning the precise spot where their children were buried, only to come back and see the entire place turned upside down by bulldozers. Zohreh, a woman whose three brothers were executed, two of them in the early 1980s and the third one in 1988, related this to me: "The red ants would have revealed the secret of this crime anyway, even without the dogs dragging out the arms and legs of our loved ones, even if we had not heard about the German journalists or had not been able to talk to some of these Afghani workers. We would have still guessed from the way these red ants were having a feast during those few months. They were really growing larger and looked as if they were drunk with the flesh and blood of our beautiful young loved ones."

Thanks to the freshness of the soil and the dogs, the drunken fattening ants, the foreign journalists, and the Afghani workers, the families learned about the dark secret of the massacre and the mass graves of their loved ones. After months of no news, their worst nightmares came true when, instead of a visit with their loved ones in jail, they came face-to-face with the shocking proof of their death in their traumatic encounter with the uncovered arms, legs, or faces of the young dead men, who had been buried with their clothes on. How many nights since hearing the story of the journalists had I stayed up, imagining myself watching through that same window, from that distance, trying to distinguish Hamid's beautiful hands and arms from those of others? How could those hands, which knew so well the way to my heart, which knew how to calm me down in the most distressing conditions by simply caressing my hair and behind my neck, be lost to me? Does one's hair know how to cry? Does one's neck feel thirsty? Mine did—it still does. I tried so hard to keep my tears hidden inside, hidden from my parents and everyone else, as Hamid's body had been kept hidden from me.

To control my emotions, I concentrated on the landscape. The cemetery was surrounded by a brick wall, within which a rectangular-shaped area was nearly divided in half, though not by any wall or fence but by the distinctive landscapes on each side. In the section on the right, the graves had tombstones; the dead were recognized by their names on the tombstones. There were also bushes with white and pink flowers on that side. On the flat, barren dirt on the left, there were only flowers scattered on the ground that had obviously been brought by visitors and put here and there on unmarked "graves." There were no tombstones, no markers, no names to signify this section as graveyard.

The left side itself was divided into two parts, again with no fence or walls between them. The section closer to the entrance looked a little more like a graveyard. A few bumps on the ground and some broken stones here and there told the story of different periods of brutality but also the story of the struggle of those families whose loved ones were executed in the early 1980s to make the deaths of their loved ones visible. It also reflected the intolerance of the state toward allowing these dead dissidents a place not so much to rest but to remain visible and be recognized as dead. The area closer to the wall of the Christian cemetery and its church was, however, completely flat with no indication of the lives that were cut short and buried under its soil.

Only on my later visits would I learn that the section with tombstones and bushes belonged to the Baha'i dead. Baha'is were allowed to mark the graves of their dead and even plant flowers and bushes, but they could not create the kind of lasting greenery that one could see, for instance, in Behesht Zahra, the Muslims' main cemetery in Tehran, especially in its Flower Garden of the Martyrs, a section allocated to those whose death the state considered as martyrdom. The cemetery of the Muslims, particularly of the martyrs, was to remind one of the gardens in paradise, which obviously the Baha'is were not to imitate. The area closer to the gate held the bodies of those executed in the early 1980s, where the families were at least given a sense of where their loved ones were buried with a single grave for each individual—since the bodies were not given to the families and they could not be present at the process of burial, there were many occasions when two or more families were given the same location for the grave of their dead. I knew of a woman who visited a grave as that of her brother, only to learn, twenty years later, that another family was also visiting that same grave as that of their loved one, who was in fact buried there. And finally, the area toward the Christian cemetery was the site of the mass graves of the dead of the massacre of 1988.

But in my first visit to this strange cemetery, I knew nothing of these details. I thus felt totally disoriented. In this remote area of Tehran, where one could see no houses, where no one walked around, the dead, my dead loved ones, seemed really lost, utterly deserted. This was not a mere cemetery but the cemetery of a cemetery, where the dead person was lost to his or her own death. Suddenly, I was horrified as I realized that my Hamid and other loved ones had been denied not only their lives but also their deaths. They were being lost to the world, denied having ever existed in this world. I felt like I was losing them not simply because of their death but because their death was a forced erasure from the face of this land, from the face of life, and from history. Imagining such a possibility, such an absolute loss, made me shiver, for I recognized my own utter loss. How could I think of my own existence while all those I had loved so dearly were being thrown into the abyss of amnesic nonexistence? What could become of me without my memories of my loved ones? I looked up and around and felt a brief sense of relief. I noticed the mountains on the northern side of the cemetery, at the base of which lay this graveyard, over which the sky had generously spread its vast and wide blanket. Strangely, I seemed convinced that Hamid, who loved the sky and the mountains so much, could not be lost to them, that somehow these beautiful mountains and this blue sky could not let his love die away or be lost.

But then I noticed my father's nervous eyes, anticipating my reaction and my grieving for my loss. Since my childhood, he never had the heart to see my tears. I thus had learned never to cry in front of him. But now he knew that I must be crying inside. I could see that in his worried eyes. This made me uncomfortable. I tried to allow Hamid, Fakhri, Shohreh, Ata, all those loved ones who lay somewhere under this undistinguished dirt, to speak to me from beneath the soil, but I could not concentrate. I could not ignore my guilt, noticing my father's anxious behavior, his even more than usual hasty walk, and the raspy sound of his sick lungs. He had never been good in allowing me the space to be sad, out of his overwhelming love for me. But now, since he knew the depth of my loss, his pain was too grave to be retained. He was escaping it, dragging me along. I knew him well and, of course, understood this all, yet I was still at once sad and angry. Neither could I allow myself to cry along with my mother, whose tears were flowing down her face in silence. I thus turned to my father and asked where Hamid and my friends were buried.

Pointing to the right side, my dad almost ran toward that section. I followed him and hoped my heart could lead me toward Hamid's grave. But I sensed no clue. It was as if I had fallen into a thick, misty night. All my senses were tarnished and fogged in. I read the names on the tombstone, but none seemed familiar. Later, when I learned that the section to which my father had taken me belonged to the Baha'i dead, I was surprised that I had not even come across the names of those Baha'is whom I knew were executed in jail—apparently my father had intentionally misled me, in his mind to protect me from the pain of my first experience in the outside world in seeing a barren land as the graveyard of my love.

Even when I asked my parents why we were the only people there, my father chose to offer an answer that instead of reducing my pain intensified it. "People do not come here that often." I was so disoriented and so out of touch with the outside world that it did not occur to me that this was a Wednesday and that Iranians visit graveyards usually on Thursdays or Fridays. Soon, I would find out that the families avoid coming as small groups or come during different hours to reduce the risk of being attacked or arrested by the government. But for now I was dependent on my parents' guidance, and my father's loving intentions had misled me.

Later, my father would make other similar gestures, all with the intention of saving me, in his mind, from living with the dead and in order to pave the way for my future. What he knew but could not allow himself to accept was that to move toward a future, I could not bury my past; my past had to be integrated into who I was today and would become tomorrow. He knew well that a rupture with my past was impossible, yet he took on this impossible struggle, which caused so many heartaches for both of us.

Thus, when he said, "People do not come here that often," something did not feel right to me. Standing on the unfamiliar names on the tombstones, I looked at the other side of the cemetery, at the barren section. A strong force was running through the air and into my cells, pushing me to that direction. But I felt paralyzed by my father's concerned eyes. I could see how hard he was trying to hold himself back and not rush out of the cemetery. I looked at my mother. The stream of her tears rushed through my heart as if it was a hot lava river. No way could I find Hamid or any of my other friends while overwhelmed with so much guilt; neither could I talk to them, not while my father was anxiously walking around and eyeing my every gesture; not when my heart was pierced by my mother's innocent tears. How relieved my dad was when I told them we could leave. We drove to my parents' house—a house I had not seen before, for after my arrest, they had been forced to sell their house in Tehran overnight and move to Karadj, a town about forty-five miles west of Tehran. As a girl, I had been so independent. I had worked and lived on my own even before my first arrest under the Shah. And now I was going to live with my parents, in my early thirties, a widow. I could not even bring myself to say the word. How could I imagine myself without my love?

As we drove away from the cemetery, I felt my heart was buried there, but not in a particular spot where I could go and look for it. It was lost with all those other hearts under and on these mass graves. How long would I carry the weight of the promises I could not even whisper in the ears of my dead loved ones through the soil? Would I be able to convey them through the air? The sky was getting darker. The first bright star appeared. I swallowed the air, and the heaviness was lightened a bit. I touched my wedding ring and whispered Hamid's name.

In the car, the music was so loud that I felt my brain was going to explode. In prison, we had to listen to the loudspeakers, which were constantly broadcasting interminable prayers, religious verses, and crying voices confessing their sins and humiliating themselves. Now I had to listen to these hysterically happy musical productions exported from Los Angeles by Iranian musicians in exile. I was astonished by the fashions of the women on the street and their garish makeup. My sister said to me, "We have to buy you a new dress. This one looks awfully outdated," reminding me how different I looked from other women.

Coffins or Machines?

The difference between me, the former political prisoner, and the out-side world made more sense to me when a few months later, in the midst of the deafening noise of several different languages and dialects, com-pressed in the minibus, in the mixture of the sweaty odor of bodies and the smell of gasoline, I saw two eager eyes inviting recognition. While the bus was wobbling and groaning under the weight of its overcrowded pack, Pori squeezed herself through the standing crowd to make her way toward me. When she reached for my hand, her eyes were shining with thirst and excitement, a look of a person who finds a spring in the desert. I was both baffled and enthusiastic, seeing her reaction. She was even paler than Soudabeh Ardavan, a former inmate, had portrayed her in her prison drawings.

Pori was one of those women taken to a severe punishment ward set up by Haji Davoud, the chief of Ghezel Hesar Prison at the time. This already notorious prison, located in Karadj, was bestowed with a new dimension of infamy because of this punishment ward, which Haji Davoud referred to as *kārkhāneh-ye-ādam sāzi*, the human-making factory, or *dastgah-e-ādam sāzi*, the human-making machine—prisoners shortened it and simply re-ferred to it as *dastgah*. The landscape of this human-making factory was a large hall in Vahed-e 1 Ward, or Unit 1, within which a large number of small cells were temporarily built by erecting makeshift wooden walls. Each cell was separated from others either by the original walls of the hall or the makeshift wooden walls, depending on its location in the hall. The wooden walls were high enough to prevent prisoners from seeing each other while they were either sitting or lying down, which was their status all the time except for brief moments when they would be taken to the restroom, for a shower, or for interrogation.

All prisoners faced the wall; again, depending on the location of their spot, they faced either the wall of the hall, if their cell was adjacent to any four walls of the hall, or the wooden wall. They were, however, entirely exposed to the guards, who could see and access them from above—these boxlike cells had no roofs and their walls were not high—and there was no wall behind them. Thus, while they faced the wall, blindfolded even while asleep, they were under constant scrutiny by the guards, who could strike them at any moment.

During the ten months that this torturous situation lasted, from 1983 to 1984, prisoners were forced to live, in their own words, in these *j'abehha* (boxes), *taboota* (coffins), or *ghabra* (graves). They sat there the entire time with no permission to speak, move, even cough or sneeze. Any noise or motion was punished by lashes and beatings, which occurred frequently and without warning. Since the prisoners were blindfolded all the time, these blows, which so abruptly struck their bodies almost always unexpectedly, carved a huge hole in their minds within which the deadly bird of anticipation hovered, constantly flapping its wings.

From six in the morning until ten at night, prisoners had to squat on the floor, motionless and silent. For several hours every day, which seemed eternity, they were forced to listen to the prison radio that broadcast religious lessons, prayers and Qur'anic verses, or their former comrades' confessions. If these lengthy hours of imposed propaganda were not torturous enough, the wretched, dull knife of prolonged silence sliced their bodies and souls into pieces, with pieces floating around in the endless, sleepless, nightmarish nights.

The fall was imminent! It came! The first soul gave in. Like Faust, the first broken woman bargained her soul, though not so much for prolonging than for escaping the continuous torment of her hellish life. The first soul's fall paved the path for many others. One after another, those who broke offered public recantations in which they confessed to sins they had only discovered having committed in their past lives while sitting in these boxes, blindfolded and under Haji's lashes. Some of them became collaborators, acting as new guards and whipping their friends alongside whom they had sat and been beaten only days before. Even the softest of the lashes by these former friends, who were now playing extra hands of evil, felt harsher on prisoners' bodies; these lashes sank deeper into their memories and burned an irreducible, enduring register of pain in their minds and bodies.

Friends turned into enemies. Trust was shattered; it survived in an abstract language, which was already eluding prisoners. Words seemed to lose their meanings. Yet, as unspeakable as this all felt, language was the means through which this surreal reality could be located somewhere within human experience. It could be remembered through forgetting and forgotten by remembering. Through language, and in the language of remembering and forgetting, some sense had to be made of these impossible experiences.

Those who had gone through this calamitous situation, be it the collaborators or the resistant prisoners, were marked by its injuries, which they carried with them to the wards where they were returned, and perhaps later, everywhere they went. Again and again, they each experienced and lived these memories, yet always in unique and new ways. Some came back hating everyone else who still appeared passionate about life. It seemed as if they had turned into the vehicle by which cruelty and hatred were traveling. To survive the pain and hatred that had been inflicted on them and turned their brain to "mush" they projected it onto those who reminded them of their past and of their lost selves and integrity. The question remained, however, what kind of survival was this, since death had captured them before they could physically die?

Like wandering souls, they sought their peace solely through squeezing the essence of life out of others. They interpreted their former friends' joy and laughter as a conspiracy against themselves. They sent them under torture by false statements; they hated any sign of resistance, for they saw it as the negation of their presently precarious existence. It was as though any resistant spirit reminded them of their past life, a life about which their most vivid memory was unbearable physical pain and unforgettable humiliation. In order to forget this pain, they not only detested but had to destroy whatever lay in that past or resembled their previous selves. But if these prisoners were still capable of functioning, albeit in a deadly and destructive manner, there were others who appeared so oblivious to their existence that even death could pass them by without noticing them or being noticed by them. Although the corpse of a stagnant life was still clinging to its vegetative being like a parasite, the prisoner had already departed this world.

Still, for others, the impact of this ferocious experience was so profound that they could not free themselves from it. They became the subject of a never-ceasing torture, humiliation, and pain, eternally reproduced in their own mind, a mind possessed by and frozen in a horrifyingly, ever-present past. Not so much paralyzed subjects, but nonsubjects, they seemed to no longer exist as subjects. Haunted by the horrific experience, their mind perpetuated that moment of horror, time and again. The person's relationship to temporality and spatiality was thus relinquished. This was a state of being in which the self was frozen, either at the time before the horrific experience or at the moment of its occurrence, as if nothing existed before or from that moment on. Either way, the possibility of remembering and forgetting was eliminated. As long as one lived in the moment or seemingly out of it, not with it, the experience was neither digested nor remembered; neither could it be forgotten, for it was lived each time anew, each time for the first time.

But a small number of prisoners came out of this human-making factory with their subjectivity still somewhat intact. Pori was one of very few women who left this place without submitting to Haji's condition to collaborate or at least renounce her past. Yet, while she refused to be broken by the regime, mistrust of her fellow inmates grew inside her. She returned to the ward but soon withdrew from others and remained in a kind of isolation that resembled her condition in the *dastgah*. This retreat to isolation was also pursued by a few others who had gone through the experience of *taboota*. It is true that some of them explained this desire for isolation as a way of distancing themselves from other inmates, who, they argued, were unable to recognize the consequences of their adventurous actions against the regime. They suggested that since we had not been to the *dastgah* and had not experienced what they had, we undertook radical resistance to prison regulations in an adventurous manner without realizing that if we were put under a similar torturous condition, many of us would end up betraying our friends, as most of their friends had betrayed them. They recounted how some of the most outspoken inmates were broken in the *dastgah* even faster than others and how they turned into collaborators who reported, menacingly, on their former cellmates.

Whatever their reasoning, the result was that in no time they retreated into a near solitude, once again, after enduring months of isolation that Haji Davoud had imposed on them. Many prisoners perceived these withdrawn inmates as cynical, as political pessimists, if not just broken. Those who had chosen to withdraw from others, in turn, construed other prisoners as politically naïve or irresponsible adventurers. For some, these differences were translated into the language of politics and different political affiliations. Some of these prisoners would realize that they had superimposed their own experiences and emotions onto the views of their political affiliations only after they were released. But while in jail, as time went by, the distance between those who were isolated and the others grew deeper. The division increased, for gradually even those who had distanced themselves from the rest of the prisoners but were close to one another began to distance themselves from each other. Most of them continued to live as single individuals, as if on separate islands.

Pori, one of these inmates who had been subjected to ten months of isolation in Haji's hell, was now living in her own self-imposed isolation. Despite her self-isolated, thus double, imprisonment, Pori still refused to give in to the regime's condition to sign the letter of repugnance for her release. All those years in jail, a short while after returning from the *dastgah*, she spent most of her days sitting silently as portrayed in Soudabeh's drawing, hidden behind newspapers and reading them meticulously, at least so it appeared. She ate alone, walked alone, and slept with her back toward others.

It was with this history in mind that when in that crammed minibus I saw Pori's reaction to me, the eagerness with which she held my hand while in her eyes the stars of joy sparkled, I was simultaneously befuddled and intensely moved. Her words made me realize how strong the bond of pain was between those of us who had experienced those years of imprisonment and the challenges of surviving in the world so estranged from it. "Seeing you feels like a gushing of light into a dark cave. I feel so lonely in this world, and I so regret that I did not realize how much we were connected there." I could sense her excitement and hear her nostalgic tone, yet I could also see her blushing, from shyness perhaps? The "we" of which she was speaking was a reference to all of us former political prisoners, with whom she now seemed to feel a deeper connection than to her own family members. This was a kinship felt not only by Pori but by nearly all of us who had survived imprisonment without becoming collaborators or without having completely lost ourselves in the process. This was a kinship built upon and around pain, loss, love, resistance, and survival.

Eventually, each of us who lived through and came out of our torment experienced and were marked by it in a unique way. In regard to Haji Davoud's human-making machine, both the experiences of those inmates who lived through it and the language with which they spoke of it varied from one person to another. There was eventually a gender dimension to these experiences and languages, even in naming the place. Male prisoners seemed to have chosen a single metaphor, *taboota*, to refer to the place within which they were forced to live for months. I am not sure, though, whether *taboota* was the men's own invention, in accordance with their experience of the place, or if, either directly or indirectly, Haji Davoud had suggested that these cells would become their coffins if they continued resisting the offer to recant. Notwithstanding its initial coinage, it appeared to have resonated with nearly all prisoners, for after hearing it from men, women often spoke of those cells either as *ghabra* or *taboota*. Perhaps no other name could have conveyed as accurately what the place was to achieve, the annihilation of prisoners' old selves. Nobody emerged from this place with his or her old self intact, whether broken by Haji or not.

Most of the names appropriated by the women were initially used in some form by prison officials. Some women simply spoke of it as Vahed-e 1, which alluded to the ward within which the wooden cells were erected. Others referred to it as *gharantineh*, or quarantine, also the name Haji Davoud and other prison officials used for the large hall in this ward where prisoners were often taken for different periods for further punishment. As the name suggests, the place was to temporarily segregate the "contagiously dangerous" elements from the rest of the prisoners, as is the purpose of quarantine in epidemics, until they were either cured or dead. Quarantine was thus an interior within the interior, a space that pushed one into a deeper and thicker isolation. Another word drawn from Haji's terminology and employed by women was *dastgah* or *dastgaha*, which was the shorter version of Haji's "human-making machine or machines." Women used several other terms, including *j'abehha* and *takhtha* or *takhta*, beds or wooden beds, to convey their sense of the place.

While it is obvious that men and women were not treated exactly the same, and even the setup of their wards was not identical, I have often thought of the ramifications of these different terms and their gendered dimension. Apparently, we all live in language; thus, our experiences are shaped by language as our language is shaped by our experiences. For instance, was the term *taboota*, which nowadays has been adopted more broadly by most former prisoners and even the larger public to allude to the presumably unisex experience of prisoners in those punishment wards, simply coined by men based on the physical resemblance between those wooden cells and coffins? Some of my female friends have suggested this, arguing that men are more practical minded and their reference to the place was derived from its physical appearance and intended function. Yet this argument rests on two assumptions: on a stereotypical view of men as more practical minded than women and a reductive notion of death that does not take the complexities of prisoners' experiences and views of life and death into account.

But in a sense, Haji Davoud's "human-making machine," a term known by both male and female prisoners, was intended to produce his desirable humans through the destruction of prisoners' old selves. Those who submitted to Haji's demand for recantation and collaborated with him against their former friends turned into the very enemies of their own past selves. Haji had in fact promised that nobody was to leave this place unless he or she recanted. Even though Haji could not break everyone and the ward was finally closed down, those who emerged were not the same as the ones who had gone in. "Graves" or "coffins" thus described the intended, the metaphoric, and the symbolic function of this place.

But assigning only one possible function to an object, or a single meaning to a word, tends to preclude other possibilities the word might entail. It also imposes a fixed outcome. For example, ascribing names like "coffins" or "graves" could implicitly articulate and reinforce prisoners' sense of death as an inevitable "destiny-ation" of Haji's project. Death, however, does not mean only a physical ceasing of existence. It could refer to a total departure from the world or the demise of an old self and the creation of a new one. Obviously, even the total departure from this world does not necessarily have to be, and has often not been, perceived as an absolute nonexistence.

Death appeared differently in the language of men and women inmates. Male prisoners used the word *zadan*, beating, to refer to execution. Why should execution be considered synonymous with beating? Isn't it true that under torture, inmates had to give up the body on which the torturer exercised his power, in order to preserve their integrity? Isn't it the case that, to save their soul, inmates had to detach themselves from their body and let the body go? This was a detachment that could not be completely accomplished unless one was physically dead. Isn't it also true that there is no life if no blood is running in one's veins? Yet prison experience proves how one might live such a stagnant, bloodless life that no thunder or hurricane could affect it. Which one of these meanings of life and death did these men have in mind when they used *zadan* to mean execution? How should one interpret the fact that women distinguish between *zadan* and *e'edām*, execution? Are these differences merely gendered languages, or did the experiences of torture differ for men and women? Can one actually distinguish gendered languages from gendered experiences?

Let us consider women's naming of Haji Davoud's invention. Although women do not use one name for the ward and the cells in it, almost every name has something to do with the official reference. For example, Vahed-e 1 simply refers to the ward in which these wooden cells

were set up; *dastgah* was Haji's word, only shortened, and *takhta* alluded
to a small space nearly the size of a small single bed between the wooden
walls where the prisoner could sleep. The word *j'abehha* was also a description of the wooden cells. Thus, even though these names may not
seem creative or rekindle the assumption about women's submissive tendency in following the authoritative ascriptions, the fact they prescribe no
fixed function to the place seems to allow for a more subjective reading of
and response to their singular condition. To refuse to name this place with
a single term may indicate women inmates' refusal to submit to a single
possible outcome or destiny.

The names could also be considered evidence of women's naïveté, as
their failure to understand the significance of this torture machine and
the limitations of human capacity for tolerating pain. It was not rare to
hear of the inadequacy of female inmates' knowledge and experience of
political activism and imprisonment. Of course, the number of men who
had experienced imprisonment under both the Shah and the Islamic Republic far exceeded that of women. However, assuming, for instance, that
women's shortening Haji's term "human-making machine" to "machine"
was an unimaginative act of mere abbreviation sounds rather odd to me.
Words were not casually utilized in prison; particularly under the Islamic
Republic, words could easily save someone or lead to someone's death.
There must have been much more than their assumed naïveté or care-
lessness behind women's usage of terms similar to those of the officials,
but amended. This raises another question: to what extent does language
speak us or we speak language? I also keep contemplating the manner
in which such "otherly" worlds and words find their way to my present
world, the way they get translated to a corresponding language in daily
life outside jail. I realize how often the impact of my experiences colors not
only my own present life but my comprehension of others' experiences.

٭

*One morning in 1999, after five years of living in the United States, as I
was driving home, I nearly jumped out of my skin from the sudden noise*

of a bus ahead of my car. This noise took me back to seven years earlier, when the bus in which I met Pori came to a stop with such a sound, reminding me of the lash that stroked the air and fell on inmates' bodies to rip their flesh off. Pori had let my hand go and said, "This is my destination," and had left, but that pale face, those eager eyes, and that deep sadness had sunk deep into my memory and become part of my existence. I never saw her again, but I looked with those eyes when in Europe I saw Zinat, my former cellmate. I lived that alienation when in the early years of coming to the United States, I went to parties where the conversation often revolved around beautiful dresses, good-looking "babes," and fancy cars. With the eyes of my soul, I looked for any sign by which this world could seem familiar to me or any path that would lead me to this "strange" world. How many times it failed me!

A few nights later, I had a dream in which, while standing up, I was tied to a metallic bed. I was in a large room with several interrogators who were speaking loudly to one another, laughing hysterically and taunting me. They all had whips in their hands and once in a while were whipping me. But I felt that the real torture had not yet started, and I was impatiently and fearfully anticipating it. It felt like all my nerves were stretching to the point of being torn apart, and my brain cells were burning with the buzzing of a thousand bees. I woke up frustrated, agitated, and nervous. The whole day I thought, what was it that helped me survive that impossible situation? How did I die without dying, and how can I live each day as if my last day? Contemplating the state of my being, only then did I realize the selves that had died within me without my recognition. I realized how silent I had become, a silence characterized by carrying on meaningless conversation and by my absurd talkativeness.

In Whose Voice?

What had happened to my promises, those that I made in the cemetery on my departure day? It is not that I have forgotten them. It is just that there is no one way of forgetting. I had forsaken my promises in the very act of living in them all the time and not being able to step back and look them in the face in order to recognize them. To be faithful to my promise and my experience, I had to betray them, to detach from them, and to move out of them. This could allow me to live with and remember them. It is impossible to provide an intact image of what happened in prison. Nobody is able to do that. I am talking about it, as others have, so I do not forget and yet to free myself from its haunting, imprisoning power. But in order not to forget, I must see it as outside of me, in narrating it, in remembering it as something that occurred in the past. The task is complicated. What I remember is my memory; it could never be an utter narration of what happened in the past, but rather what I remember and experience today as my feelings and memories of then. Yet it is the life that my mind and body remember and of which I herein write.

But for whom am I writing? Is it possible to find a space and a language that are faithful to the experience? How might I avoid essentializing the particular experiences of political prisoners in a specific moment of Iranian history yet also avoid reducing the experience to the act of cruelty of an Islamic state, as has often been done by the West and even many Iranians? What would be the best way to personalize the event without ignoring and detaching it from the larger sociopolitical and historical context within which each person has come to experience it? In what form and style might I relate my own story along with those of others, wherein their voices could be heard as powerfully as but distinct from mine? Is it even possible for others to have a voice of their own while their experience has to pass through the filter of my subjective memory and my writing? These questions will continue to haunt this text.

Writing about prison is not an easy task. It is challenging to attempt to describe these intense emotional and physical experiences in a nonsensual and abstract piece of writing. Such writing often turns an intimate personal experience into a public matter, into objectified evidence, one more document, to prove the state's atrocity. There was yet another dilemma with which I wrestled: how could I write about certain aspects of this experience while leaving the rest untold? What would the ramifications of this selectiveness be in my own immediate life? As I began thinking about writing, the ghostly presence of those prisoners who had gone mad became overwhelming. My waking hours were filled with their memories, and my dreams became the stage on which their "otherness" was enacted. I was tempted to convince myself that I was writing to give voice to those who were voiceless. But I asked myself, if so, why not write about those who have been executed without having the chance to write their last will? Why should I think that I am able to give voice to those whose deaths could speak for them much louder than my life and my physical existence? How was I going to be faithful in giving voice to these others from whom I had been so painfully removed and subsequently estranged? I could have easily been buried beside them in 1988, if not earlier.

The debate about the mass executions of 1988 has always been very rancorous among Iranian political prisoners and activists. They argued over whether or not the prisoners knew that they were being taken for execution in the last moments of their lives and if having the knowledge would have made any difference in the way they answered the few questions in the court that determined their life or death. Many of those male prisoners who had accepted the regime's conditions, and therefore had escaped their "destiny," attempted to convince others that the knowledge of imminent death would have changed the strategies of the condemned. These survivors had their own integrity at stake. It was seemingly essential for them to prove that their cooperation with the regime was an informed decision, based on knowledge, and not a betrayal or a gesture of weakness in their resistance.

On the other hand, the women who had lived and gone through long periods of torture in prison, both physically and psychologically, and survived the loss of their loved ones, insisted that their resistance and refusal to submit were not merely emotional, irrational, womanly behavior or a stubborn or sentimentally heroic gesture, as suggested by some male political prisoners and sometimes even their own families. It was rather, they argued, a necessary response to a situation in which their submission would turn them into vegetative beings.

Whatever the essence of these subjective debates, both sides based their arguments on the assumption that death and silence are inexorably correlated. This assumption appeared perplexing when accepted by prisoners who had themselves so often experienced blurry boundaries. Many political prisoners had faced interrogation and torture, wherein silence defined the essence of one's existence. Death, on the other hand, sometimes cried out with an eloquence that opened up a far greater space of communication than physical existence could have. Prisons are to isolate the unfit, inappropriate, and nonconformist other from the rest of society. Yet within the interior, isolated world of prison, a plurality of otherness is brought into existence and a simulated hierarchical society is created. The interrogators' relationships to the prisoners vary depending on the quality and level of the prisoners' involvement in the opposition movement, their position in their organizations, resistance to torture, gender, class and ethnic identities, and even physical appearance. The hierarchy, however, is neither limited to the prison officials nor to these variables. Prisoners draw many other boundaries that erect invisible walls between them within the prison walls.

Executed prisoners belong to a terrain that we cannot enter unless we give up on our lives or perhaps our sanity. Surviving almost always insinuates suspicion about the survivor's compromised integrity—at least an assumption that if not executed, she or he did not pose a serious threat to the regime as a dissident. The survivor herself usually lives with guilt even when she is aware that inmates' lives and deaths were so often determined arbitrarily, sometimes simply based on gender, political and religious affiliation, or family background.

While the world of death shuts its door on the living, madness ruptures the soul as the body continues its existence. Madness touches death's fiery fingertips, flies on its wings, and climbs up its doorstep but does not totally enter into its world. The dream of death fills the gap in a shattered world and the pieces through which a mad person travels. That is how madness and death come face-to-face at the crossroads of an unknown other world. Yet sheer physical existence distinguishes death and madness in a relatively radical manner. We see the strange behavior and make judgments about it, but our knowledge of what is beyond death adds up to almost nothing. I am on this side of the world where I can still be seen, be judged, and judge. I have met death face-to-face but have not been allowed—luckily or unluckily?—to set foot in its mystified "garden." The ominous thought of falling into the darkness of this endless well captivated me as I watched those who were so severely isolated from the rest of us, and the possibility of opening any space to speak from that well was dramatically diminished. Neither my parents nor I was more horrified of death than of crossing the line into the strange world of madness. The only way I convinced my parents not to force me to submit to the regime's condition of release was to tell them that it would drive me crazy.

I did not submit, nor did I go crazy, but I felt the burden and the responsibility of giving voice to those who were, in one way or another, lost. Evading entrapment in the lives I was touching, sometimes perhaps briefly living within their world or visiting their threshold, I distanced myself from madness. Nevertheless, the potency of its shadowy presence chased me, made my body shiver, shook me to my bones, and smashed my shell. A year and half after she was released, two months after my departure, Mahvash, a physician who was imprisoned for nine years, committed suicide. I sensed the danger then. I, however, did not completely comprehend its significance and normalcy until I heard more news of suicide by those who were "free."

Comprehending these attempts to complete the job that the interrogators had left unfinished seemed a very challenging task to undertake. Far more challenging was the way in which I was, somewhat unconsciously, identifying with them. I did not fathom the enigmas of this outside world any more than they did. I realized that I was not writing, or dreaming, about my experience, or more accurately, did not know what I was dreaming about; nor was I aware if I was even dreaming at all. It was a state of despair, a space of silence and lost voice. I was no longer even singing to myself as I used to. Horrified by this realization, I reluctantly began to write, and my writings were saturated with the ghosts of the dead and the spirits of the mad. Roya was setting her table again in her little corner of the cell while barking and crawling in the hallway the next moment. Marjan's wrists were cut, and I was getting her undressed over and over with her beautiful eyes staring at me fearfully and angrily. I was saving her from death but forcing her deeper into a continuous hellish agony, fright, and melancholy. It became apparent to me that I could not tell my story unless it incorporated all these other voices and worlds, as giving voice to anyone else would inevitably involve my own story.

Another dimension revealed itself to me in the process of thinking and writing about my experience. I read what I had written a few years ago about my experience of emerging from prison and compared it to what I was writing now. I noticed an astonishing disparity that could be explained only by the relationship between experience, memory, and temporality. Bitterness had become the dominant flavor of my recent voice, which was almost absent in my earlier writings. I was fully aware that I had not lied about my feelings, yet there was such a contrast in these two ways of telling the story. None of the experiences were artificially created, but both were my perceptions of the moment that I had lived, and was reliving, them. However, I had not consciously intended to produce a certain tone. Rather, my retrospective differed in relation to various historical contexts. It became clear to me, as I wrote and reflected on my writing, that in light of temporality, the seemingly rigid, icy walls between past, present, and future melt and fade away. My recollection of the past creates a new life of its own, different from every other moment. While the past intervenes in my present life with a new color, flavor, and shade, the "I" who is living that past in the present is no longer the same as the "I" who experienced it then. The subject and the object are manifested differently in these temporally shaped instants; the past intrudes in the present, and the present reshapes the past and the future.

It is at this juncture and with these questions in mind that I am writing my story. Although the gaze will be mine and therefore the shade of my perception of the reality will dominate other shades, I intend to let others speak through me or, rather, let my multiple selves tell their stories.

2

Roya

THE THRESHOLD OF
IMAGINATION AND PHANTASM

The savage danger of madness is related to the danger of the passions and to their fatal concatenation.

—Michel Foucault, *Madness and Civilization*

A barzakh, writes Ibn-al-'Arabī, is something that separates two things while never going to one side, as for example the line that separates shadow from sunlight. There is nothing in existence but barzakhs, since a barzakh is the arrangement of one thing between two things . . . and existence has no edges.

—Stefania Pandolfo, *Impasse of the Angels*

When the man laughs, he already laughs with the laugh of death.

—Michel Foucault, *Madness and Civilization*

Begging to Remain a Human

Stop it, please! Stop it! I wished I could tell Roya to stop, but I felt totally mute. All I could see was her skinny, delicate body crawling like a beaten, injured dog in the midst of hundreds of feet. The ward was so crowded that I thought she would be crushed under the feet of other prisoners, who I was not sure had seen this fragile body. Even her barking wasn't heard since prisoners were talking to one another and the ward was filled with noise. But my eyes were fixed on her as she crawled, barked, and begged Sister Bakhtiyari to allow her to stop barking and crawling—"Sister" was the title by which prisoners were to refer to the women guards; all the male prison personnel, from guards to interrogators, were to be called "Brother." Refusing to refer to the prison officials as sisters and brothers was itself another reason for punishment.

Roya was still barking and asking Sister Bakhtiyari, a notorious guard in Gohar Dasht Prison, to let her stop. I wished I could help her to stop. I wished I could make her understand that there was no guard there and no one was asking her to bark or crawl anymore, but I could not. Why didn't I hold her in my arms, comfort her, and assure her that she was safe, at least in that moment? Why couldn't I? Had I become paralyzed while I was walking? Was I afraid of her? But how could I be scared of such a harmless, beautiful young woman who was in such enormous pain?

I wonder whether the fear and emotional intensity with which Roya was living were not in fact reminding me of my own fear, pain, and worries. If Roya had actualized her anticipation of the torture so that there was no distinction between imaginary and real torment, for many of us the world of our nightmares had turned into the terrain where this perplexity played itself out. Many inmates screamed while sleeping but kept themselves busy during the day and managed to act normally. Torture and humiliation in prison are brutal hunters waiting for an opportunity to seize their prey; our nights could simply turn into reality the day after, sometimes in the same night.

The fear of losing it, of not being able to disengage ourselves from this horror that was haunting us at night, could also lead us to the endless agony in which Roya was lost. For her, the experience of the past, the past in which she was forced to bark like a dog, and the possibility of its recurrence in her mind now and in the future were turned into one seamless reality. It was perhaps the realization of this similarity between our own nightmares and Roya's reality that rendered her status so horrifying to us. We tried to keep our distance from what appeared to be the threshold of madness.

Roya was still crying and promising Sister Bakhtiyari that she would be a "good girl" and never again would violate the rules, that she would not tap on the wall of her cell to talk to her neighbor in another cell. She was begging the sister to let her be herself again, a human being, not a dog. Haunted by her traumatic experience, she was reliving the torture repeatedly. The wound was inflicted not merely upon her body but also her mind. Roya was repeating her torment in her mind, as she kept crying, screaming, covering her face and her head—apparently from beatings—while crawling without a direction. She was circling around, back and forth, side to side, in a desperate gesture of trying to escape the torture.

ﻉ

paradox of children, solemn savagery

—Yacine Kateb, *Nedjma*

I was six years old, I remembered:

The dog was sadly wailing, running around with its eyes covered by the black scarf that the boys had forcefully taken from my head. It was a very cold winter, and the snow was over my knees. Four or five elementary school boys were holding big sticks in their hands, chasing the dog wherever it ran and beating it while hysterically laughing. The dog's voice was growing coarser as this sadistic game continued. The snow had turned to bloody red wherever the dog walked. It was on its knees, on its side, on its back, and they were still beating and laughing. My voice had almost disappeared as I screamed to stop them. I was smaller than them and only one against four. Over and over, I begged them to stop, but they wouldn't. The largest boy was taunting me while beating the dog even more hysterically. Others followed him in beating the dog and taunting me. They even repeated his words, as if parrots. One of the boys said to me, teasingly, "You idiot, you are crying for this dog? Don't you know that dogs don't feel or understand anything?" I wondered why he beat the poor dog if he thought it was not feeling anything? Was he lying to himself or to me?

ﻉ

How many times have I heard this in prison, that we were nothing but brainless dogs? It was not surprising that Bakhtiyari had forced Roya to act like a dog. Under both the Shah and the Islamic Republic, the torturers forced the prisoners to play different animals' roles, especially dogs and donkeys. One of the torturers' hobbies was getting a ride from these prisoner-donkeys.

"Roya was my student in high school: such a sweet and brilliant student she was," Aki, one of the inmates, told me, during one of those insane evenings when Roya had once again crawled and begged not to be a dog for an hour or so. But now she had stopped crawling and was back in her cell, squatting in a corner with her arms tightly holding her knees. It was amazing how little space she occupied. I can still vividly recall the first time that I saw her in the yard. It was 1984 when seventy prisoners, I among them, were taken from Evin Prison in Tehran to Ghezel Hesar in Karadj. During the last few months, many of us were taken for interrogation and repeated torture. We had to listen to the confessions of prisoners, many of them our close friends. These were prisoners who had gone through Haji Davoud's *dastgah* and had agreed to collaborate with the interrogators. The information that they produced pushed many of us back into the torture rooms. During these melancholic months, the omnipresent shadow of fear had become the flavor of our food, of any sip of water we drank, the invisible force that woke us from our sleep, and the exhaustion that pushed us into ceaseless, nightmarish battles.

The rumor was that a place existed, *dastgah*, and that whoever was taken there came out broken, defeated, either crazy or a ruthless collaborator. Then one day it was our turn to go. The prison officials threatened that they were taking us to *jāei keh Arab ney andākht*, a place where a legendary Arab had dropped his *ney*, a flutelike musical instrument. This expression implied that we were going somewhere from which there was no return, so remote and deserted a place that it would be as if an Arab had dropped his *ney* in a desert. Finding a *ney* in the desert, no matter how attached to it an Arab might be, according to this story, is nearly impossible, perhaps because it is so hard to find directions in the desert and because the dust and dirt would soon cover anything that falls on the ground. The expression was to warn us that where we were being taken was so deserted that we would be lost to outsiders as if we were a *ney* under the dust in the desert.

After being transferred from Evin to Ghezel Hesar, for three days we were kept in a big hall to be taken to that "nowhere." During these days, we breathed the air of *barzakh*, sat so close to hell that it barely separated us from hell's fire. We nevertheless ate, slept, talked to one another, laughed, sang, and continued to live our lives. Survival in prison—surviving the madness, suicide, and collaboration—requires holding on to hope when it seems so remote and so unreachable. Sometimes torture stops when you do not or cannot see any end to it. Against this hope, interrogators try to create an atmosphere of the eternity of horror so that the prisoner loses sight of any possible ending. Yet there are times when the end comes, precisely at the moment one may not have expected. The joy of the end is, however, often tarnished by the terrifying question in the prisoner's mind, what if the end had not come? A woman who was in jail during the 1980s explains these precarious moments between her own state of despair and the end of torture: "Half consciously, I thought if these interrogators were not such idiots, they would have known the state of mind of a prisoner in each moment. If they did, how horrible the outcome would have been! They would have gotten what they wanted much faster. Of course they were not idiots all the time. Probably those prisoners who were whipping their own friends, or participating in their execution had been caught in the state that I was last night."

All of a sudden, our anticipation for the torments that were awaiting us in the *dastgah* came to an end, though our pondering of the "what if?" question continued. We were not taken to "nowhere" since the whole process stopped as a result of prisoners' families' pressure and the conflict within the regime over this system of punishment. Instead, they took us to a ward that was already overpopulated. Entering that ward was one of my most grotesque experiences in prison. As soon as the metallic door was opened and we were pushed in, we were squeezed into a small hall where we saw hundreds of women jammed behind the bars, like animals in their cages. The bars separated this small entrance hall, called *zir-e hasht,* from the main hall, in which twelve cells, six on each side, were located. The cells were also separated from the main hall by similar black metal bars, which made them appear more like cages than the rooms or cells in which I had lived in different wards in Evin Prison.

While we were jammed in this *zir-e hasht,* where the warden's office was located, waiting to be assigned our cells and to be added to the list of prisoners in this ward, women on the other side gathered behind bars; some even climbed the bars to watch us. I wondered which of us looked more bizarre, they or we? We in the *zir-e hasht* were just emerging from three days of surreal life, waiting to be thrown into hell, but had suddenly found ourselves in a place that appeared more like a purgatory (somewhat like a *barzakh*). At the time, we had no idea why we had not been taken to the *dastgah.* Neither did we know what was awaiting us in this new ward. Were we about to be tossed into a hell from here, or could there be another "destiny-ation," a salvation perhaps, either here or some way out of this place? We had no idea! From where I was standing and eyeing the other side, the place awaiting us looked more like a madhouse. In a few days, however, I would forget this image since I would be immersed in it; I would be inside it, making my own noise.

At the moment, of those on the other side of the metal bars in the main hall, I knew very little; thus, I returned their eager, anxious stares. In shock, I watched these women who, one after another, in small and large groups, hurried out of their cells, as if bees out of their hives, toward the metal bars behind which we were compressed in that small space. It took a long day, or at least so it felt under the eyes of so many people watching, to be sent into the ward.

In the ward, there was no guard because the collaborators from the *dastgah* were doing the guards' work for them. Only rarely would a guard, male or female, depending on the situation, come to the ward or to the office. The head of the ward was a former leftist, Homa Kalhor, who used to be a close friend of one of our fellow prisoners. She was the one who asked us our name and information, including questions about our past political affiliations and present ideas, and entered them all on her list.

She told us about the rules so authoritatively that it was as though she had been a warden all her life. The absurdity of the rules made any person of a right mind wonder how someone with her background could even speak of these rules, let alone oversee their implementation. But soon we would learn what it meant to be a collaborator in Haji Davoud's *dastgah*.

Those prisoners who had been in jail longer than I had begun to recognize faces among the ones on the other side, some of whom had clearly become collaborators. One's scream of joy for recognizing a friend was interrupted by another's deep sigh followed by a squeeze of a friend's hand to hold her fearful silence at the sight of a collaborator who was once a friend. Uncertainty about who was a friend, emotional confusion, and exhausting anticipation were all mixed up in the cacophony of noises and erratic movements. Seeing Homa Kalhor as the head of the ward shocked our friend so much that she became very pale and began to vomit. Her migraine attack was getting the worst of her, and she could not stand on her feet. We tried to create a comfortable space in this impossibly crowded and noisy place.

Suddenly, in the midst of all this chaos, I noticed a woman sitting in a corner of the *zir-e hasht*, motionless as a statue. I could not understand why she was separated from the others and why she was sitting with her back toward them, so immobile that one could find no trace of life in her except that her eyes were open, though I never learned whether she saw anything with those frozen but open eyes. I noticed that she was breathing very slowly; her face had the appearance of a dusty ghost, while her disheveled hair seemed like that of someone rising from the grave. The pungent smell of her unchanged clothes gave me a headache. How easy it was to go mad in this peculiar place!

Melancholic Evenings and Madness

It was in this bizarre place that I saw Roya for the first time, on one of those evenings when the prisoners were pouring out of their cells like lava from a volcano. In prison, evenings are the worst part of the day. They are a time of restlessness, loud conversation to escape madness, and a descent into madness. Evenings in prison are filled with worries, fright, pain, and boredom. Evenings are the beginning of a beginning and of an end: the end of a day with all the conflicts and struggles to keep—even if just the mask of—courage, resistance, and vitality alive while a long night of battle is just beginning. At night, one enters the realm through which the bird of unconscious desires and passions freely flies. These flights are extremely terrifying, especially during the interrogation period. What if you talked while you were asleep and somebody heard you? What if you demonstrated some inappropriate behavior or desire while you were asleep? These were concerns that deprived prisoners of sleep.

The trauma of evening extends beyond prison so that it affects prisoners' feelings about this time of the day for years to come. I still remember my childhood in our village when people would mysteriously talk about this ghostly time during which all the jinns and witches would wander about, seeking their victims. I remember how fascinated I was with my grandparents' and my aunt's tales. The invisible monstrous evils hid in the trees, especially in the large ones, waiting for the ignorant, careless people who sleep under them in the evenings. The morning after, they were found dead, for late at night, the evil beings blew their heavy breath on them and put them in a deadly sleep from which they never awoke.

On such an evening I saw Roya in Ward 7 in Ghezel Hesar, where we had been taken after waiting three days to be sent to Haji's *dastgah*. As on most evenings, everybody was walking restlessly, bumping into others, and speaking loudly. Suddenly my eyes caught sight of a frightened deer in the shape of a beautiful young woman. Roya was trying to escape the crowd but seemed entrapped. She looked like an angel in a fairy tale, with a face so beautiful and so perfect, as if painted by a master painter. Her large, frightened, innocent eyes stared at everyone yet seemed to see none of us. She was arrested before she was eighteen. Nobody knew exactly what had happened to her in prison. All we knew was that she was kept in solitude, in the notorious Gohar Dasht Prison, for a long time.

Obviously, she had been severely tortured. We knew she had been put in a cell without any light for several nights, a common punishment in Gohar Dasht, from which she had come out mad. What was this young, fragile-looking, most likely middle-class woman thinking in those long, dark nights, away from her family and friends, with guards punishing her for any violation of the rules, as trivial as coughing?

乄

Almost as obsessively narrow and repetitive as the pain on which it models itself, torture can be more easily seen because it has dimension and depth, a space that can be walked around in though not walked out of.

—Elaine Scarry, *The Body in Pain*

And I remembered:

The interrogator opened a small metallic door and pushed me into a small cell. "You have two seconds to tell me who you are and what orga-nization you are involved with," he whispered with a strange tone in his voice. I had just begun to say that I had already told them who I was, but before my sentence was finished, I was on the floor vomiting. It happened so fast that all I could remember was a sharp pain in my belly. Something burned inside me. It felt as if a monster had opened its mouth in my ab-domen, a huge hole that swallowed all the evils of the world that induce pain and devastation. His boot was still on my chador, and I vaguely remembered his fast, severe kick that felt so deep inside me. Before I could get up, he kicked me in the head. I tried to take refuge in a corner that he could not reach. I hid my head and face in my hands and made myself as small as I could, so as to give him less surface to strike. But now there were two interrogators; when did the second one come in? I did not know. They had caught me in the corner. My body had become a punching bag, a target for them to hone their sadistic skills. Every punch made me let go of my hands to protect some other parts of my body, but I was always slower than the blows.

乄

Prisoners' desperate and vain attempts to move to the corners to avoid beatings are reinforced and taken advantage of by the torturers who surround and trap them, as hunters catch their prey. That Roya often retreated to the corner of her cell, from the agony of her memory of torture, which for her was not a memory but a living reality her mind perpetuated, reenacted this scene of hunting. Her retreat to the corner of her cell was a walking into, rather than out of, torture. She lived her torture in a span of time that stretched and tied her past experiences to the present moment, in such a way that it was neither past nor present. She could not live a different moment in the present, for her mind was reliving her torturous time in Gohar Dasht, while the past was still felt as an experience of the here and now, an experience of the present.

The stark contrast between our modern perceptions, which rely so heavily on precision, clear distinctions, and dichotomies, and the world of delirium in which the boundaries and borders are blurred, is further accentuated in prisoners' remembrance of their traumatic experiences in which memory and reality are fused. For the rational mind, time is fixed in a rigid frame with its linear direction from past to future; reality is perceived to be distinct from imagination and remembering. In Roya's reliving Sister Bakhtiyari's punishment, the past appeared in the present, and the present became the past; places, Gohar Dasht (Meadow of Jewel) and Ghezel Hesar (Golden Fence), were mixed up. With the sense of time lost, neither past nor future existed. Roya lived in a present that was not really a present.

The only moment relived out of this hideous all-present past was the state of suspense in which Roya awaited the dreadful return of Sister Bakhtiyari to once again force her to bark and crawl like a dog, all playing out in her mind. What kinds of emotions did this forced behavior invoke in Roya that it stayed with her even more colorful, vivid, and present than the torture that had forced her to submit to these humiliating acts? Or was the pain so deeply, intensely, and enduringly engraved on her body and mind that she had to bark and crawl, hoping that it would stop, as when she had barked and crawled so Sister Bakhtiyari would no longer beat her and inflict pain? It was this space of suspension, this *barzakh*, where the blaze of the past still burned the injured body of the tortured person, where the flame of the upcoming hell scorched the mind before it reached the body in which we lived from one evening to another.

It was this uncertainty with which a prisoner had to come to terms and live. Failing to do so could result in being imprisoned in the torturous moment, in one's inability to move out of it, which would mean to lose the capacity to create and live with history, memory, and imagination. Without a past, one has no sense of history; without a space for remembrance, forgetting does not take place, for the past becomes a subject of possible forgetting only if it is separated from the present by being transformed into a memory that can be recollected, remembered, and hence in some ways forgotten. A frozen present, like that in which Roya was imprisoned, blocks the possibility of imagination and precludes the possibility of differentiating between reality and illusion. The imaginary becomes, albeit elusive and illusive, reality.

Torture generates an impasse. The extensive pain inflicted on a person's body and soul throws one into a state of vacillation and confusion, between memory and experience, that tarnishes the person's ability to separate the frontiers of imagining and seeing. Under torture, time seems unimpeded, an eternity; there is no memory before or after that. In the climax of this calamity, the world vanishes, and all that is left is the unlimited pain extending forever. Of this destruction of all distinctions in the face of the pain of torture, a former Iranian woman prisoner, also in the 1980s, remembers: "Counting, cursing, or imagining my loved ones' faces no longer had any effect in reducing the pain of the lashes. I could no longer even tell where on my body the lashes were hitting. Each blow was running through my whole body as an electrical shock, a sharp pain all over my body." Under torture, even death with its grinning smile—how often it is longed for!—does not exist for the person for whom life no longer offers anything but pain and suffering. In the absence of a past, or in the present that has been obliterated by the past, memory becomes obsolete, nonexistent. Imagination loses its reality—a paradoxical phenomenon—

for while the world of delirium is reduced to the world of the imaginary, the nightmares in the act of imagining draw the real out of the subject's world. This impairment in perception clouds the space between anticipation of torture and its real occurrence.

A Party in the Clouds

The cells, about 1.5 to 2.5 square meters in size, which were at the moment occupied by at least ten people, had the capacity for three people at the most. There was not enough space for all of us to be in a cell at the same time. Some of us therefore had to walk, sit, and sleep in the hall, which was always overcrowded. Once in a while when nobody else was in her cell, Roya would prepare for her imaginary guests. During these occasions of privacy, she sometimes sat on the first level of the three-tiered bed in a dark corner, while her eyes fearfully looked around, as if waiting for something horrible to happen. At other times, however, her eyes sparkled with the delight of some imaginary loved ones' imminent arrival. She pretended that she was cooking and preparing a cake, and how delicately she would enact this cooking ceremony! She would put her imaginary pots on a nonexistent stove, gently and graciously, and while now and then checking the food, she would mix her bread and dates with water to make a cake.

She would then set the table meticulously. The manner in which she arranged the flowers, the silver, and the plates on the table demonstrated her urban middle-class background. Sometimes she was apparently expecting more than one guest, since she would put out more than two plates and sets of silver, while on other occasions she would set the table evidently for one person. During these hours of preparation, she appeared to experience such an extraordinary peace as if nothing existed beyond this little world of hers and her guests. She worked cheerfully, and when she was done, she stood at her doorsill and waited, sometimes for such a long time that she grew impatient. There was a haze of sorrow on her face and in her beautiful eyes every time they disappointed her by not coming.

However, on those occasions when they did arrive, she became as revitalized as blossoms in the spring. She would invite them in, sometimes very formally, and other times very intimately and informally; obviously some were distant friends or relatives and others close family members or dear friends. She would seat them and passionately engage them in conversation, which none of us could hear. These conversations varied from friendly and loving talks to serious discussions and even arguments, which we could distinguish from one another by her facial expressions and her body postures. She would then kiss them good-bye after an hour or so. I wonder why I don't recall what she usually did after they left?

Day after day, I sat in the corner of my cell and watched her through the bars, fascinated by the precision in her preparations, and the passion and eagerness in her behavior. I was puzzled by her varied emotions and demeanor during these different episodes. Although it seemed as if she were different persons in different moments, a similar thread was weaving all of her actions together. There was an innocence in her character that she may have been carrying from her past, or it could have been a return to a childlike state as a result of trauma beyond her capacity to bear. Was she a well-nurtured, if not overnurtured, child of a wealthy, loving family where she was always taken care of and had not felt the need to grow up? But where did she get her talent to host guests? Was the trauma an element of a swift journey to the time during which things were not so complicated and where a loving mother and father were always there for her?

Roya herself seemed to perceive her situation as a consequence of torture, for in her conversation with her former high school teacher, Aki, the only prisoner she ever talked to while in Ghezel Hesar, she suggested that "they [apparently the guards] melted my brain so that there remained nothing in it except water." This conversation with Aki occurred on one of Roya's lucky days on which her loved ones had come. When Aki told her that she was her high school teacher, amazingly Roya recognized her almost immediately. I wonder if this remembrance and the following conversation were not in fact evoked by the place she was in, an imaginary present, yet another past in which she could host the guests and was a high school student. For the first time since our coming to this ward, she calmly walked alongside others and conversed with Aki about high school; suddenly, she seemed to be jerked back into the site of torture. Aki did not know what had engendered this sudden change of mood, but Roya had begun speaking, no longer calmly and coherently but like someone pulled from a comfortable place, someone about to be drowned. In fragments she spoke to Aki before departing the present moment with another flight to Gohar Dasht.

"Full of cockroaches and mice, everywhere, my cell, I screamed, begged. She is very bad. The cell is dark, very dark. I cry; I beg. My brain was melted. She did it. She hit me on my head over and over. I know I am stupid because they destroyed my brain. See, touch it. It is only water. Oh my God, only water is left. She hates me. I do not want to bark, but she beats me. Please, please, Sister Bakhtiyari, I won't be bad again. It is dark, very dark. Sister Bakhtiyari, please, please let me out. I will not do it again. Please let me out."

Aki had tried to keep Roya from falling into that space again. She had tried to get her to talk. She had asked what she had done that was so bad. But Roya was vacillating between two worlds, struggling not to sink in.

"Oh, I was a bad girl. But don't hit me on my head. Please, Sister Bakhtiyari, I won't tap on the wall any more. I didn't mean it. I was just bored, lonely, Sister Bakhtiyari. My back is hurting. Please let me stand up. I'll be a good girl. You know what they did [obviously, now she is talking to Aki]; they put a device in my head that sucks out all my brain's contents. I know when I sleep they insert a pipe to fill water in my head. That's why my brain is so swollen. There were scars on my head when I woke up. It was dark, very dark. Mice were walking on my head, tasting my blood. You don't tell them I have told you this, do you? They'll kill me. They want me to bark again. Please, Sister Bakhtiyari, I have been a dog today for a long time. Don't hit me; OK, I crawl and bark. They melt my brain. I know I'm crazy. They took my brain away. I begged and begged.

They hit me with a big stick. My head is rotten. I know. That is why I look so stupid."

She had already almost departed the present moment when Aki asked her who those people were who were melting her brain. She had first remained silent for a while, as though thinking and looking for an answer, but then had emerged momentarily only to say: "Oh, I have to go. If they see me with you, they will put me in that dark cell again." The entire evening after this conversation she had squatted in the corner of her cell, tightly holding her knees.

We, other inmates, talked about Roya and watched her curiously, sympathetically, but always from a distance that seemed so immense and yet so slight. When she was preparing for her guests, we recognized our own games in hers. Didn't we all play such games to keep our spirits high, to be in touch with something rather than the horror of torture, and to remember the innocence and the joy of our childhood?

Prior to every Iranian New Year, we took days to clean up our cells as though they were our own homes. We embraced the risk of stealing soil and seeds on our way to the clinic, to interrogation, or to our family meetings, so that we could plant our New Year *sabzeh*, the green plants we grow for the New Year as a symbol of growth. We reshaped the plastic dishwashing detergent containers into a vase and planted flowers. With great pleasure we took all the risks to prepare the items we needed for a perfect celebration of New Year or other similar occasions. What was it then that defined Roya's behavior and her game as abnormal and ours as creative and reflective of our resilience? What were the decisive factors allowing us to perceive her theatrical reenactment of cooking and hosting guests as delusional and ours as an imaginative and politically solid act?

On one level, the resemblance between our games and those of Roya seems striking. Despite their theatricality, both of us, the resistant prisoners and Roya, considered these ceremonious acts to be deadly serious. An essential element of resistance in prison is the refusal to let torturers take over one's life and turn its every moment into another source of pain.

Prisoners insist on their humanity and struggle to assert themselves as social and creative beings. Regimes of surveillance, however, despise and confront any insinuation of resistance to their totalizing and individualizing systems. Prisoners gather all their personal and sociocultural resources to engender an atmosphere of joy, creativity, and rejuvenation, whereas the torturers target any potential sign of happiness and imaginative creation of lively moments among prisoners.

IT IS IN THE FACE of this resilient creativity, not merely of artistic production but of artistic ways of upholding one's spirit of joy and life, that torture loses its ability to destroy. No wonder that in all these years in jail, both under the Shah and in this regime, I realized that prison officials treated any indication of sympathy for someone and any refusal to comply with authority as a criminal and rebellious act, for which prisoners deserved to be severely punished. In fact, the event leading to the establishment of Haji Davoud's *dastgah* was a minor event undertaken by a group of prisoners who simply cared about their integrity and about one another.

In Ghezel Hesar, prisoners were forced to attend regular public confessions given by other prisoners. The goal of these confessions was twofold: to humiliate both the speaker and the listener while annulling prisoners' trust and confidence in themselves and one another; and to give the regime another opportunity for demonizing any opposition organization. More important, Haji Davoud claimed that he was concerned about the immorality of his prisoners, who, he suggested, were a deadly danger to society. He accused the leftist prisoners of being nonbelievers—sex-crazy, corrupt individuals who lacked any values or morals, who shared their women with one another. For some unknown reason we were accused of being spies for both the United States and Russia, either knowingly or unknowingly.

Listening to these confessions was so emotionally disturbing for other prisoners that they preferred to resist attending them and hence be seriously punished than to suffer the pain of bearing witness to these humiliating recantations—an attempt that wasn't always successful since they were usually dragged to the confessions. In this quarrel against the forced witnessing of the humiliation of our former comrades, we challenged the regime's attempt to shatter our integrity. This was a quarrel against participating in the despicable show of brutality that subjected our comrades' humanity as well as that of our own. Our resistance renounced the ruthless demonstration of technologies of power exercised on human flesh and souls.

On a normal day in 1983, a day not worse than any other day in prison, a guard came to one of the women's wards and announced a new session of confessions for that day. She also ordered the group responsible for the day's cleaning to take carpets to the hall where all the prisoners would sit and watch the show. Cleaning the ward was usually a voluntary job organized by prisoners in our ward. But now, this newly imposed duty created conflicts and various reactions among prisoners: some believed that fighting against Haji Davoud's order would be too dangerous since his reputation for punishment was well established. Others argued that complying with the order implied our collaboration in the regime's attempt to destroy us as free subjects. The volcano erupted when the day's work group announced that they did not believe it was their responsibility to prepare for the confessions and refused to do it. Haji Davoud's blood rushed to his face as he heard the prisoners' response. A new phase of anticipation began, and until late in the evening when Haji was through with his show for the day and came to the ward, prisoners experienced a life of *barzakh* again. Haji announced the names of thirty people whom he considered instigators of the movement. The beating started, and before long, some of the prisoners were wrapped in blankets and rolled over like a ball from one guard to another while being beaten brutally and violently.

In contrast to claims that suggest we cannot feel others' pain, my experience is that watching other prisoners being tortured is extremely unbearable. I strongly relate to the words of a woman inmate who was jailed at the same time I was under the Islamic Republic: "When it was

your turn to be tortured your body was in pain, but when it was somebody else's, it was your soul that was being tortured." Even though I
think when one is tortured, never merely one's body but also one's soul
is inflicted with pain, I still think the way one's soul burns while one
witnesses others' pain differs from being tortured oneself. What Haji
Davoud labeled as a preplanned rebellion was a natural reaction initiated by one of the prisoners who, unable to continue watching her
friends' suffering, protested the beating by simply saying, "Don't beat."
Her words were contagious, mainly because the feeling was commonly
shared. Other prisoners also began saying, "Don't beat," and in a few
minutes all the prisoners in the hall were repeating, "Don't beat." Haji
Davoud found this incredible. "How could you dare to protest under my
authority and in my prison? You'll pay such a high price for this; just
wait and watch!" They were sent back to the ward with broken heads,
arms, ribs, but this was only a sample of what was on its way. The fire of
hell was just being ignited.

IT IS THIS DYNAMIC of power relations that was exemplified in prisoners' untiring attempts to preserve their connection to rituals, tradition,
innovation, and creativity as part of their humanness, to keep their sense
of empathy alive, qualities that were the object of suppression under
the regimes of surveillance. Trying to justify our unspoken but ongoing
struggle with the prison officials over such "trivial things" as our New
Year tradition would be impossible unless it is explained and seen in its
symbolic and temporary contexts.

According to Iranian culture, New Year is the time for a fresh start,
and we must remove all the contamination of the old year in every way,
materially and spiritually. Cleaning up, dusting, and trying to solve old
problems with family members, neighbors, and friends are some of the
tasks taken up before New Year. The idea that if you haven't cleaned
your place, the whole year you will be a mess was considered a funny
idea and somehow superstitious for many of us modern intellectuals before we were imprisoned. However, once in prison, keeping this tradi-

tion alive was a determining element in feeling connected to our larger community and its social life. It also gave us incredible relief and a sense of renewal to work hard for ourselves and feel the energy of our free will in our veins.

When we first began to celebrate the New Year, it was probably a natural reaction to our cultural background and an effort to feel connected. The action taken upon our celebration intensified our energies and stimulated our persistence as if it were a matter of life and death. One of the ways in which the guards would confront us was by pouring dirty water in our cells right after we had cleaned them up and just moments before the New Year, so that we could not have time to clean it up again. Hot water would usually be shut down right before the New Year. For two years, the guards inspected our ward to discover the plants we had grown specifically for the celebration. We planted and trimmed them in a way that they would grow in different shapes, such as migrating birds, stars, the moon, and the sun.

The struggles over these plants were extremely emblematic and symbolic. Both the prisoners and the guards were sharing the same symbolic culture according to which plants personified growth and vitality, depending on the context in which they were being metaphorically used. Designing these plants in such shapes, instead of their usual form, was to communicate another stratum of this symbolic representation that was more overtly political, although in prison every action taken was extremely political. *Freedom*, that illicit word in prison, was invisibly yet clearly inscribed in the wings of our plant-bird who could fly in the blue sky of our free imagination to release us from the imprisonment of our spirit. This was the reason that the guards would break the wings of our plants to illustrate that no wings would survive in this jail. When I once told my interrogator that they could not prevent the bird of my imagination and my spirit from flying beyond the imposed boundaries, he replied, "Forget about flying. We cut any wings that do not fly in our direction."

In Persian literature a migrating bird was metaphorically used as a messenger of spring. Thus, if a bird alluded to *freedom*, a taboo word, then a migrating bird, a bird that would fly to a warmer place during winter and fly back in spring, suggested an even stronger confrontation to the system. For the regime it indicated the prisoners' blunt proposition that winter would be over and spring with its generous smile would embrace every tortured body. "You are prisoners, and you are supposed to be in isolation. The changes of the season are not your business. Don't stick your nose in something that does not have anything to do with you, and don't assume that we are stupid and don't understand what you mean when you say the freezing cold winter is leaving and it has to give way to spring with its beautiful, generous, sunny smile." These are almost the exact words of Meisam, the head of the Ghezel Hesar ward in 1985, in response to the prisoners' complaints that their letters were not sent to their families. He indicated that we were only supposed to write our greetings and just formally say how we were doing. The irony of the censorship illustrated itself in the creativity of the prisoners in exploring new ways to resist, new symbols to employ to convey their message, and innovative tools to communicate their desire and emotions.

The embodiment of the deeper meaning of every action and reaction in prison was what made life in prison so intensely stressful and exhausting, immersed in pain and grief yet so saturated with marvels and exploration. Ordinary life could be charged by such intense political implications that the struggle to preserve it appeared existential.

It is in this light that our effort to celebrate New Year was considered so significant both for us and for the prison's officials. It is also this very act that, on the one hand, indicates an all-important resemblance between Roya's party and our games, while on the other hand distinguishing Roya from Donya. Donya, the woman who sat in the entrance section of the ward in Ghezel Hesar, motionless and totally withdrawn from the rest of the prisoners, seemed to have died before death. One saw in her no indication of life, dream, or imagination, no delusional pain or imaginary party, no reaction whatsoever such as that which Roya seemed to experience. Nothing appeared to exist for Donya, nothing inside or outside her. It was as if she could feel no pain or had no memory.

Unlike her, Roya was alive, even though in a world that was often out-side her present situation; she still felt and experienced emotions. Despite the resemblance between our creative acts and the imaginary party guests she hosted, however, her very imaginary, delusional parties separated our worlds, for she took them as real and we created them as a way of con-sciously resisting social isolation. Roya's imaginary guests connected her to another world, but still kept her, to some extent, connected to others. Roya was hence closer to "normal" since she still felt the desire to so-cialize and have conversations with others, a desire that had been lost to Donya. Paradoxically, this was exactly what typified Roya as "insane," probably even more so than Donya was. Where was this line drawn? Roya and the rest of us had the desire and the need to feel connected, to love and be loved by others, and still were able to feel emotions, cry, feel pain, fear, and disappointment. Donya lacked these qualities, at least as far as we were capable of understanding her—how does one understand a liv-ing person having turned into a statue? Sanity and insanity are categories, albeit with no fixed meaning or boundaries, that require each other in order to exist.

The world of civilized humanity, especially in the West, is the world of dichotomies and clear-cut distinctions: the physical or material world and the spiritual; the imaginary and the realistic, which is directly con-nected to the material world; as well as the emotional and the rational. The imagination is acceptable and sane only to the extent to which it reflects and is instantly related to the world of the real; otherwise, it is an illusion and an indication of insanity. Roya, though capable of feeling human need, desire, and emotions, at least to some extent, was basically detached from the real world. Instead, in her illusory world—because of the lack of connection to the exterior world—innovation, though it existed, appeared invisible. Except for her one conversation with Aki, she made no attempt to reach out to others in the ward. She had turned to her interior world, in which her mind would produce and reproduce a life of its own. She would suffer the lashes, beatings, humiliation that had no existence in the moment except in her memory and imagination, yet for her they were probably the only reality she was able to experience.

We, on the other hand, refusing to be detached from our fellow inmates, sought new ways to communicate with them even in our solitude. In the ward, our efforts concentrated on creating a life as cultural, social beings while accepting the reality of our situation in prison. Roya and Donya, however, had submitted to this isolation by disassociating themselves from it. This distinction between our world and Roya's was exemplified even in our relations to the objects we used for our social gatherings, parties, and celebrations.

We played the game by giving it a physical existence through either reshaping or creating objects that were required for such an occasion. Stealing seeds, making vases out of dishwashing containers, even making tools such as knives out of empty cans and sharpening them for hours were ways in which our imagination flew down from the clouds and from its haziness to the world of clarity and objective existence, to the world of creativity and productivity. Roya, however, played this game with her imaginary objects. She kept living in the clouds where, according to folk tales, dead people go. Roya was living in the world from which her mind had already departed. The world of death was crossing hers somewhere in the foggy sky.

One day in the middle of Roya's crawling and barking, the guard called out Roya's name. While leaving the ward to I don't know where, her skinny body, her pale face, and her distracted eyes looked so misty that she seemed made of vapor. While she walked toward the door, I felt that she was going to vanish before my eyes, not by going through the door but by evaporating into the air. Her deerlike eyes passed us, and I wondered if the image of any of us left any trace in them. Was she going to invite any of us from her imagination to her parties? Did these past months of her life in this bizarre ward have any impact on her? Was her world in any way affected by us? How far was she from the world of death? I never learned where they took her and what happened to her.

She came back to my dreams a couple of years ago with her innocent eyes staring at me, chasing me in my dreams, sometimes in my waking hours, and I asked myself over and over, Why didn't we try to approach her, find a way to communicate with her, and feel connected to her? Were we afraid? Afraid of what, and why?

Fozi

LOSING IT ALL

> If one knew in advance that everything, including one's self and the current state of affairs, was bad, what would there be to learn? What would be the sense of acting? Why think? A life without the possibility of error would not be conceivable. One might say . . . such a life would not be alive.
>
> —Paul Rabinow, *Essays on the Anthropology of Reason*

Lean as a lath, naked as a newborn baby, wrinkled as an old woman, with the earthworms marching over her skinny body, asleep or unconscious, Fozi had lain down on the wet floor of the bathroom. It was morning, a time of the day that we needed the bathroom more than ever. But Fozi had not left it for eighteen days now, and there was only one more bathroom left for about three hundred women in the ward. This had prevented us from using or cleaning it. The building was old and humid, and we had to wash and sterilize the bathrooms with chlorine every day in order to get rid of the worms. Now they had taken over the whole place—the walls and the floor were covered with them—and they were climbing over Fozi's slim body as though climbing a hill. During these days she had neither eaten nor drunk, and her face was so still and dusty that death would be frightened at the sight of her.

It all started when some of the prisoners tried to help her take a shower after weeks and weeks of sitting and lying down in her own dirt and blood. She sat in the hall on the side of the entrance to the yard, in front of the room where two little children and their imprisoned mothers were living—children were a conflicting aspect of prison life, simultaneously a source of joy and pain. In the early 1980s, there were sometimes more than thirty children in a ward. In 1983, for instance, in the ward where I lived, there were twenty-eight children from a few months to eight years old. These were children whose parents did not have anyone outside to take care of them and did not want to give them up. Later the regime made it mandatory for these children to be sent out of the prison. Thus, in 1985, we had only these two children whose parents had been arrested less than a year earlier. Every morning, Yashar, a two-year-old boy, with his bright greenish blue eyes, would stare at Fozi while she was sleeping, and the cockroaches and flies would have their feast across her bloody, dirty body. They were almost eating her "dead" face and her closed eyes while she was making no movements—so soundly asleep as if long dead. Sometimes Yashar would go closer to her to brush the flies away from her face; adults were trying to stay away from the rotten smell of her malodorous body.

Before taking residence in the corner of the hall, Fozi was assigned to one of the rooms occupied mostly by other prisoners who had been arrested for their affiliation with the Iranian militant organization Mojahedin-Khalgh-e Iran, called Mojahedin by resistant prisoners, and Monafeghin, or hypocrites, by the regime and collaborators. She was not yet completely silenced then. In fact, during the several months since she had been brought to our ward, we witnessed her situation worsening every day. Watching her rapid changes, those prisoners who had known her since her first arrest were more shocked than the rest of us. She was a beautiful young pregnant woman when she was arrested for the first time in 1981. She gave birth to her daughter in prison and pretended to be a devoted collaborator. Earning Haji Davoud's trust by giving information about the members of other organizations in prison, she became the head of the ward. Still connected to Mojahedin, she sent them information about prison, thus actually working as a double agent for the regime and her own organization. Within less than two years, she was able to convince Haji of her faithful support for the regime against its opponents and was therefore released.

The break she had because of this clever game did not last very long. She was arrested in one of the Mojahedin's secret houses with some well-known members of the organization, hence in a more serious situation than the first time. She had, however, sufficient confidence to play the same game for the second time, albeit with greater generosity to collaborate and offer information to Haji at the expense of others. This was obviously necessary for her to yet once again earn his trust. What mattered for Haji was, of course, more about what he was gaining in the exchange than his trust in her. But as is said, history does not repeat itself; instead of being released, this time she was caught and paid a high price for her cleverness.

In 1984, through the information given under torture by one of the members involved, an underground network of the Mojahedin organization in prison was discovered. All the members connected to this network or who even knew about it were taken to a *dastgah*, although to a different one from that built for leftists. The leftists had been forced to sit and sleep in individual wooden cells while blindfolded throughout the day and night, with the guards and Haji Davoud watching over and beating them. Mojahedin, on the other hand, were thrown into a big hall, also in Vahed-e 1, but along with interrogators, who were dressed casually as though living in their homes. There was not even a moment of escape from interrogation, never an instant to breathe in privacy.

Every day these *mojahed* prisoners were obliged to read and memorize Islamic texts or political propaganda and to listen to the prison radio's special programs for several hours. As though the prisoners were in school, the interrogators played the role of their teachers and would test them on these materials, except that here a failing grade would be punished by severe torture and humiliation. They were compelled to either whip their own friends or be whipped. Only two, out of more than fifty women, came out of this situation unbroken, one of whom committed suicide a year later. The other sat in her corner for days and nights with her eyes wide open until one day she began to speak nonsense.

COLLABORATORS IN PRISON are the fulcrum of the systems of surveillance, as they were in Iran, especially under the Islamic Republic. They assisted in the process of arrest, interrogation, torture, and execution with a wide array of motivations and circumstances. Some initiated their activities to gain personal advantage, while others were driven to the process to escape torture or were within the throes of psychological chaos. Collaborators are a crucial element of the panopticon of the state and the modern system of penal surveillance.

For prisoners, collaborators embody lost souls who remind them of their own potential moral degeneration, tempting them to submit and find relief. For the prison officials, the collaborators are part of the machinery of the laboratory with which they improve the effectiveness of their methods. Collaborators supply unique forms of knowledge to increase productivity and further rationalize and intensify the policing procedures. Collaborators have a strange relation to those who resist; they hate them, since the very existence of resisters proves the collaborators' pariah status and continuously symbolizes the possibility of victory over cruelty. The intense humiliation and shame induce the perception of themselves as so unworthy and outcast that they must continuously deny any connection between themselves and other prisoners.

This feeling of radical otherness between themselves, their past, and their former friends leads them even further toward a pathological identification with their torturers' absurd reality. This increased existential gulf between the collaborators and other prisoners undermines the legitimacy of their suffering in the eyes of other prisoners and blinds them to the fact that the collaborators are also subjects of these technologies of power. This terrifying image of a collapsed or imploded self and its monstrous shadow menacing other prisoners reminds them of their own possible fate, alienates them from these monstrous others, and excludes the collaborators from their community as morally flawed.

FOZI'S COLLABORATION with the interrogators reached such an ugly and disgusting level that her infamy spread to all the wards and even to the outside world. Her husband, who was able to flee the country and was exiled in Europe, sent her a message of repudiation and abrogated his marriage to her. Her parents stopped coming to visit her for months until she became mentally ill. The whole world had turned into an enemy for her. The regime and Haji no longer trusted her, no matter how hard she tried to earn their trust. She had used up all her chances. She was already disliked by the leftists and other prisoners not allied to the Mojahedin, and now she was hated by her own friends, among whom she found her worst enemies. Stuck in the mud and dirt of this strange road, she could turn nowhere. All the roads were dead ends with her enemies' blazing, hateful eyes watching her everywhere she looked. With her mind restless and confused, with her body aching and fatigued, and with her soul so shattered and lost that she could find no pieces of it, she collapsed in a world of despair. Swallowing its poison inside and out, she became unable to pass through all the labyrinths of this world. She completely lost her way.

What happens to a person who is chained to a world that appears so hostile and from which no escape seems possible? Moreover, where can one escape if one's own self emerges as the most dangerous adversary? You feel surrounded by a world that is in an undeclared battle with you, a world in which you are doomed to be defeated. Every day, you feel more and more humiliated, yet no possibility of death or release appears in sight. Sisyphus would feel lucky watching you since he would at least have some sense of accomplishment when he took the rock up to the top of the hill. If his disappointment comes with dropping the rock, your punishment disallows any chance of achievement. Is there a way out of these dead-end paths where the shattered soul can put its pieces back together?

SHAKAR WAS ONE OF THESE LOST SOULS, also affiliated with Mojahedin, who found her way to salvation. She, a nurse whose job was taking care of injured and sick people, ended up in prison and in Haji's *dastgah*, where she inflicted pain on her own friends' bodies and was herself also beaten by her friends. Atefeh, a leftist woman, a former colleague of Shakar's in the hospital where they had both worked as nurses, was still in shock days after we saw Shakar in Ward 7 in Ghezel Hesar. "She was one of the most responsible and kindest nurses I had ever worked with. How could she become who she is now? What have they done to her to turn her into this disgusting, antagonistic person?" Atefeh wondered.

What had they done to her, to this petite young woman with her yellowish brown eyes, which looked even more yellow with such fear and fury burned into them? Her blond hair only served to make her look more ashen, to better fit her damaged body and soul. Sitting, almost always, on the same corner of the second story of the three-story metal beds in her cell, she would either read the Qur'an or look at us with hate glowing in her eyes. An empty can was her main possession besides her clothes; she would carry it everywhere, and once in a while she would vomit in it with amazing indifference, which occurred frequently during the day. Was she throwing up all the hate inside her to find some sense of relief? If so, it was not that effective. Anytime she looked at us, we shivered to see how much abhorrence was reflected in her eyes, especially when she heard our laughter. Shakar's soul was saturated with anguish and animosity toward the whole world. I was unable to tell who she was more loathsome toward, herself, her interrogators, or us. But if Shakar would somehow rescue something of herself, though at the cost of her life, Fozi had already died, while living with no possibility of redemption.

FOZI, COVERED IN HER BLACK CHADOR, was pushed into our ward on a dismal early evening in 1986. When she was thrown into the narrow hall of the first floor of the two-story Ward 246, into the midst of hundreds of prisoners who were walking hastily as though headed somewhere, I heard the whisper among Mojahedin prisoners, "Oh look, she is Fozi, that awful monster, the evil." Fozi was already in action before anyone had the chance to react to her arrival. As though sensing the hatred of her former friends, she began knocking at the bars, while screaming, cursing the guards, and demanding they let her out. At this early stage, many of the Mojahedin were convinced that playing mad was another one of Fozi's tricks and that she was merely trying to fool others in order to escape the consequences of her actions. There were others who argued that even if mad, she deserved her misery, for she was paying for the horrible harm she had inflicted on other prisoners.

Whether crazy or not, Fozi was still screaming and repeating the same words over and over: "Stupid pimps, get me out of here. You cowards, let me out." She said these words in exactly the same order, even in the same tone, without ceasing. The whole ward was disturbed by her constant repetitive curses and knocks on the metallic bars, which made an extremely annoying sound. It was driving us all crazy, but it seemed that the guards had chosen to ignore her. Like an old, lame person climbing the hills, the evening was laboriously moving toward the long, feverish night. Fozi was still screaming, and her voice was getting coarser and more difficult to tolerate. A guard came to the gate and opened it. Fozi stopped screaming while the guard was beating her up, but as soon as the guard closed the door and walked away, Fozi began all over again. Then it was Fati's turn, a young leftist woman whose very tall, robust body was supposed to scare Fozi off and make her stop. Fati yelled at Fozi to "shut up" and told her that her voice and knocking were disturbing the children in the ward. But Fozi did not budge. She went on screaming the whole night.

Fozi kept shrieking for three days and nights: a constant, incessant cry and curse with the same endless repetition. A few times she was interrupted by guards who came and beat her in order to force her into silence, but their beatings only induced her to scream louder and with more rage in her voice. Obviously, the prison officials were entertained by this situation, which had disturbed the whole ward. The children had become restless, and nobody could sleep, especially those of us in the front rooms closer to the gate. Fozi, however, standing on her feet the entire time, without eating or drinking or even using the bathroom, having grown extremely pale and almost at the point of completely losing her voice, did not seem to feel anything except rage, or was it a feeling of entrapment so overwhelming she could not feel anything else? Finally, apparently, the guards had had enough of the "show," since they came and, after hitting her one more time and harder than before, held her by force and gave her an injection that put her into a long sleep.

꙳

*April 1999: Last night I had one more of those dreams in which I was sur-
rounded by so many people; many of them I knew—either my family members or my Iranian friends. I began having such dreams several months
ago, and they kept repeating themselves, sometimes with slight changes
in the locations or people involved. The main theme and the emotional
content are essentially the same in all of them. People are fighting, and
I am trying to convince them that what they are fighting over is a very
trivial issue. I do not remember what the arguments are about; all I know
is that they are over something so ridiculous that even a child could realize its lack of importance. But they keep fighting as if their entire existence
depends on that subject. I feel extremely outraged, desperate, and helpless,
and my voice is lost in the midst of all the screams and shouting. I beg
them to stop for a second and listen to what I have to tell them. If I could
tell them where I have been and what I have seen, they would know how
frivolous their conflict is, I think to myself.*

*But they are too busy yelling at each other, and I am doing exactly
the same thing, trying to speak louder just to be heard, as though my
words would make a difference. My throat is sore, and my voice is gone.
All sweaty, I wake up and turn the light on. Hamid is looking at me with
his beautiful, gentle smile from that small photo frame. On the other side,
Fakhri, one of my best friends, who was executed in 1981, still looks at me
with sharpness and confidence in her eaglelike eyes. I am up and silent.
I recall how much Hamid and I used to communicate with one another
without words. And here I am in my dream, screaming louder to be heard!
Why did I believe that I was any different? I wonder how I can learn again
to speak through silence in such a noisy world where too many words
circulate so that silence is rarely heard.*

꙳

Fozi went to sleep while many of us restlessly contemplated the incredible capacity human beings have of becoming so different from one an-

other. Why is it that there are people who risk their lives to ease others' pain, although their own suffering may be even greater, while there are others willing to rescue themselves by walking on the injured shoulders of others? How should or could we compare the reactions of those who participated in executing their own friends to those who put their lives in danger to protect their beloved ones from persecution and torture? Prison is the stage on which these different scenarios and their characters are enacted, albeit in a wide continuum.

What Madness Now Keeps Me?

What madness now keeps me
from becoming totally mad?

—Rumi

"Behrouz was bathing in his own blood when the interrogators untied him from the ceiling of the torture room where he was hung for the last several days. The torturers were taking turns, but he was being interminably beaten, either hung from the ceiling so that his feet could not touch the floor and his arms were stretching to the point of being torn from the joints, or on the torture bed or on the floor, where all of them would attack him as if he were a dangerous animal. Although he was no longer walking but crawling, the red streams were imprinting his existence everywhere his feet, with their gaping wounds, passed. The whole time, however, he was more silent than the silence itself. There was heavy breathing or moaning once in a while, but no language was spoken by him to the torturers. Instead, it was the language that was speaking him, so transparent he had become, yet so unreachable."

Nahid's deep, dark, sad eyes were shining with pride as she was listening to the story of her husband, Behrouz, told by one of our fellow inmates, Soudi. It was a year after Behrouz's death under torture, and we were having a secret memorial ceremony for him in the ward. Everyone who knew Behrouz or had heard anything about him was talking about him. Soudi, who had spent several days in the torture room with Behrouz, had much to say. She had come to know Behrouz and felt extremely close to him, paradoxically, while they were both going through hell in the torture room, a place where nothing is supposed to exist for you except pain and its agony. Soudi's words about Behrouz brought him into our midst and our heart more than many who were physically alive and "really" there.

"I learned more about love and care in those days than ever before, merely by watching Behrouz," Soudi related to us about the time she spent with Behrouz. "Since the first night that I saw him through my blindfold, I felt his loving energy was reaching me in that terrifying room, and he became the source of my inspiration, courage, and strength. During those several days and nights he used every chance to encourage me and to remind me that my situation was not going to last forever, and I was going to be fine. At night, when they stopped torturing me and untied me to go to sleep, he was still hung up, and I could hear his painful sighs, which he tried so hard to keep inside. Every time the interrogators left us alone for a brief time, he sang for me through his injured lips. The words of the poems he recited came out of his mouth adorned with his broken, bloody teeth, immersed in my soul, washed in my bloody tears. He knew he was going to die since he was determined to keep his mouth shut. Already disappointed by not getting any information from him, the interrogators were desperately trying to force him to say that he was defeated by them, or say something of the kind. His candid speech of silence was a slap in their face, so humiliating that it drove his interrogators crazy."

Such a strange irony that torture's main purpose is to drive the tortured person out of her or his mind, while, in fact, torture itself is a crazy game in which both parties play deranged roles, especially if they both take it to its extremes. The torturer speaks his power through the torture devices. His integrity, as he perceives it, is dependent upon winning this game by the means of physical and psychological pressure inscribed on the body and soul of the victim. For the interrogator, the person under torture is cut off from her or his subjectivity; instead, she or he becomes the subject of the torturer's task to claim his, and therefore the torture's, victory. Through the violence, the interrogator exercises personal power while at the same time fulfills a task. By objectifying the person under torture, he invests his own self, for to be able to perform such a monstrous job, one has to be persuaded that there is at stake—beyond a state duty— a search for the redemption of one's own crushed identity. The manic re- action of the torturer is only justifiable through the inherited insanity of the torture itself, though it is rationalized as an unpleasant yet necessary act to protect the well-being of society.

The tortured person who resists confession, however, subverts all the rationale behind a normal response to the body in pain. If the normal response to severe pain is to avoid it through eliminating its causes, one's persistence in keeping silent, an act that results in continuous pain, could be categorized as abnormal. This abnormality manifests itself in the ways in which the tortured person takes pride in her or his strength to push the torturers into madness. One of the joyous moments that the most resistant prisoners experienced occurred when their torturers got furious at them, called them names, and beat them more severely; it meant that they had accomplished the goal of their resistance. Their torturers were unable to get from them what they were after. Yet isn't this behavior defined as sadomasochism in psychological terms, if one forgets the sociality of this resistance, its relationship to the other within oneself and the others?

ONE OF THESE INSPIRING STORIES for resistant prisoners was about Reza's resilience. Reza was a leftist activist who was arrested in late 1982 and went through a long period of severe, relentless torture, even though like nearly all the leftists, his activities posed no threat to national security. Yet in Iran, under both the Shah and the Islamic Repub- lic, any involvement in thinking, reading, discussing, and writing about ideas other than those in agreement with the government was considered threatening. Since 1970, the Shah's government had had the excuse of the armed struggle of the two militant organizations, Sazeman-e Cherikha-ye Fadayee-e Khalgh-e Iran and Sazeman-e Mojahedin-e Khalgh-e Iran, to justify its harsh persecution of all the dissidents, even those with no rela- tion to these organizations.

Under the Islamic Republic, too, since 1981, only Mojahedin had been involved in armed struggle, along with a very small fraction of the leftist Ettehadiyeh-ye komonistha, the Communists Union, and even they were involved in only one particular incident—a failed attempt to capture the city of Amol in the north of Iran in 1981. The rest of the leftists had no involvement in armed struggle. Of course, the government blamed the leftists for fighting alongside the Kurdish people against the government. But only a very small portion of the left did so, and that also occurred mainly in the early 1980s.

Dissidents like Reza, or many of the rest of us in prison, had never been engaged in, nor did we believe in participating in, any armed struggle against the regime at that historical moment. Thus, when subjecting us to torture, especially those of us who were arrested after 1982 and were affiliated with the leftist organizations that by then had been dismantled, interrogators knew very well that we had no sensitive information to offer them. The main goal of this torture was therefore not really to obtain information, though torture is never only about obtaining information, but even more so here it was to force prisoners into humiliation, self-annihilation through forced confessions and recantations. Reza, however, refused to play a part in this process by embracing his death under torture. Later, when I was arrested, Rahim, who had been Reza's main interrogator, became my interrogator. Time and again he attempted to terrify me by reminding me how I, too, could die under torture if I refused to talk, as had Reza or others like him. Yet every single time he told me the story of Reza's death, he grew furious, even at the mention of his name. He cursed Reza for having died without giving his interrogators what they wanted. Although he pretended to be concerned that he died as an unbeliever, the real source of his agony was revealed to me in the expression of outrage that "in dying on me this wicked man was trying to prove that his will is stronger than the power of my lashes." Interestingly, he seemed to feel an urge to mention Reza's name rather frequently, as though haunted by his ghost. His outrage was not so much about the subversive knowledge that Reza had taken to his grave but rather about his undefeatable character.

In his dying moment, Reza had opened his bloodied eyes to look at his torturers' angry and disappointed faces, victoriously smiled, and through his broken jaw and injured mouth said, "Sorry, you lost; your torture lost; I am dying, utterly free; good-bye." With a glorious smile on his deformed and smashed face, he closed his eyes, sighed with relief, and died while the torturers were insanely waving their hovering whips over his dead body. Reza had "crossed into a country" into which his interrogators "could not enter." Reza had entered the land of freedom. Who belonged more to the category of the lunatic: Reza, who conceived of his death as his victory, or the torturers, who sought their identity in defeating a helplessly bound person undergoing unlimited pain?

Reza's rebellion was against the kind of death that denied his desire to know and share his knowledge with others, and to remain present to himself and his community. As a modern human, he cultivated in himself the attitude of daring to know and question. He defied the power that deprived him of active participation in creation of his world. He believed that he could emerge as a dynamic participant in making and remaking his present only through the exercise of his free will, which entailed the possibility of questioning, criticizing, and resisting what restrained his creativity and dynamism. Ironically, the very same conduct that defines the integrity of a modern human being simultaneously puts the person's sanity into question when she or he wills to live and, if necessary, die accordingly. Reza's surrender, which appears as a natural reaction for survival and avoidance of pain, would have destroyed the very essence of his humanity, his free will, and his presence to his community, as he perceived it. Death, in this sense, is viewed less in relation to the prolongation of life than in how that life is lived. Reza radically refused to live a life in which his curiosity was stifled, his will to know suppressed, forced to deny even his very humanity, which undermines an ethical responsibility toward himself and others.

SOUDI CONTINUED HER NARRATION. "I would never forget Behrouz's incredible generosity. It was one of those rare occasions that they had left us alone. He was lying down on the torture bed with his feet tied up and his hands open.

"As he reached toward me, I heard him say, 'Please take these and eat them. You have to stay strong.' I stretched out my arms and discovered that he had saved his sugar cubes for me. He had already given his food to me several times. I refused to take the only source of energy he was able to consume since he could not eat food with his injured mouth. He said very convincingly, 'I don't need them, but you do.' His eyes were telling me good-bye.

"He taught me how to massage my feet after being beaten by cables. It was the last time I had the chance to talk to him. When they came back and hung him up again, it was for the last time. Less than half an hour later, he was down on the floor, silenced forever, but alive in the language of love to the end of the world. I am bewildered by how people are so different in their response to catastrophe. Look at Fozi; why has she become who she is? Despite the inhumanity of the torture, what else breaks us down or holds us intact?"

Soudi's questions were those of many of us in jail. Nobody could really know precisely what made some people care so deeply for and about others, while others thrived in inflicting pain. But what was certain was the fact that for Soudi, Behrouz's resistance had generated a sense of hope and showed her a power beyond the destruction of torture that not only allowed her to survive the torture but taught her the art of living and dying. Refusing to bargain with his dignity and humanity, he confronted the system of individualization according to which all a person cares about is his own pain or happiness. Behrouz's attitude indicated how his ethics of care for the self was linked to his care for others. The self, in this perspective, is inseparable from the larger exterior world, whether it be other humans, nature, or the society we live in. Since he conceived of his existence as an indivisible unity, his physical being lost its significance when his sense of self was lost. It is in this light that his death connects to and reveals so much about life, more than so many others whose lives do not seem to embrace others in any meaningful sense.

The Price of Learning the Sacred Word

After months of not being allowed to go to the yard, while in Ghezel Hesar in the summer of 1984, one day the guards took us to a beautiful yard and let us enjoy the fresh air for a few hours. Oh, how exquisite everything looked, and how delighted I felt then. The bright white clouds were gliding over the blue sky so gracefully. The gorgeous birds, real birds, not those of our imagination, were flying in the heart of the blue sky. Pouring its rays down upon us, the sun was generously healing our frozen, aching bones and offering us a pleasant sense of relief. We were fascinated by the beauty and colorfulness of the flowers; laughter and joy had enveloped the yard. Shakar, a survivor of Haji Davoud's *dastgah*, was, however, bitterly cursing us while walking without paying any attention to any of these wonderful emblems of life and the beauty of nature. Anger sank deeper in her eyes every time she heard us laughing, speaking, playing, and chasing each other. She remained extremely outraged and continued ceaselessly vomiting. Mozhdeh, an inmate with whom I was walking at the moment, said, "She is totally repulsed by any suggestion of life. Her resentment toward us is because we remind her of the difference between who she was before and who she is now."

I wondered if she was throwing up in disgust and anger, destroying her insides, or if these were symptoms of the last vestiges of life she had suppressed inside. Even though, thinking back, I wonder if I could have ever truly comprehended her complex emotions; I still shiver at the thought of the miserable life that she lived in such a radical disconnect from it. Somehow this reminds me of a poem by the late contemporary poet, Ahmad Shamlu:

> They had told us: "We will teach you that sacred word.
> In order to learn it, however, you have to endure a severe ordeal."
> We tolerated that severe ordeal for so long
> that the sacred word escaped our memory.

IT WAS AFTER 1988, after the bloody war between Iran and Iraq ended, after those freezing, snowy days when after every meeting with our families, wives would return to the ward as widows, for from their families they heard about their husband's execution. Sisters would learn about their brothers' executions, and many of us would hear of the loss of our best friends. It was after we had our new color TV, which was brought to the ward in the aftermath of the news of the mass execution of our husbands, brothers, and friends. It was after we watched, on this new TV, the remaining male prisoners marching in the streets of Tehran, announcing to the world that "Evin is a university, not a prison. There is no execution or torture in Iran's prisons" and that "we are devoted Muslims redeemed from our sinful past." They sent messages to us: "Stop fighting. They will break you, too, and will make you dance like a monkey with any rhythm they want, as they did to us. Save your lives. There is no point in fighting; they will win." It was after those men and women who accepted the regime's condition were released that few of us remained imprisoned.

In the evenings, if we still felt like talking, we would sit and recall those early years of our imprisonment, so far and yet so near, when we did not have any space to even sit in the ward. Now our numbers were shrinking every day. How lonely the world was for those of us who lost parents while still behind bars. Newborns were strangers to us, as we were to them. The memories of the past were fading away, and new people were rarely arrested, nor were they brought to our wards if they were; so our connection to the exterior world was diminishing. The former prisoners' handwriting on the walls was the only trace left from those thousands whose friendship, laughter, whispers, screams, pain, fear, madness, and even betrayal once filled these jails with life and death. Now it seemed that death had consumed this place, and loneliness was the color with which everything was painted.

And it was after our women friends returned to the wards, from that hellish period they spent in solitary confinement, where they were whipped five times a day, at prayer times, until they would say they were Muslims and agreed to pray. It was during the summer of 1988, when the entire world had been closed to us, when all the visits with families had stopped, newspapers and television were taken away, and we had lived in a state of constant suspense not knowing what to expect and when. While waiting our turn to be taken to the court and tried, while knowing our friends were under lashes, we were perplexed as to what to wish for. Wishing for their return meant hoping that they would give up on their beliefs, which also meant the arrival of our turn for torture, while desiring any delay in taking us would favor the prolongation of their suffering. How would we resolve this confusion?

Most members of the first group returned. It was after we watched Mahin, one of these women who had returned, walking in the yard with tears washing her face, which she made no attempt to wipe away, and repeatedly reciting only a couple of verses of a poem, the entirety of which almost all of us knew by heart: "O love, O love, your red face is no longer apparent. / O love, O love, your blue face is no longer apparent." She did not recite the rest of the poem:

And the coolness of an ointment on a blazing wound.
Not the joy of flame on the coldness within.
O love, O love, your red face is not apparent.

Night after night we also cried with Zari, another inmate who like Mahin was forced to utter her *ashhad*, profession of her belief in Islam—which, ironically, Muslims also recite at the moment of their death and for the dead. She had been mournfully crying for the past few nights since her return from solitary confinement in Āsāyeshgāh, the Place to Rest, after she had agreed to profess she was a Muslim and that she would pray—in fact, they had forced her to pray in front of the guards. She had submitted mainly to stop remembering the constant hovering of lashes, the pain of which was even more excruciating in the interval between times they actually cut through the skin of her back and bottom.

To us, on the third floor, the echo of her moaning cries coming from the first floor of the three-story building, called Amoozeshgah, the Place for Education, sounded like the wailing of ghosts. These emotions were apparently also present among men. Nima Parvaresh, a male inmate in the 1980s, narrated a similar story: "At the noon and evening prayer times they lashed us, forty lashes, twenty for each time. They came back for the night lashes, . . . continued torturing us beyond the prayer times. Now it was no longer just the pain of the lashes, but it was the pain of the defeat of accepting to pray that we felt."

Yes, it was after all this. Soon we were mixed with common criminals, for the first time in the recent history of the political prisons, where we would see young teenagers blossoming in prison only to be raped by the interrogators. We would witness how these devout Muslims lashed the bodies of the women whose behavior was considered inappropriate.

And it was after Mahin cut her wrists and her neck, and I undressed her while my hands were immersed in her blood. And then in the evening, we ate our dinner, as on any other evening, explaining to ourselves that we should keep our spirits high and not let the guards think we were disheartened. We washed our faces in the mornings to hide our red, tearful eyes from the guards and each other, for we did not want our comrades to lose heart. We laughed, played games, and lived our lives as if nothing had happened. Yes, it was after all this, after hunger strikes, starvation, loneliness, and solitude, and after hearing our friends' cries when they were being beaten that I began to fear becoming indifferent, forgetting how to care. How distraught I felt even at the thought of it.

ﻙ

But then I remembered:

It was a snowy early morning, and I was twelve years old, when with my eyes still sleepy, I opened the door to a sudden loud knock. My classmate and friend Azizeh was at the door holding something covered in a worn-out blanket. She asked for my father, who came to the door, uncovered the blanket, and there it was: her little eight-month-old sister, blue and swollen. My father checked her pulse, and with a deep sigh said, "She's dead." The tears in Azizeh's eyes did not reach her cheeks. I went to see her mother who, while softly crying, told me that she was happy for her little girl since she escaped the suffering of the poverty and starvation the family had to endure. She was frozen on the night they ran out of charcoal, their only source of heat in such a cold winter. I held the baby's little cold hands in mine and stared at her gaunt face. It was a moment in which I promised myself that I would fight for a world in which no family would consider their child's death a blessing for the child and the family because of the cruelty of their lives.

Later that winter, Azizeh was slapped on the face by our math teacher because she had not done her math homework in a new notebook, which she could not afford to purchase. Standing up to my teacher and taking the issue all the way to the principal of the school and to the parents' meetings, I learned that if I chose to resist authorities, I had to be ready to pay the price. That year, for the first time, I did not receive an A in math. Yet I felt satisfied since something more meaningful than my grades and my insignificant interests was at stake. I had refused to watch my own integrity and that of my friend be crushed. We had won our little battle. The teacher had apologized in front of all our classmates for his behavior.

I swore to myself then that I would never pass by indifferently when someone was in pain, that I would never live my life without being conscious of other lives besides mine. It would not be truly a human life if I forgot that I was part of all of existence and not an isolated, disconnected self. In fact, a self could not exist without links to the rest of the world. It was after all those years and those oaths that now I had become truly frightened of losing my sensitivity toward the pain and suffering of others. I was concerned that I would watch injustice and pass by, that I would get used to undressing others like Mahin after her suicide attempt and then have a casual dinner. What would become of me then? Would I become another Shakar, who returned from Haji Davoud's dastgah *so full of hatred that she vomited her hatred into a can she carried with her all the time; or like Fozi, who had become more frightened of her former friends than of the wardens? I had been witnessing pain, suffering, and torture for so many years now that I was terrified of becoming numb to them. Even now, this thought makes me shiver to my bones.*

✒

I am pushed into a room when suddenly I am not blindfolded anymore. The interrogator says, "Now you'll see how pathetic your heroic man has become." In the middle of the torture room, Hamid is tied up to a metallic bed surrounded by four interrogators, all of whom are holding cable whips in their hands, beating him all over his body. He is blindfolded, unable to see me. I hear him breathing heavily and rapidly. His feet are swollen, and blood has turned his beautiful thick brown hair into red. As soon as he feels me in the room, he tries to breathe normally. I am confused about the appropriate reaction in such a situation. Should I stay quiet and nonchalant in order not to give them the power over my emotions, or should I resist watching my beloved being tortured in front of me? Should I stay calm and cold, or should I scream?

And suddenly I am nine years old again. My hands are so cold that I cannot hold the pencil. Hassan, one of my classmates, is in front of the class again with his cold hands open to the teacher's lashes. How were his freezing hands feeling with those sharp lashes cutting through them? The teacher calls me forward and asks me the math problem that Hassan could not answer. Should I say what the right answer is? If I respond to it correctly, I then have to spit in Hassan's face or beat him, and if I refuse to do that, I would be beaten myself. I am standing there in front of everyone wondering what to do while the teacher is staring at me with his wild eyes and the lash in his trembling hand. "Go ahead, Shahla, tell him the answer. I'm sure you know it. You are an excellent student. Don't have sympathy for this stupid jerk." What should I do? Should I spit at him, or should I be beaten? What should I do?

Still undecided and in shock, I am standing in the middle of the torture room where Hamid's feet are getting more and more swollen with every blow of the cables. After a few minutes, an eternity, I begin to yell at them, not because I have come up with the rational choice but because my soul is hurting too much, and I cannot take it anymore. So I scream: "Don't beat him. Why are you torturing him? He doesn't know where my sister is. None of us do. Leave him alone. He has nothing to say."

The torturers attack me, beat me all over my body and curse me: "You bitch, you mother . . . don't guide his response. We'll make you as miserable as he is. We'll make you remember things from the time you were in your mother's belly."

Hamid's feet are untied while his hands are still tied. They force him to stand on his injured feet, still blindfolded. One of the torturers is holding me to make sure that I do not miss their every gesture and act of brutality they inflict on Hamid. Later, after this is all over, I would suddenly become a nonrelated opposite sex whom they would not touch. They would give me a pen, which I would hold on one end and one of them on the other to direct me to the cell, while I am blindfolded. But for now, all the rules of Islamic piety are suspended.

Two or three—I am not sure—guards (or interrogators?) join the other four, so now there are six, or more, of them passing him like a ball, kicking, whipping, and throwing him back and forth to one another and to the walls, while laughing hysterically. "You wimp, what kind of man are you? How were you going to protect your wife while you are not able to stand on your feet?" Hamid is under their feet, his face covered with blood. But he is so quiet that my heart wants to scream with all my might for and on his behalf. Why does he think he needs to be this strong for me, yet he is on the floor, under their feet? I try to imagine his eyes behind his blindfold. Suddenly I miss his eyes. Where are his expressive, bright, lovely eyes?

Oh Hamid, what has happened to those beautiful teeth and that determined jaw of yours? It was this very contrast between the kindness in your eyes and the determination implied by your facial structure, especially your jaw, that impressed me first when you smilingly walked toward me in that crowded street on which you and I met for the first time, on that gorgeous spring day of 1980. What has become of your athletic body, the chest I so adored and loved, the very chest that offered me the greatest comfort at times when the entire world was being shattered in and around us? It was your chest that warmed my heart when the news of the execution of our closest friends was sucking the blood out of my veins, during those gruesome years from 1981 to the time of our arrest in early 1983. How strangely protected your love made me feel during those disastrous years during which newspapers had become the cruel messengers of the news of our comrades' lives cut short, announced and lost in a long list of other names who were others' loved ones. How rapidly it had all passed, and how strangely life had changed around us between that lovely spring day when I had first met you and the spring day of our arrest, yet how deeply you had grown in me that I could not remember the time I had not loved you. Still, it was only three years since I had first seen you.

But such a different time it was then. The Iran-Iraq War had not begun yet, and the "spring of freedom," lasting from the Revolution of 1979 until the Iran-Iraq War in September 1980, though rapidly fading, was still alive. Hamid, how soon you had made me fall in love with you; and I had fallen in love first and foremost with that beautiful soul of yours, with the way you used to listen to me, with your sensitivity, the way you so unabashedly cried for others' pain without worrying that your masculinity would be undermined—how much I loved you for this confidence that was such a rare quality for most men then. Remember that day when you and I visited your sister in the hospital when she had begun bleeding while pregnant, and you cried with and for your sister because she was missing her two-year-old son she could not be with while in the hospital? I had been arrested on the street while walking with one of our male friends. To avoid being arrested for walking on the street with someone of the opposite sex who was not related, which could have led us to Evin and our death, I had to tell the guards he was my cousin. I thus brought them to your sister's house so they would believe my story.

Your sister, five months pregnant, played along really well, but after the Revolutionary Guards left, we noticed she had begun bleeding. Remember how in order to show the guards that you were a real Muslim brother who knows how to put his wife in her proper place, you yelled at me in front of them and told me off, only to hold me tight that night, kiss me on my eyes again and again, and apologize for being rude, explaining why you had to do so, knowing that I understood and yet needing to explain? It was two days after that we went to visit your sister in the hospital, for they could not stop her heavy bleeding, and I was feeling so guilty for having caused this, but you sat there and cried with her. She had missed her little boy, and I thought to myself how every day I discovered something new in you that made me fall in love with you all over again. Your sensitivity was one of your characteristics that I so admired, that you could fight for the entire world, yet a little injury on your sister's finger, for instance, could make you cry.

But now, here I was watching Hamid fallen under the feet of these interrogators who were trying to humiliate him for not being man enough. If the pain had allowed me to think then, I would have known in my heart that, unlike them, Hamid would not feel humiliated for a "defect" in his masculinity. He would be feeling devastated for not being able to protect the love of his life, as he would later write me in a letter in 1986: "You are my love; the harvest of my life, and all I want is to protect you and see you blossom." But now, I was watching you under these men's feet. How long I have been watching this scene! And I remember when my third-grade classmate Hassan's hands are bleeding from the lashes of our teacher, I am being pushed to choose either his or my suffering. How could I scream loud enough so that all the perpetrators of violence would know that such a distinction is impossible? How many years have I been watching these scenes and been pushed to make these impossible choices?

Did He Cry?

Oh my hands, my hands, how much my hands hurt! I feel I want to cut them off, but they throb as if they have turned into two aching hearts. What were my hands doing that day when I read and imagined how Yousuf (the biblical Joseph) was violently separated from his father, Yaghoub (Jacob). I was there among Yousuf's brothers when they threw him into the well, then killed a sheep, covered his clothes with its blood, and returned to their father to claim that he was killed by a wolf. I was there when his innocent look begged for mercy, but his brothers washed the blood from their hands. How awfully my hands are hurting! How stiff they have become! What were my hands doing when Ibrahim (Abraham) took his son Ismail (Ishmael) to the desert and put the knife to his neck while Ismail's little heart was beating like that of bird? Yet how surprisingly content he was that his father had to prove his love for his God by killing his dear son—poor sons and poor fathers who were themselves once their fathers' sons. What were my hands doing when the pulse in Ismail's neck was racing, as he waited for his father's knife to cut it through? Where were my hands then? My hands, my hands.

༝

When I was born, that Yousuf and his brothers were long dead, as were Ismail and Ibrahim. But I remember being simultaneously in the positions of Yousuf and his brothers and detesting myself for that. In my instance, the archetypal Yousuf was named Masoud, and we were not his siblings. But Hussein, a thirteen-year-old son and brother, was as hurt and as angry as Yousuf's brothers for the attention and love Masoud was getting from his parents. Masoud was the five-year-old son of a neighbor, whom everyone loved and adored. Perhaps this was the reason that on that dreadful morning Hussein tricked Masoud and six other children in the neighborhood into following him to a remote meadow. My heart jumped into my mouth. Knowing Hussein, I feared that something horrible was bound to happen, but what did occur was beyond my wildest imagination. In a heavy silence, trembling and overwhelmed by fear and anticipation, we sheepishly walked behind him until we got to the meadow.

Where was the well into which the incarnated Yousuf was to be thrown? Masoud was still politely smiling, vaguely scared perhaps because of the unusual seriousness and silence, but obviously unaware of the kind of game Hussein had in mind for him, in which we were to be the unwilling actors. Like those of all other Ismails and Yousufs, his eyes looked so innocent that any sensitive heart would be moved by them. I

think when Yousuf was thrown into the well, at least one of his brothers
must have quivered at the sight of his innocent gaze. At least one of them
must have begged for the others' compassion. At least one must have. Hus-
sein did not listen to our begging for compassion. He pulled out his belt,
and instantly we were shocked and stunned by the force of his blows on
our bodies. An early school for torture training—how fast and how early
we had to learn! The little commander, Hussein, ordered two of us to grab
Masoud's arms and legs, and the rest had to beat him up.

Did Masoud cry? Did he scream? Why can't I recall? All I can see is
Masoud on the ground, surrounded by the children he used to play with,
and their hands beating him all over his body. Were Masoud's eyes open
when Ali, his best friend, was hitting him? I do not remember. Our hands
hit him, for whenever they stopped, our bodies became the surface on
which Hussein's anger and jealousy found a way of expression through
the strikes of his belt and hands. Oh, our dirty hands. I do not remem-
ber my hands. I vaguely recall Masoud's eyes, which to me seemed more
puzzled than frightened. He must have been totally bewildered about his
strange experience. I still ask myself how he made sense of what hap-
pened to him. Did he ever wonder what he had done to make Hussein
so outraged? Poor Masoud, did he ever learn that the simple fact of his
being a "nice" boy exaggerated Hussein's already established position as
a troublemaker? We participated in Masoud's beating to avoid our own
pain, though some of us, if not all, cried, begged, screamed, and even tried
to resist beating him. But Hussein's fists and belt, which kept slashing over
our bodies, were stronger than our tolerance and power of our resistance.

What am I doing, justifying an unjustifiable action? How did I live with
myself after that day when I chose to use my hands for destruction instead of creation? Why am I tempted to explain that I acutely resisted,
that I refused to actually hit him, that I was beaten much more than I even
touched him, that . . . ? What about my hands; can I cut them off? Oh my
hands, how much they are hurting me. What will erase the memory of

that day from those children's bodies, when their minds have no memory of it? Hussein totally denies having any recollection of the event. I phoned my brother Naser, who is younger than me and was also a participant in that incident. "Do you remember anything about that day when we took Masoud to the meadow?" I asked him. "Who is Masoud? No, I was too young to remember anything about that time," he responded.

During all my life since then, the image of Masoud's body on the ground, his puzzled and frightened look, and several hands beating him have haunted me in my waking hours and in my sleep. I cannot tell my own hands apart from those of others. I cannot recall where on his body and how many times I hit him. I cannot remember my hands beating, but I was there, and they too were there, among other hands. Yes, I resisted, but I fell short of refusing to hurt someone else only to save myself from being hurt. I have forgotten the pain of the belt on my body, but my soul is still bleeding for Masoud's confusion, fear, and torment.

I looked with Masoud's eyes when we were attacked and beaten up by the collaborators. None of them cried, as we had then; instead, they seemed to sadistically enjoy inflicting pain on others. Yet, like Fozi, there were those who later crossed that line into the world of madness. Shakar, whose hatred was manifest even in the change in the shade of the color of her eyes, would later seek redemption through death. I heard of those who committed suicide, or attempted it, after they were released. Could it be because their bodies remembered their pain while their souls refused to become conscious of it? Could it be that they could no longer carry around the body that was saved at the cost of their own soul and others' suffering and it thus had to be eliminated, either through madness, where the soul loses touch with history and memory, or through death?

Since that day in the meadow when my hands became the hands of a criminal, when I participated in beating Masoud, I have been forced to watch many fathers beat their sons while the sons in turn beat their sisters and wives. I have seen these wives and sisters who hid their black-and-blue bodies from their neighbors and bragged about their men's masculinity. Bearing witness to the cruelty of children to one another and to animals, I have been horrified to realize how deeply rooted torture is in our daily experiences, collective consciousness, and historical memory. I have nevertheless been unable to figure out what makes people reflect on their experiences so differently.

Watching the cruelty of my third-grade teacher, who put a pencil between two of Hassan's fingers and squeezed them so hard that they began to bleed, I felt the urge to fight for a different relationship between people. Years later, Hussein, the thirteen-year-old boy who, like Hassan, had himself been beaten by his teachers and who orchestrated and executed the beating of Masoud by forcing our participation in it, told me that he had promised himself that he would become the fiercest teacher. I never learned what happened to Hassan. I remember, however, that I would feel dumbfounded by the way he would scream as his fingers bled, but the instant the teacher turned away, he made comic gestures behind his back that made the entire class burst into loud laugher. Of course, the teacher would become furious and beat him again. He would scream and beg him to stop only to ridicule him again, on and on. I remember I could not even laugh at his comic gestures, for I knew what would follow them, his suffering, which seemed not to concern him. What kind of pain was he trying to suppress inside himself that compelled him to bring, albeit unconsciously, this much injury and suffering onto himself?

Since that day of collective cruelty in the meadow, I had promised myself that no matter how much pain was inflicted on me, I would never participate in causing pain for others. I had sworn that I would no longer silently watch anyone's subjection to torture. However, time and again, I found myself in situations where, though not directly, my presence intensified the torture inflicted on others. Neither before nor since that day have I ever hit anyone. Yet later, in prison, my presence pushed Soosan, a woman inmate, to take a more outspoken stand that may have caused harsher treatment by her interrogator.

During my interrogation soon after my arrest in 1983, Rahim, my main interrogator, was trying to break my resistance by bragging about his merciless treatment of those prisoners who had not given in and had thus died, either under torture or by execution—though he could not hide the rage and disappointment lurking under his apparently victorious tone. He claimed that anyone who had survived had given in to the pressure and become a collaborator, and that even those who were not directly collaborating did not dare to speak their mind. To prove his point, that particular day he called me for interrogation, where I met the woman whom I would later know as Soosan. I would also learn that Soosan had been a mere supporter of, without any affiliation with, a leftist organization before her arrest in 1981. Nearly two years after her imprisonment, she was still refusing to publicly recant and renounce her past.

That day, Rahim had called Soosan and me for interrogation in the same room to use each of us against the other. Neither of us knew the other. Both blindfolded, we sat awkwardly in the interrogation room while Rahim began his show first by asking Soosan whether or not she had changed her mind about *mosahebeh*—an interview, but in fact, it meant public recantation—and was now willing to appear in the *husseiniyeh*, the large hall in prison that was mainly used for prisoners' public recantation, to utter her renunciation of all the dissident organizations.

I heard Soosan's soft tone responding no, and Rahim's absurd questioning began. "Why? Don't you want to go out? You don't like being free? You like to be executed? You know that you will be if you don't accept the renunciation interview. Don't you? Why do you have a death wish? You don't like your life? Do you have a stepmother? You are not happy with your life? You prefer dying than going free?"

I could not really believe that he was in fact expecting responses from Soosan to his condescending, absurd questions. Soosan's replies were limited to the very softly uttered yes or no. But then Rahim began going on and on, now lecturing me about how Soosan's case proved that those prisoners who pride themselves on maintaining their stand against the regime and act courageously among themselves are in fact cowards when facing the interrogators; that they do not dare to speak and stand up for their beliefs because their beliefs are based on fake materialistic ideals, which cannot endure the power of Islam and the brothers' lashes. In the end, he had gotten Soosan to say, in a loud and clearly angry tone, that she did not want to and would not recant in the *husseiniyeh* or anywhere else, for she did not believe in doing so. Later I would be taken to the same ward as Soosan, and I would realize that the game Rahim played that day about her choice between execution and freedom by merely accepting or denying all dissident organizations and ideas was not a mere show; that in fact she was to have been executed but was given twelve years' time only because the circumstances changed from 1983 and the execution sentences were less summarily given, at least until the massacre of 1988.

After I was released, I would relive these experiences in different ways. My sister-in-law would tell me that I could have convinced Hamid to survive execution by submitting and answering yes to the interrogators' questions about whether or not he was a Muslim, if he was willing to pray as a Muslim, and if he supported the Islamic Republic, the three questions that determined the life or death of the leftists in the summer of 1988. My brother-in-law would look me in the eye and ask if I thought a belief was more important than a person I loved more than my life. How was I supposed to respond to him? How could I explain to him that my resistance was not so much about an ideology as such as about the kind of subjectivity in which one is forced to bargain that very subjectivity? How was I to elucidate this obscure point that it was not merely about life and death but about the kind of life and death that one has to choose? How could I convince him that Hamid could not survive without his ability to resist submission? That such submission would have made his life impossible? But for my brother-in-law, this would all be incomprehensible, for perhaps unlike me, his body and soul did not ache with the memories of humiliation, the pain of which is more excruciating than all the physical injuries that one's body endures under torture. And my body remembers the humiliation of that evening in 1986.

It was eight in the evening when the guards rushed into the ward and forced us out of our cells, even out of the bathrooms. We were taken to *zir-e hasht* and made to stand up facing the wall so that we could not see the guards behind us. With our eyes blindfolded, we could not predict what they were planning for us, as they had us wait for about half an hour, during which time coughing, sneezing, or any motion was punished by sudden blows by wooden clubs that were taken from dismantled fruit boxes with their nails still on. Then the real show started. The guards announced that they would be calling roll, but we had to respond precisely in the manner they ordered. Soon we learned that the calling of our names, supposedly taking attendance, was a mere pretext for beating and humiliation. Each prisoner had to wait to be beaten on her head while she pronounced her name. But it was up to the guards to determine when they were satisfied by the tone and the volume in which we uttered our names. They beat us, teased us about our names, and laughed at our parents' names; in short, humiliated us in any way possible. We had no chance to discuss the situation and make a collective decision, so we each reacted based on our own instincts and feelings. Although our decision was seemingly personal, its impact went beyond ourselves. Complying with this game would put the pressure on others who decided to resist, and vice versa.

The first person played the game, then the second, the third, on and on. The tone was set for the others; so it went on up to number 297. The clubs were being broken on our heads as we participated in this ridiculous spectacle all night long. Each of us made varying degrees of efforts in delaying our compliance with our own humiliation. Some responded according to the guards' desire after a few strikes, while others endured far more physical pain to reduce the pain of humiliation. The guards, too, had their own preferences as to how soon or late they accepted the tones and the responses as desirable enough to stop the beating and move to the next person. But when the guards came to two *mojahed* women, Souheila and Mina, they resisted going along and refused to utter their names. We all stood against the wall, silent, while the guards broke the clubs on the two young women's heads. The guards yelled at them, breathing heavily out of exhaustion from beating as hard and as fast as they could and out of rage about their resistance. But Mina's and Souheila's lips were sealed. The guards continued beating them until they both passed out and were taken to the clinic.

The place had turned into a battlefield with one side's weapons being only their bodies, which while receiving the beatings in turn exhausted the guards. The guards were drained of energy, after hours of beatings, especially by the resilience of Souheila and Mina. So many clubs had been broken on our heads and bodies and thrown on the floor that the guards tripped over them while walking around. Finally, when the guards' exhaustion overcame their rage, they told us to go back to the ward, while cracking the remaining clubs on us as we passed them to enter the ward. I was feeling dizzy because of the beatings and the physical and emotional exhaustion. I could not make sense of my feelings.

I had supposedly made a logical decision, along with many other prisoners who also refused to sign the renunciation form, not to spend my energy on small fights with the guards. I, of course, did not believe that we should not fight the rules and regulations the regime was imposing on us. I believed that we needed to be wary of falling for the daily tricks that officials played to keep us on our feet all the time, with no chance to think, and develop ideas, meditate, and reflect on our lives. Considering the constant pressure the regime imposed on us, we figured that it was essential for us not to constantly distract ourselves by engaging prison officials over insignificant issues they intentionally threw our way. The idea was not to waste our time on small matters and preserve our strength to stand up for the more important concerns, for instance, refusing to renounce our ideas.

My dilemma, however, was over separating the ordinary issues from those we deemed more consequential. I presumed that we had reached a logical conclusion regarding our capacity to tolerate the torture, but I was hardly satisfied with the rationale. I knew prisoners who, unable to endure more pressure, decided to sign the renunciation form. They honestly admitted to their fellow inmates their failure to endure the hardship any longer and were either released then or played safe until they could be released. Among them were, however, inmates who behaved more ethically and sensitively toward others than some of the seemingly more resistant inmates whose conflicted emotions were projected onto others and made their lives miserable.

I could not convince myself to live with endless humiliation and the violation of my own and others' dignity, justifying such compromises as necessary for resisting something more essential. What could be more essential, I wondered, than to protest the infliction of pain and suffering on others, to which one had become an unwilling witness? Was it not as, or even more, important to not get accustomed to living under torture, violence, and degradation as refusing to submit to the regime's condition for release? I began to believe that our energy to resist and to live humanely is initiated and reproduced by our belief in justice for ourselves and others, and these are inseparable from each other. Nevertheless, the question of how I was going to deal with my damaged soul remained.

That morning we returned to the ward, like beaten dogs, with our heads swollen and injured, our feet and legs bruised and trembling, and our souls shattered by the pain and humiliation. We gave massages to each other, but what could we do for our damaged souls? Some prisoners ignored the pain of their souls, as if nothing had happened, while others hated themselves, and still others turned the pain into rage toward the regime. Although tempted to push my soul into the corner or become outraged, I realized that I had to face myself directly. Despite all these meditations, these moral dilemmas repeated themselves in impossible situations where any decision was harmful one way or another. Since I have been out of jail and in the United States, I have come to think of nearly every decision as a matter of life and death; therefore, I avoid making decisions until I am forced to do so. This attitude, I recognize now, is a way of living the traumatic experiences of my childhood and prison, each time anew.

ى

My experience with Naser, the exhibitionist boy in our neighborhood in a small town in Azarbaijan who chased me around for several months and exposed himself to me, was another occasion for my confusion. How was I supposed to distinguish between all those complicated emotions of guilt, fear, and curiosity and react to them appropriately? As a ten-year-old girl, I was old enough to know that telling my father about Naser's improper behavior would cause a violent fight between them. My father had had a serious surgery, and Naser was a strong, six-foot-tall, eighteen-year-old boy. Refusing to tell my father overwhelmed me with guilt, as if I were sinful, especially considering my shameless curiosity to comprehend Naser's deviant sexual behavior. I sat by the window where Naser would stand in our backyard and put himself on display. Scared to tell my father about it, I felt both abused by Naser and an accomplice to his shameful act. My concern for my father's safety forced me into an impossible situation of constant fear, pressure, and shame. In my mind, keeping Naser's secret, even if for my father's sake, with no consent or participation from him, constituted an immoral act. How many times did I ask myself, even years later, what should I have done? How many moral and ethical dilemmas have led me to perpetually ask myself a similar question: "What should I do?"

The air was thick with the perturbed sighs of prisoners who with their eyes wide open witnessed Fozi's inappropriate behavior—she had taken her pants off in the room she shared with more than forty other women and was inserting a bar of soap into her vagina. Many of the prisoners looked frightened and agitated, while Fozi showed no sign of awareness of others' presence. Even if she knew, she seemed not to care. Lying down naked in her bed, touching herself in front of everyone, she was undermining an extremely sensitive aspect of the Iranian political prisoners' unwritten moral and social code of conduct. This was the point where everyone could tell she had really gone mad. Her madness was undoubtedly confirmed, for no political prisoner in her right mind could ever have done what she was doing, getting naked in front of others, but even worse, touching herself. From the prisoners' perspective, she had violated all the social rules of propriety that made us political subjects. In our minds, she had crossed all the boundaries that distinguished a human from an animal.

With her abnormality confirmed, she was removed from the category of collaborator to the world of insanity. In this new position, instead of being viewed as a traitor and consequently the target of hatred, she was perceived as a sick person who needed to be confined and taken care of. This new status, however, did not grant Fozi the same sympathy from other prisoners as it had for Roya, the young woman in Ghezel Hesar who relived her punishment of being forced to crawl and bark like a dog and host imaginary guests. This had partially to do with Fozi's infamous background as a collaborator. Many Mojahedin were still quite hostile toward her and therefore reluctant to care for her as they would for others.

Fozi's particular way of being abnormal, which was more outward and aggressive, especially in its early stages, and manifested itself in her sexual expression and "animalistic" characteristics, reinforced this resentment toward her. If Roya's remaining connection to the normal world introduced her to us as a person of delicate taste and manners, Fozi's behavior affirmed her dysfunctionality even as a normal person. During the period in which we were in the same ward as Roya, her sense of reality was never so clouded as to influence her basic social behavior. She dressed normally, used the bathroom like others, brushed her hair, took showers; in short, her adaptation to the primary social codes remained intact. Her physical beauty, social class, and neat appearance created a more sympathetic attitude toward her. Fozi's past reminded the leftists who knew her of her rigid religious beliefs and her adherence to the Islamic view that considered unbelievers as unclean. Anything that the leftists touched with their wet hands was rendered polluted, according to prison officials and many collaborators, including Fozi, before she was insane.

The sexual expression of Fozi's abnormality was perceived as more animalistic, while her irregular ways of eating, talking, and sleeping were no less erratic, since she "had lost it." The only difference was our perceptions about these activities, since for us, her sexual behavior was conceived as an assault on our collective morality, secular or religious. Fozi would go without eating for days, but then she would suddenly eat the food prepared for forty people. She would sit or walk for days without even taking a nap, and then she would go to sleep for such extended periods that she appeared dead. These strange patterns extended to almost every aspect of her life. Sometimes she was very aggressive and would attack us if we approached her or even looked at her; on other occasions she would be very calm and timid. We began to observe her different moods in order to clean her bed, change her clothes, and wash her. Until the final stages of her disintegration, she was performing some sort of religious rituals, though she was no longer praying or fasting. But suddenly it all stopped.

We were in Ward 325 in Evin, to which we had recently been moved. Ward 325 was one of the strangest wards during my years in prison. Even though some three hundred women and two young children were compressed in a small space of only five rooms that had been occupied by no more than forty people under the Shah, we loved its yard with its beautiful old trees, with water occasionally running in its streamlets. We loved the fact that we could stay in the yard most of the day, and that in the evenings we could hear children's shouts and laughter from Luna Park, the closest children's park to Evin Prison. Perhaps it was this daily access to the yard and its beauty that rendered Fozi's presence at once more tolerable and yet more disturbing, for the ward was often humid and suffocating.

It was here that one day, after eating about forty or so cooked eggs, she lay on the floor right by the door between the yard and the ward and stayed there for days, apparently asleep, while her urine and menstrual blood made the ward unbearable. The flies and cockroaches were having their feast but also making the ward a generous host for epidemic skin problems and other diseases. On one of these days Atefeh, our leftist friend who was a nurse outside the jail, took Fozi to the bathroom to give her a shower. She stayed calm the whole time and let Atefeh wash her. After Atefeh dressed her, Fozi went back to the shower with her clothes on and performed her ablutions. Obviously, she was still conscious of her previous religious belief that being touched by an unbeliever made her polluted, and to eliminate the pollution, she had to perform a specific kind of ceremonial washing of the body called ablution. What she did not realize was that she had her clothes on, or could this be her way of insinuating that even her clothes had become polluted and needed washing?

Atefeh took off Fozi's wet clothes and tried to put dry clothes on her. Fozi refused to get dressed and lay down on the bathroom floor where she stayed for eighteen days until the guards came, beat her skinny, un-kempt body, and eventually took her out of the bathroom. She was finally delivered to her family and institutionalized in a mental hospital. I never learned what happened to her later. The Mojahedin outside prison did not have to take the risk of punishing her betrayal by killing her. She was already dead, even if she could still breathe. Her lost soul never found its way back, at least as far as I know.

SHAKAR, the woman who returned from Haji Davoud's *dastgah* as a hate-ful, broken soul, on the other hand, changed the course of her life and her destiny. She died, but her death had a significant impact on others. Her death was a way for her to become alive again, or at least validate her past. After years of living in agony, she came to her senses. I do not know how. All I know is that she eventually stopped vomiting and began to smile. Color came back to her face, and her eyes started shining with life again. One day she promised her friends that she was going to make up for her sins, her betrayal, and her wrongdoing.

In 1988, when they called Mojahedin women to the court and asked whether they wished to collaborate or be executed, Shakar responded with joy and certainty that she would not collaborate, or so her surviving friends relate. It seemed as though she embraced this chance to salvage some meaning, pride, and solidarity in place of the long, miserable, an-guished life she had been living since her return from the *dastgah*. She was executed, while those who survived remembered her better days and felt sympathy for the torment she had experienced. I still ask myself how can it be that a woman must exhibit such extraordinary courage and pay such a price just to be considered a human being? Why should she go through all of that and eventually have to die in order to live one meaningful mo-ment? Yet this one moment was the essence of life that distinguished a sheer existence from living a life. But how long should we pay such a price just to be human beings?

Mass graves of dissidents in Khavaran

شماره _____ تاریخ ۱۳، ۹، ۴۵

نام و نام خانوادگی: حمید ـ حیدری، مادر جان، سلام، جمعه در ستهای سربازی سربازی، باباکم و سید وحشیسی

کلیم را نشار نگاز نمیکنم، امروز بهسترام برایتان نگفته میشود، پیش از شب جمعه، شب تولد سمعانخ عبدالدهار رفتگ، بیا

منکم، دعای جوری بنی سال خواهد بود که سر درد از عزیزانم ویبا دعوت تولد سید و لذهن فراغ رفت، درسای جمعی شما سمی

میلاد، شب طولی و سرد یا پیشد را نگرتنم که بادرس درمینا درانوار شدی، برگم طبیعت کم او وسایم شب منزر جانه ما خواهد به

از صبح زود را ساع از هخ، ابتیا باد رها بود و رتبه بایا، درتبه بایا، سر درد و غیر با، با سر خرو غیر با با ندشب سخی با سمی میشود، بالاخره با ها

نیک کستر و امیده شب یکرت می بینند، با دفعی کشید، مادرا سر ودند نار کدام میگرد، دو نند، یا بهرو یسه و هر رنگ اراز

وقت مادر جان از مرگ خم تر کسیر، پا بیدر خود مایی موم جمع بنونی، دنیا رنور خلیم، بارگ که با نش تی و کتاب بیا، بهلو و رب، یا

در بل احتیاج جادری بی شود و خلیم سود ویهودم، بیا کم مادره، بیاب سرتود، و تک خی و بارا ازرو خوان، و هران، و منه تلی

سلام، و دتک، خی، عزیزی کسیم، ابراکم، با اسلام، منط کردم هتم، قربیان شما حمید

آدرس فرستنده: _____

(پاسخ پشت صفحه نوشته شود)

ن ـ ۶۲/۲۶۱

Hamid's letter to Shahla's mother (translation opposite)

My dear mother, Greetings,

With no introduction, I kiss your kind hands and offer my heartfelt greetings and affection for you and all dear ones. These days I miss you more than ever. As the night of the solstice arrives, my dear Shahla's birthday, I find myself in a different mode. This would be the fourth year that I will be celebrating Shahla's birthday away from my dear ones and with all of you in my mind. Each year on this night, I try to imagine the long cold night of autumn in which the cold winter wind lashes madly at nature's body and the darkness of night tries in despair to forestall the dawn, but in spite of all this, there are mothers who burn in the fever of labor and heroically bear a night of hardship. Finally, the dawn in its full beauty prevails, and the night fades away, the wind subsides, the mothers calm down in triumph, and children come to the forefront of existence. And you, my mother, that same day you see a beautiful narcissus at your side, light like the morning, and pure as the snow on mountain tops that, with the flowing of the spring sun, along with the translucent streams, flows into society. May Shahla's birthday be a blessing for all of us. I offer my greetings to grandmother, dear father, all brothers and sisters, their spouses, and all the relatives, and I kiss all the children, particularly Nasim. This year too, I will be waiting for photos.

May I die for you,
Hamid
Evin, Hall # 3, Room 66

A wallet Hamid made from the thread of his socks during the period of his interrogation. His feet were still so badly injured from torture that he could not wear socks. Instead he decided to put them to a better use and made this wallet for me.

This necklace and bracelet are both made of date seeds and colored by
tea that Hamid made for me for the anniversary of our wedding.

Kobra

THE GAZE OF DEATH

When you have known the rapture of burning

You will never again be patient even to keep from the fire.

—Hafiz, *The Green Sea of Heaven*

When we arrive at the site of burial and put the corpse down in the direction of Mecca to pray the salat l-gnaza in front of it, the prayer of the dead, as we contemplate the corpse, the gaze of death slowly takes hold of each one of us. There is a moment of silence, when sitting on the ground we see Death, and we are colonized by its overwhelming thought. We forget our families, then, our children, our property, . . . and we lose ourselves in the infinity of that vision, where everything becomes indifferent. Dunya, the world and its affairs, disappears for us.

But the angel comes. . . .

An angel comes, flies over us and sprinkles a handful of earth over our heads. It is the earth of forgetting and makes us blind, once again, to the paralyzing vision of Death. Again we can see the world, set back into its boundaries by our blindness, and again we find ourselves caught in daily affairs.

—Stefania Pandolfo, *Impasse of the Angels*

Roudabeh: Deceiving Life for the Sake of Death

The angel, however, did not show herself to Roudabeh when she was taken to see the corpse of her brother and was seized by the gaze of death. An eighteen-year-old woman, Roudabeh used to admire her older brother and follow in his footsteps. When her name was announced on the loud-speaker of the prison ward, she was walking in the yard with her friends. The guards took her to her brother's cell, where she saw his battered body, his smashed face, and his swollen and infected feet, heavily and irreversibly possessed by death. He had saved himself from the viciousness of the unbearable torture by hanging himself from the door of his cell. Looking at her brother's lifeless body in that somber cell, where probably no angel would dare to come, Roudabeh experienced the encounter with the absolute other.

She walked back to the ward, ate her dinner, brushed her teeth, and went to bed, but she performed all these activities as if they were some residual habits from a world to which she no longer belonged. Her feet were still imprisoned in this place, while her soul had already stepped out, and in so doing, she had lost the means of utterance. She no longer spoke to anyone, though her body still required her earthly attention. Her spirit hung in the air awaiting her body's release from the agony of this prolonged anticipation. She lived with the strangers she once knew as her fellow inmates. Was she aware of her imprisonment in Evin Prison? Even if she was, what difference could it make when the whole world was a prison for her from which she was interminably trying to escape?

A few days after her encounter with death, Roudabeh's repetitive suicide attempts began. A strange insufficiency characterized these constant efforts that we were unable to fathom. With a broken glass in her hand, which she didn't even hide from us, her ghostly body would walk in the yard while the scratches on her wrists and hands were lightly bleeding. Stolen pills, which she would take at night, were not enough for her imprisoned body to fly out of this alien world. Were these attempts her struggle to call back life through experiencing physical pain, or were they her way of trying to cross the line into her brother's world, that other territory, a desire her confused state of mind did not allow her to draw to its ultimate end?

We took turns watching over her to rescue her from death, by which she was already possessed. Yet we were baffled by her behavior. If she were already captured by death, and trapped in the everyday world she shared with us, why couldn't she be more vigorous and successful in her suicide attempts? Some prisoners perceived her behavior as an indication of her need for attention, thus insincere and pretentious. I disagreed. We could see no sign of reaction to whatever attention she got from us. In fact, she appeared to be totally oblivious to our reactions toward her, or even to our existence. She made no effort to communicate even with formerly close friends.

Some of my fellow prisoners believed that, despite her alienation and depression, she was still more in touch with life than death so that she could not seriously hurt herself. They argued that her inability to severely damage herself implied a deep connection to life and her sensitivity to pain and fear. I, however, felt that, while disassociated from this world, she was no longer able to play by its rules. She lacked the force and the energy required to effectively take action. Her eating, sleeping, and other habitual activities were performed in a dispirited manner, as though they were solely conditioned behaviors. Roudabeh's experience seemed like neither living nor dying, but a state of *barzakh*, where one is neither alive nor dead, unable to live or die. This is a realm of extreme deprivation where life and death have both perished. Taking one's life necessitates a drive and energy that can spring only from life. Roudabeh's soul had already departed life, so that type of force no longer resided in her. Her attempts to discard the body were doomed to fail, for she was not able to die.

The gaze of death by which she was haunted had virtually transformed her into a ghost, without the dramatic fear such an apparition normally provokes. In this *barzakh*, the rules and impact of neither reality would apply. Melancholy and despair overtook her, and before we knew how, we had identified her place as in the world of the insane, the threshold of that land of the absolute other but still occupying an edge of life. It is the irregularity of this domain that presents itself as indecisively other. Perhaps it is this position of at once falling into the domain of the absolute other while keeping a foot in this world that renders insanity so troubling to us.

Roudabeh withdrew to that other territory where, even while living so close to us, there was no common language with which we could cross the line between us. The estrangement grew deeper. She kept attempting futile suicides, and we devotedly "saved" her until the prison officials considered her abnormal and ill enough to interfere in her anguished life. The torturers were now supplanted by the psychiatrists, who evaluated her condition and gave her medication. She returned to the ward acting normal. For an entire month there were no suicide attempts or more strange behavior. She would not initiate conversation, but if asked a question, she would briefly respond. Everybody seemed satisfied that she had changed. She was anesthetized enough not to be a political threat to the regime. The psychiatrists were content that their treatment had been effective, and we were happy that we no longer needed to take turns watching over her. Having her come back from that terrifying world of madness could reduce our fear of its strangeness.

A month after she was cured, however, we woke up one morning only to find her dead in her bed. With her face so peaceful and her body so relaxed, it seemed that she had died with no struggle or pain. She had obviously preplanned everything, taken all her medication at once, and gone to a sleep from which she knew she would not awaken. Although we felt surprised and sorrowful, a sense of embarrassment pervaded us. It was as if we had been tricked by her gesture of playing normal, followed by her sudden, powerful act, an ironic living for the sake of death. In a game of mutual deception with the psychiatrists, Roudabeh had won the game. In exercising her power over her life and death, Roudabeh's only weapon was her life, and she had reclaimed it by eradicating it.

There was no angel in jail who could sprinkle a handful of earth over Roudabeh's head to return her to the world and its affairs, after she was seized by the gaze of death at the sight of her brother's body, to which she had been an unwilling witness. Instead, the psychiatrist gave her a handful of pills. Roudabeh was, however, bewitched by death. Through her, death spoke and utilized its power to consume life while her living, if one may speak of it as such, had become practice for dying death. Because of this drive for death and this possession by it, Roudabeh deceived and used life to destroy it. After death, her face presented the enigma of a strange peace, a victorious smile so unfathomable to us then that the irony confused us.

Living in the Face of Death

> I have never been afraid of death
>
> Even though its hands were more fragile than triviality
>
> My fear is, however, of dying in a land in which
>
> The grave digger's wage is worth more than a human being's freedom.
>
> —Shamlu, "The Grave Digger's Wage"

In 1979, in the midst of the stormy demonstrations in which gunfire produced piles of human bodies on the streets of Tehran, I ran into a young man whose bloody eyes and strange behavior seemed like that of a drunk person. I was surprised by this peculiar encounter—how could someone be drinking during a time like this? I stopped to find out what was going on. The revolution in Iran had created such a peculiar situation that every aspect of people's life was affected by it. People were so intoxicated by the movement that coming across a young man in the midst of all the killings who appeared as if drunk on alcohol seemed very unusual. But when I walked closer to him, all of sudden I caught sight of his bloody fist. "Are you injured? Are you shot? Is something wrong with your hand?" I received no answers to my questions. He had leaned his head against the trunk of a tree. I held his arm and helped him turn toward me, which he did mechanically. He looked at me with red eyes but as if in sleep; he slowly opened his hand.

And there it was. What he had been so tightly holding in his hand was part of a smashed brain covered with blood. Silence, the only possible language for such an unspeakable situation, spoke to us. In shock, waiting for him to break the silence, I stood there suspended as if in an eternal moment. Now that his fist was opened, he seemed just to have realized what had happened. He began to shiver, burst into tears, and finally, while sobbing, in fragmented speech he described how he and his best friend, Mahmoud, had arrived at the rally and how the events leading to that present moment had transpired. Guards had shot Mahmoud before his eyes, and all he could save was Mahmoud's smashed brain. "How can I go back to Mahmoud's mother and tell her that I broke my promise and could not take care of him, that I watched his brain splash under my feet? How can I compensate for this only son, who was his mother's sole breadwinner? Should I give these pieces of his brain to her? Tell me how I should go to her," he lamented. Now I was the silent one.

But this silence was far from inactive. Grief and rage were boiling within me as I stood there for a few minutes. Suddenly all I could think of was to organize another rally right there and then. Was organizing another rally right on the spot and at that very moment, and shouting out the slogans with all one's might and defiance, a meaningful response to this man's and his dead friend's mother's loss? Events like these directed our rage toward organized riots for freedom and against the life and death enforced by a dominating system under which, as Shamlu, my favorite poet, would have said, "the wages of grave diggers outweighed the worth of human freedom." I did not see another way to channel my rage against such brutality and its consequent tragedy than to speak out.

Years later, however, when I was released from my second imprisonment, my mother-in-law looked me in the eye and asked, "How could you go to prison with Hamid and come back without him? How could you let him go?" I knew she was not really accusing me of letting him go. Her words were merely expressing her own grief and actually her sympathy for my pain. I understood, logically, that she was simply imagining herself in my shoes and that her question was an expression of her bafflement as to what it must have felt like to go to jail with the love of your life and return without him. For she herself had lost the two most significant loves of her life, her son, Hamid, and her husband, my father-in-law, who had had a stroke and died while we were still in prison. Her words were thus articulating her own heartache in facing the world without the ones she loved, first her husband, and now her son. I knew all this, yet my heart bled with pain as I heard her words. Was she really expecting a response from me? I had none. There was no demonstration then in which I could cry out my rage and grief. There was no visible movement, and we were not on the street but in my parents' home and under the worried, scrutinizing eyes of my father, who had never been good at seeing my tears and witnessing me upset.

In silence, I swallowed my grief and hid my emotions whenever I heard these kinds of questions about my husband's death, as if I could have saved him; as though somehow I could and should have convinced him to choose life over death. My first encounter with one of my brothers-in-law after twelve years, since he had left Iran and resided in Europe and I had been jailed, was another of these incidents that endured in my memory. It was December 1993, and I had just left Iran for Paris, from which I would soon leave for the United States. He had driven on snowy roads a long way from another European capital in order to see me. No longer a teenager, this grown man was now telling me how painful it had been for him to hear of his brother's execution not from his own family but through a friend's phone call, on one unforgettable early morning.

"Imagine being awakened by a phone call, and there is someone on the other side of the line asking you if a particular first and last name is in fact that of your brother, and when you inquire why he is asking this question and confirm that the name is in fact that of your brother, he sighs and tells you that your brother has been among those executed in Iran whose names had been announced by Radio Israel. Can you believe this? The Israeli radio should be the source for me to learn that I no longer have a brother with whom I used to go to the public bath; to learn that the brother who cared for my injuries is no more. I was so angry at my family that I did not talk to them for a while."

I tried to imagine his pain and anger—I could not have reminded him how I had learned about all my losses, not only of Hamid, but of my aunt, my father-in-law, my cousin, . . . all those loved ones I had lost while in prison, always belated, always after the fact, always months, if not years, after all the mourning processions had passed. I tried to contemplate how particularly agonizing this must have felt for him since he was abroad, safe and sound, not knowing his family was grieving for his brother's death and now he had to grieve without them. He must have, of course, been very outraged, at the injustice of his time, at the brutality of the regime, at himself for having been enjoying his time with his girl-friend while his brother was taken for execution, while his mother was mourning. Who else could he have directed this rage toward but his family, the only ones who could have loved him, regardless of his attitude?

Sounding somewhat angry—was he still angry at me, too?—he asked me what ideology was worth a human life. Before I could say anything, he repeated the question now in specific terms—"What ideology is worth my beautiful, kind brother's life?"—assuming that Hamid had died for Marxism. I could have ignored the political massacre of 1988 that had cost the lives of thousands of political prisoners, including Hamid, and told him that he had died to refuse submitting to a bare life. This would have been true. The truth was that Hamid and I, and many other prisoners, believed that to surrender to the regime and to denounce our past, regardless of what we presently believed, was to allow ourselves to be reduced to a merely organic life, a life in which one's survival comes at the cost of one's subjectivity. One survives, so we thought, by giving up being a thinking and social being. It was hence true that I could not have convinced Hamid, even if I had had the chance to talk to him, to be reduced to this bare, organic survival.

Yet my brother-in law could have argued, and rightly so, that the very question of whether or not a bare life is worth living is hinged upon a set of beliefs or a worldview and is therefore ideological. And this, too, would have been true. For people live believing in something; we all have a sense of ethics or an idea of justice, whether we live accordingly or not. For some, life may be a ride on the shoulders of others, while there are individuals who strive to create a beautiful symphony of love, friendship, and community to render their life meaningful. Most of us, however, live in between these two realities. We make a wide range of complex and contradictory choices that vacillate between these two extremes.

I, too, try to remain present to myself and my community. It is my constant preoccupation to bear witness to the injustices of the world around me and to respond, in the best way I know how, to the calls of our disjointed time. Yet time and again, I have found myself lost in the labyrinth of strange worlds I have come to inhabit since my release from jail, both in Iran and later in the United States, my place of residence since 1994. Each and every time, my urge to reawaken my senses, and my urge to seek justice have demanded of me to recultivate my ability to listen to the voices from the graves and their echoes in the future.

IT WAS 1999, and I was extremely heartbroken following a failed romantic relationship for which my inexperienced heart had no preparation. My only previous experience of romantic love was with Hamid, whom I had lost so violently. And here I was with no regime to take away my love, yet I had lost him without knowing how to make sense of this loss. I was not prepared for the games of this world. I was too loyal, and words meant much more than they meant to an American with such a radically different life background. I was going through a very painful experience and had no resources for surviving it. Friends could not understand how someone who had been through hell and come out of it still a joyous and dynamic person could be in such despair in the face of something as simple as a failed love. It seemed that the image of this vulnerable woman did not match that of a resistant political prisoner.

I, too, felt ashamed, not for having fallen in love or even for feeling despair for failing in love, but for not being able to fight for love, for not being able to show that love can survive all the disasters of the world. Suddenly, I saw it. It was not merely the loss of a person, or a romantic love per se, but all that I had believed and lived for my entire life, especially during my years in prison, that love is the cure and the savior, the power and the might that overcomes everything against all odds; this belief that had helped me survive all obstacles, even the absurdity of my own survival, was now being crushed in front of me.

And then I realized that I had begun to feel somewhat envious of those friends of mine who had been executed. I envied Hamid, who lived such a meaningful and devoted life and died with so much love and admiration from his family and friends. I contemplated my own life now in the United States, where I had to begin everything anew from point zero. Already nearly in my late thirties, living in a new and strange cultural world, I had come to feel a lesser person. Paradoxically, just three years before at the Iranian Women's Studies Foundation Conference, I had argued, in response to a former political prisoner who used the metaphor of animals in a zoo to speak of our experience of imprisonment as being victims of the regime's atrocities, that we were neither animals nor helpless victims but the subjects of our own will. But now, I had caught myself feeling like a victim, something I had always thought I would refuse to accept.

Since then I have come to realize that overcoming and surviving traumatic events like the ones I had experienced could never be a foregone conclusion. It is a constant process that entails a never-ceasing struggle through and against the vicissitudes of life's ups and downs. The idea of a psychotherapeutic overcoming of trauma, I have come to learn, is an illusion. One might only work through it, in ways that sometimes paradoxically reproduce trauma, but other times one finds innovative ways of dealing with it in one's life. During the 2004 earthquake in the old city of Bam in Iran, for instance, I saw how my own experiences became constructive while I was working with the survivors of this heart-wrenching disaster. To work through trauma means to live one's life always in quest of meaning, to strive to create meaning for one's life and, of course, death, without which there would be no meaning to life.

But in 1999, I caught myself asking, albeit without words, why should it be I who had to suffer all the time? I felt embarrassed for even thinking this way, yet there were times that I could not help it. Night after night in my dreams, I confused Hamid with the person whose love had hurt me so deeply in the recent months. Unable to make sense of my experience of this failed love, I contemplated the reasons for this strange confusion in my dreams. And then one day I surprised myself by telling one of my friends how lucky Hamid was for having been executed. He did not have to be challenged by the absurdity of this kind of life we could never learn how to live.

Neither Hamid nor I thought of love as something trivial that could be purchased and consumed in the market like a commodity, the way I felt it was by many people in the United States. And now Hamid was gone, and I was left with a heart that was too loyal and too young and naïve for a woman of my age, while the world around me was so complicated. How did I age so quickly without having experienced situations that might have prepared me for these kinds of challenges? Did I survive all the horror and humiliation to come to live such a trivial life? What was I doing in this country anyway? After going through all those complexities of life, how could I be so naïve? How was I to live a life in which no sacrifice seemed possible, for everything seemed to be so easily purchased with money, where people changed their feelings faster than their shoes? Why was I even alive anyway?

> My darling. Brush in the garden
> Untie your hair and brush it in the garden
> In the Garden, because of the flower,
> They have hung the nightingale.

These verses were embroidered on the wings of two birds that Hamid sewed for our fourth anniversary, while separated from one another within the walls of different wards. We had lived together only to celebrate our first anniversary outside prison. For every other anniversary after the first year, until his execution, we were separated from one another, while both imprisoned. For the occasion of his birthday, I, too, embroidered a poem on a fabric folder I made for keeping his letters:

> By the magic of love, I am now a clear riverbed
> Find a way toward me through the valleys of the mirror.
>
> —Shamlu, "Mahi"

In one of his letters, which passed the prison inspectors' filtering, he wrote me: "From you I learned how to apprehend being together while living separated," and I wrote him back: "Every day of living with you and now thinking about you has been the source of inspiration, strength, and new ways of loving. Every moment with you is a new birth." In another letter he said: "How could I clearly explain that you are my life, my love, and that your happiness is the goal of my existence? I wish I could absorb all your pain. How consoled my soul would feel then." Was it the power of this incredible love that helped me through those tunnels of horror at the end of which I was still able to smile?

He wrote in yet another letter after our first visit in about four years: "I finally saw you, though behind those thick glasses, and under the eyes of all those others and so briefly that I could not even overcome my excitement to say something—Oh how long I had waited for this moment!—before I knew it, it was over. Like a shooting star, that incredible, splendid moment so rapidly vanished, but the image of your beautiful smile submerged in me. This is how you are, the Shahla I knew, the one who smiles in the midst of disaster and laughs at pain. You were always like that, and I loved you for it."

In 1983, ten months after our imprisonment, I was called for interrogation. While waiting to be sent into the room, I heard the guards and the interrogators whispering about Hamid's death under torture. I slightly pulled up my blindfold and saw someone covered in a bloody blanket. My knees were my worst enemy in that moment, for their trembling was betraying my fear and my weakness to the interrogators. Later that day, my interrogator was sadistically trying to enjoy himself by telling me the details of the way Hamid had died, and I, in turn, was challenging him by hiding my emotions. "You could not kill him. He is alive in me and all those people who loved him. If you kill every one of us, he will live in love itself until the end of the world." I was bluffing, while my heart was bleeding. My body paid a high price for my blunt comments that day, but it felt much less painful than my sorrow.

That evening, in the ward, I looked through the bars to see the moon and the stars, seeking to find an empty hole in my heart in his absence. There wasn't any. The sky was as beautiful and the moon and stars so bright that I somehow knew that if I was still capable of seeing all that beauty, he could not be dead. I went to my room. A program about Sufism and poetry was on TV. As I walked in, I heard someone on TV reciting a poem by Kalim Kashani:

> You were leaving and my heart's blood was pouring down on my way.
> The blaze of hell was pouring down from my sigh.
>
> You were coming and from the joy of your coming
> Lapfuls of flowers were pouring down from my eyes
> into the Friend's flower garden.

Joyous tears washed my face; he was not dead. Somehow my heart knew that he was alive. Two weeks later, I learned that my interrogator was just manipulating my emotions, and Hamid was still alive. However, someone was killed that day, as Hamid was a few years later. Someone else felt that empty hole in her heart that day, as I did a few years later. But during those years, Hamid's love melted the freezing hatred by which I would otherwise be haunted. His love and trust in me softened my heart. Despite our physical distance, with his love he provided me loving shelter, his generous shoulders offered me rest from my exhaustion, and he held my hands whenever my knees gave way under pressure. He was my angel who, instead of blinding me to death, unveiled the horizon for me through which I could face the gaze of death and the beauty of life simultaneously. He evoked a passion in me that motivated me to live my life fully and irrevocably, as if every day was my last day. In the light of this love and this passion for life, we were able to discover the space between deaths and ways to reveal the criminality of the law to which we had been subjected. I fought, lived, and survived with him, for him, and because of him. Was that what Roudabeh had lost when she saw her brother's dead body?

> Remember the day of union with the friends.
> Remember those times, remember.
> From bitter sorrow my mouth became like poison.
> Remember the revelers' cry of "Drink."
> The friends are free of the memory of me
> although I remember them a thousand times.
>
> —Hafiz, *The Green Sea of Heaven*

I was doing the dishes when I saw that lucid image of Hamid's execution. He was standing with his eyes open, and his blue shirt was covered with blood. A shivering cold pervaded my body. It was the summer of 1988, during the period of total isolation from the rest of the world, with no connection to other wards. I was in the dark about Hamid's situation. In the afternoon, while taking a shower, I saw the image again, even more

vividly than the first time. Was it a nightmare? But how could it be? I was awake. Was I dreaming without knowing it, or had I gone insane and begun seeing images? The thought of it made me tremble. Somehow it seemed so real, as though I were witnessing Hamid's execution while he was trying to reach me beyond the physical distance, perhaps to say good-bye. He always had his powerful ways to communicate with me. Was this one of them? Was he really leaving me forever?

Shocked and confused, I attempted to ignore this sign. But it contin-ued reappearing to me more forcefully. Hamid had stretched his arms and hands toward me. His lips were moving as though talking to me, but I could not hear him. I closed my eyes to stop seeing him, a useless effort. He kept looking at me, and the blood on his chest was spreading more widely. His face was so pale that it seemed he was already dead, but his lips were still moving and his eyes were looking at me as deeply and lovingly as ever. I resisted seeing that image any way I could, perhaps scared that if I admit-ted its presence, it would speak its reality. I turned the water to cold, closed my eyes, even tried to sing. Nothing helped. It kept reappearing and every time slightly differently as though I were watching the event with brief in-tervals. My heart was incapable of sustaining any more. Hamid was mov-ing away while he was still talking to me, and I was unable to hear him. But suddenly, I heard my name through his bloodless lips on the face so pale as if drowned in fog. His low gentle voice whispered my name and . . .

When I regained consciousness, I was in the room surrounded by my cellmates. I did not tell them what I had seen; was I afraid that talking about it could make it real? But my heart knew; it was communicating his departure to me; I was, however, refusing to accept it. That evening, when I was lifting my bag of clothes from the shelf, my ring was stuck in the shelf; its diamond fell down, and despite my efforts, I never found it. I had worn the ring since my wedding; during the last seven years, I had never taken it off my finger, and this was the first time it had been damaged. My heart was so tightly clenched, and I had such an enigmatic sense of loss, a loss that you are not aware of, but you nonetheless feel so profoundly. A melancholic grief overtook me. That night, I climbed up to the window, watched the sky and the moon, and thought about our shared memories. And finally I felt it; it was there, after all those games they played with me, but each time since I had not felt it; I somehow did not believe his loss, but now here it was, that hole in my heart. But my heart was so filled with love and our shared experience that I felt him inside and tried to convince myself he was still alive.

Three years later, when I was released, I met a former male prisoner who was in the same ward with Hamid at the time of the mass execution. My knees gave way as I heard that the day Hamid was taken was exactly the same day I had seen those images of him. Remorse filled me, realizing how I had refused to say farewell to my beloved when he had reached out to me beyond all the boundaries. I should have known that then, and I blamed myself. He had an extraordinary connection to me that my mind was incapable of comprehending. He wrote to me in his letters about specific days or even hours that I was sick or cold and that he had felt it, and his feelings were always accurate. Why didn't I interpret that image as his desire to see me before going away forever? Did he feel disappointed that I wasn't responsive, or was he able to relate to my refusal to witness his death? Which fear was more paralyzing to me, the fear of insanity if I admitted that the images were real, or the fear of letting the event become real by accepting it as so? I was physically far away from Hamid, and I missed the power of his love that was breaking all the walls of time and space to reach me. I missed such energy. How can I justify this ignorance caused by my rational, narrow mind and my rigid dichotomy of sanity and insanity?

I am still bewildered by these questions. Whatever the reason, I let the chance of bidding farewell to him pass me by. I continued to live while carrying him with me. Yet the burden of the responsibility of living in accordance with the meaning of his life and death felt heavy on my shoulders. How could I live as beautifully as he had? How could I live as though I were living his life? I scrutinized every step of my life so critically that in the end I lost confidence in ever being able to live up to my expectations. Was I, too, like Roudabeh and others, seized by the gaze of death, by the image of his moment of dying, without being conscious of it?

Kobra: A Shattered Image

Kobra, however, was caught by the gaze of her dead ideas. She took the journey to the world of the insane, from which she had tried to stay so remote. A tall, broad person with a coarse voice and rough skin, she had a masculine appearance that somehow matched her behavior. Kobra was born and raised in a modest, religious family whose members had achieved high positions under the Islamic Republic regime. Her assertiveness and her nonreligious views had apparently pushed her to withdraw from her family and relatives. Her conversion from Islam to Marxism made her perceived by both collaborators and the prison officials as even worse than those nonreligious prisoners whose families were not religious. She was almost disowned by her family for becoming a leftist, and her imprisonment worsened this distance between her and her family.

The idea was that someone who lacked exposure to religious beliefs and practices was less at fault for being a leftist than someone who had prior exposure to religion. The interrogators were extremely hostile toward those leftist organizations whose previously Muslim members had become Marxists. Kobra was doubly criminal because of her personal background as a Muslim who had become a leftist and her affiliation with an organization that had shifted its ideological position from Islam to Marxism. Having known about Islam and then rejecting it made her an unbeliever whose heart was sealed to God. In addition to the pressure from the prison officials, the guards, and collaborators, she was also almost deserted by her family since she refused to submit to the regime's conditions for her release as her parents demanded.

Kobra was arrested in 1981, when the wards were extremely overcrowded and prisoners of different ages, organizations, and tendencies were squeezed into the same ward. She was one of a few people who did not perform prayers and refused to speak or eat with the collaborators.

This deviance contributed to her seclusion in the ward. She persistently fought against her isolation and refused to alienate herself from others to the extent to which her principles would allow her. For resistant prisoners, the struggle against this isolation was a very challenging yet essential task.

From 1981 to 1985, the collaborators were dominating prisons and creating an extremely unbearable situation for other prisoners by scrutinizing every move they made and reporting them to the interrogators, thus putting the prisoners under more severe torture and heavier sentences. The regime's brutality along with these difficult conditions in the wards led many of the prisoners toward a tactical retreat. These prisoners would pretend that they had converted to Islam and that they were no longer activists. This tactical maneuver, in turn, intensified the collaborators' power and perpetuated collaboration. Kobra, however, was among a minority who avoided this tactic and directly spoke their minds.

In 1983, when I was arrested and sent to this ward, I was forced to live in a room in which everybody was either a collaborator or pretended to be one. At the time, among about five hundred prisoners, I was the second person in the entire ward who did not pray and took a direct stand against the regime. I was considered a profane unbeliever and not allowed to touch anything with my wet hands, which meant that I could not wash our dishes. Those who spoke with me put themselves at risk of being reported by the collaborators as my allies. This was harder on the mothers of young children in jail. The ward to which I had been sent had twenty-eight children from infancy to seven years old. These were children who were either born in prison or arrested along with their mothers and had no one outside who could take care of them. I always loved children and could play, sing, and take care of them with joy and ease. In jail, too, I became very attached to them, and they also felt the bond. I used to give showers to several of these children on the day that was our shower time. I still vividly hear the scream of a little girl who wanted me instead of her own mother to take her to the shower, since I let her play there. After I had showered her a few times, however, her mother was warned that if she did not stop this, she would be punished. While embarrassed, the mother asked me to let her cleanse her daughter after I washed her. I could not agree with her request since it would mean condoning their ideas about my pollution.

As time passed, those prisoners who had survived execution and madness, at least for the time being, learned more about themselves, their strengths, and new methods of resistance. The antagonistic relationship between the adamant prisoners and the collaborators eventually led to increasing divergence among prisoners. Those between the two extremes of the continuum were forced to choose, an act that intensified the conflict. This encouraged the prison officials to begin their policy of segregating the resistant prisoners from the rest. The emotional impact of being reported on, or beaten by former friends and activists, was diminished by this new policy. As a result, the tension in the wards was relatively reduced, since the guards were unable to scrutinize the prisoners' lives as closely as the collaborators did. Having thus lost their importance in prison, most of the collaborators were released.

Despite the changes that occurred in the wards, the conflict in prison remained intense. The prisoners were demanding better treatment while refusing to accept the regime's imposing rules in prison and the conditions for their release. These actions, which often included hunger strikes, refusal to attend forced public recantations, or other occasions that mandated prisoners' presence, were severely suppressed, and prisoners were often brutally punished. The defeats and the extreme pressure that followed incited many prisoners toward less direct actions and opinions. Every failure generated an atmosphere of disappointment, a lack of confidence in collective and individual resistance and trust for one another.

After experiences like the *dastgah* in Ghezel Hesar, from which very few prisoners emerged as noncollaborators or sane individuals, it became even clearer that one's resistance under torture in the early stages of one's arrest did not necessarily guarantee its continuation under more extreme and prolonged conditions of hardship. Among those who had given in and turned against their comrades after their experience in the *dastgah* were those whose resilience under torture at the time of their arrest bought them great respect in the circle of their fellow inmates. This collaboration sometimes cost prisoners' trust of one another, the lack of which influenced every aspect of their lives and relationships to one another.

Kobra passed through all these phases, fought, failed at times, but refused to give up. From 1984 until 1986, several movements by women prisoners were crushed, and many of the women agreed to the regime's conditions to recant and be released. A sense of disheartening despair was floating in the air, and those who were still directly resisting were taking a dangerous risk of being the target of increasingly intensive pressure. Kobra was among those who chose to state her opinion directly whenever she was asked.

Kobra's theoretical perspective on the postrevolutionary era in Iran went through a peculiar transformation. As the government was establishing its technologies of power more solidly by suppressing nearly all the opposition groups outside and inside prison, her analysis of the situation was becoming more radicalized. Despite a countervailing reality, she was arguing that the political climate in Iran was moving toward the "revolutionary phase." The idea that Iran was undergoing a revolutionary phase was upheld by some leftists and Mojahedin for a short period in the early 1980s. It was, however, criticized by most others as a misreading of the Iranian political landscape. Advocating such an idea, especially in 1989, as Kobra did, was no longer seen as a simple political misreading but as an indication of her delusion. Paradoxically, the more indifference others showed toward her ideas, the more rigid and dogmatic the ideas became.

The process of her delusion was aggravated by her thyroid problem, a source of great stress and discomfort for her. She had a difficult time sleeping in a room with other prisoners, many of whom would speak, scream, or make other noises while asleep, especially during and after the summer of 1988. Sleep deprivation, the prison's constant pressure, and her failure to face reality pushed her further into withdrawing into herself. After a fight with one of the guards, she was sent to solitary confinement, where she was deprived of her thyroid medication. Her condition worsened, and consequently, she sank into madness.

When Kobra was returned to the ward, her abnormal behavior, which had begun while in solitary confinement, entertained the guards so much that they could not deprive themselves of the opportunity of watching our reaction to our first encounter with it. She was brought back to the ward a few days after the first group of women, who were being whipped during prayer times, returned. She appeared shattered and delirious. With a rancorous smile, the guards were still standing at the door when Kobra entered the room. Staring at her fellow inmates, she cried out: "Why aren't you ready? Why aren't you packed? People are coming to open the prison gate, and you are sitting here so passively?" Confused and surprised, we tried to calm her down, while the guards closed the door, taunting and laughing at her hysterically.

Yet Kobra looked deadly serious and enthusiastic about the revolution behind prison walls, as she imagined it. Annoyed by our passivity, she was yelling at us to join those who were trying to release us. Her organization, she claimed, was leading people in this movement. "How could you not hear them? You are ignoring them, since you have been so afraid for so long that you prefer to stay passive and imprisoned. You are deaf and blind to the revolution that shakes all the foundations in this society and turns everything upside down." Her tone was that of a political agitator. Her best friend tried to convince her that she was confused because of all the pressure on her and also from the lack of sleep. Kobra became outraged, claiming that her friend had betrayed the revolution and had become like the rest of us. That evening, she screamed, kicked the walls and the door, and repeated revolutionary slogans against the government. The guards, who had had enough of the show, took her back to her cell, beating her as they walked her away.

Two months afterward, some of the inmates returned from their solitary cells, where they had heard Kobra's voice and the guards' conversations about her. She had become precisely what she so resented the most. She was singing the songs that she had always thought of as vulgar. She danced, got undressed in front of the guards, and demonstrated what she would have outrageously renounced as inappropriate sexual behavior had she been in her right mind. These actions had given prison officials an excuse to beat her up. She was constantly beaten and chained to the heater in her cell. She was left in the dark for days and nights without food and medication. Finally, she was driven to the point where her insanity was proved to prison officials, and she was hospitalized. In 1989, when she was totally out of control, they delivered her to her family, who sent her to a mental hospital, from one type of imprisonment to another.

I left Iran when Kobra was institutionalized for the third time. I saw her a few weeks earlier when she was released from the hospital and seemed fine. She had been given a job at a private company where a few other former inmates were also working for a previously leftist political prisoner under the Shah's regime. In between those periods of insanity, when others thought of her as normal, was the time for her to remember her episodes of madness while in jail. The shame was too overwhelming for her to bear and continue living. In 1998, four years after I had left Iran and was living in the United States, I learned about Kobra's suicide.

Kobra had rebelled against the rigid moral and social codes to which her extremely religious family adhered. However, some of these deeply rooted norms were reappropriated in her rendition of Marxism. Even though she was a Marxist, she, like many of us in the leftist organizations, upheld very firm ideas of propriety. Her knowledge of the self and her gendered subjectivity were constructed both in her mind and through the ideas and practices that emerged and reinforced themselves in the Iranian collective consciousness. It was unfortunate that we could usually recognize the vitality of the struggle against the kind of subjection that attempted to control us in direct ways, but so often we remained unaware of our own subjection to rigid identities and prescribed gender roles. The shattering of these ideal imagined subjectivities and identities led us, more often than not, to the loss of our self-respect and pride. It threw us into melancholic self-deprecation and turned us against ourselves or others whose humiliation seemed a threat to our own sense of dignity.

From an early age, moral standards are imposed on us so that we are deeply embedded in them through disciplining techniques of social institutions. While in prison, our adequacy in living up to these standards was constantly questioned. Our seemingly personal knowledge and habits are always shaped by overarching institutions such as family, religion, education, and the state. Kobra's relatively masculine appearance, her activism in a leftist organization, and her assertiveness were so contradictory to her family and social upbringing that, in order to compensate for this paradox, she became more observant of certain gender rules of propriety than even some of the devout Muslim women. Being treated as a deviant obliged her to prove that her resistance was not a result of her craziness but was an intellectually formulated and well-thought-out decision. Ironically, this tendency became a driving force pushing her further from the mainstream and hence toward further imprisonment within the boundaries of these norms.

According to a Persian proverb, *mār az pouneh badaesh miyād, dar-e lounash sabz mishe* (the snake hates the pennyroyal; it appears on the snake's door). The proverb implies that what one dislikes often appears close by. Kobra wanted so much to prove that she was not crazy, but she finally ended up proving her family right. Her embarrassment grew, especially since she saw her fall in the eyes of those who had once deserted her but were now caring for her as an insane person.

Every memory she gathered of her insane behavior in prison pushed her one more step toward her "ultimate fall from existence." The mirror she had held in her mind was shattered when she saw how far she had wandered from her ideal image of herself. What instead gazed at her was the corpse of her ideals and her ideal self. She could not bear to live with this reality, so she killed herself. But it was the other that she faced within herself, the other that had now become her, having lost her previous sense of identity, that she killed.

This is the paradox of modern societies, and Iran in particular, in which subversive political views could coexist with such conformism to cultural and social norms. Rebelling against the regime and even many aspects of the mainstream culture does not necessarily extirpate the heavy shadow of our religious and cultural backgrounds, which often looms over us. Despite our close relationship to our leftist male comrades, sexuality was constrained and downplayed. In fact, for the very reason that we were swimming against the tide and therefore were accused of lacking morals, we felt the need to prove our high moral values. We were adamant to prove to others and ourselves that we could spend days and nights with our male comrades without engaging in any sexual relationship. But this was not enough.

For many of us, we needed to prove to ourselves that our relationships were so pure that unless we were married to, or in love with, a comrade, even the thought of sexual difference or attraction did not enter our minds. Until I fell in love with Hamid, despite my regular contacts with male friends, even living with one of them for a while, not even once had I thought of our relationship in romantic or sexual terms. I took much pride in the fact that when my aunts and uncles complained to my father about allowing me to spend nights with friends or stay in the mountains for the night along with male friends, my father would say, "I can send Shahla among one thousand men with no hesitation while positive that she will return pure every single time. That is how much I trust my daughter." We sought this trust from our family members, relatives, friends, neighbors, and finally the larger society. When my mother said, "The neighbors say Ms. Talebi has six young daughters, but none of the boys in the neighborhood can say a bad word about them," this was the ultimate success of our self-disciplining goal to be unveiled, outgoing, politically active, yet considered morally respectable.

Achieving this level of success required much more restrained and desexualized gender relations. We could live with our male comrades, travel and work with them as closely as we wanted, but sexuality was not sanctioned outside marriage. We would dress differently from the rest of the women in Iran; but even though our dress was to signify our politically and socially conscious character, we remained cautious about our dress and our behavior appearing sexually suggestive. Kobra's suicide makes sense with all this in mind. Those of us who had known Kobra's

earlier attitude toward social and sexual propriety and heard of her behavior during her insanity, when she undressed in front of the guards
and acted in sexually suggestive ways, taboo behavior among political
prisoners, the enormity of her humiliation may be deciphered, and hence
her suicide. For Kobra, from madness to death, the leap was too short.

The connection between madness and death seems strange; they appear so close and related yet simultaneously detached from each other.
While both of them are disassociated from this world, their separation differs significantly in regard to the relationship between the body and the
soul. Could we argue that the reason an insane person does not commit
suicide is the result of this very connection that exists between madness
and death? Could it be true that an insane person is already separated
from this physical world and hence unable to actively think about eliminating life? This question preoccupied me and other fellow inmates since
often insanity seemed to have been cured only to lead to the person's suicide. Whatever the reason, I never came across a case of someone in the
throes of madness successfully committing suicide, while I could enumerate a list of those who were treated by professional therapists, only to
take their own lives later.

Marjan: "The Fall from Existence"

Marjan never completely inhabited that strange world of the other, though
she crossed the line repeatedly. A beautiful, gentle, delicate woman, she
had a graceful, feminine appearance, almost too delicate for prison. Yet
she was a woman of strong determination who had survived severe torture and passed Haji Davoud's tests in the *dastgah* and had not been defeated. However, like Pori, she also gradually lost trust in other prisoners
and joined those few prisoners who had gone through the *dastgah*; for she,
too, had seen her friends' betrayal, and her faith in others had faded away.
She put all her trust in Sanaz, who had survived the *dastgah*. For a while,
they seemed inseparable, but in the worst possible time of crisis in the
prison, the summer of 1988, their friendship seemed to have fallen apart.
Most prisoners believed that it was Sanaz who was ignoring Marjan, and

that Marjan was still pursuing her friendship without a positive response. From outside that seemed to be a more credible story, but none of us knew what was really going on between the two. All that appeared clear was that Marjan walked around alone, constantly following every move that Sanaz made. Either unable to trust anyone else, or embarrassed to return to those she had for so long avoided, she remained alone and did not take the hands that tried to reach out to her.

In the spring of 1988, the eight years of bloody war between Iran and Iraq ended. The end of the war was immediately followed by an attack on Iran's southern border by the Mojahedin, now based in and supported by Iraq. Considering the overall conditions, the attack was doomed to fail. It resulted in nothing but bloodshed and destruction. While the attack brought nothing for the Mojahedin but a humiliating defeat, for the Islamic Republic it provided an excuse and opportunity to solve the persistent problem of political prisoners, an opportunity that the Iranian government had impatiently anticipated. In fact, one of the prison's high officials bluntly told us that they got rid of the problem itself instead of wasting their time waiting to resolve it otherwise. He was referring to the execution of thousands of prisoners following the attack. For the Islamic Republic, political prisoners were the embodiment of a complex dilemma, since their very existence was a challenge to the totalized divine system the regime claimed to represent. Yet neither infliction of pain on prisoners' bodies nor theological persuasion was effective in returning some prisoners' souls to God, which for the regime really meant to acquire support for the Islamic Republic. The interrogators' consistent refrain was "Do you think your beliefs are stronger than God?" Effective resistance to their God challenged their totalized ideology.

Immediately after the attack, all visits with families were banned; no letters were allowed in or out. Utter isolation was imposed. The majority of prisoners who were affiliated with the Mojahedin organization were immediately called from the wards, summarily tried, and executed in large groups. Regimes of torture were intensified against the rest of us, assuring either acquiescence or execution for the vast majority of Iran's remaining population of political prisoners. They then moved to leftist men and tried and executed many of them. As we learned later, apparently the disagreements between Khomeini and Montazeri led to changing the plans about leftist women's execution. Instead, they began calling women in small groups and trying them together in trials of no more than a few minutes' duration, except that the sentence was to be whipped five times a day, five lashes each time, until the person agreed to profess her faith in Islam and agreed to pray. The lashing was to continue as long as resistance continued. The choice was either to be whipped till death or agree to pray.

As the prisoners were ushered into court in random sequence, each of us had to contemplate the consequences of our individual and collective decision to convert or to embrace death. After ten days, most members of the first group came back pale, baffled and broken, embarrassed at themselves and ashamed of their friends. Then another group was called: the order was based on no particular logic but the room number. How long it would take to reach me depended only on how many rooms were ahead of mine and how long those ahead of me would resist. What did it really mean? If I hoped that my turn did not come, I was in effect hoping for my friends to be beaten longer; yet wishing for an end meant to wish for their defeat. We wondered what to hope for. We had to reexamine many of our beliefs and employ new ethics that could explain the ironic meaninglessness of our destiny. If the methods of discipline and surveillance were being transformed, we had to learn new ways to confront them and preserve our integrity. What was at stake then was the necessity of new practices during these impossible months, while anticipating a disillusioned future. How, as political beings, could we use both our biological existence and our pending death to our advantage?

Unable to bear the pressure of this impending risk, Marjan developed severe paranoia, an exaggerated form of the fearfulness that was quite rational under the circumstances. A fellow prisoner, Monireh Baradarn, who initially wrote under the pen name M. Raha, poses the following questions in regard to Marjan: "Had she believed the horrifying events that we could not get ourselves to believe? We did not cry for all the losses, since we could neither believe they were gone, nor that we were alive." Marjan seemed to think that she could hear the lashes all day long. Repeatedly, she ran to the ward's gate to see whether her name had been called. After a while, she became nearly obsessed, perhaps not so much with the fear of death than with the horror of torture. She could no longer eat or sleep. Her beautiful eyes looked so fearful, as if she were being chased by ghosts all the time.

Every noise, object, and space hinted at the possibility of imminent torture and hence augmented her torment. She heard the strikes of the lashes in the sound of the pots in which food was carried to the ward. In the opening of the gate to the yard, one of the few pleasurable sounds in jail, Marjan's ears heard the echo of gunfire that killed prisoners. The sounds of gunfire that we heard in the early days of summer, when they took Mojahedin out of the wards, which we thought were shot only to create an atmosphere of terror, sank into Marjan's psyche and now were emerging from within her, as was the roar of the lashes. Her existence had been taken over by the presence of dreadful ghosts. No longer was she able to recognize that the dreadful was in fact emerging from within her. From this internal and internalized fear no escape was possible.

Although Marjan's imagination played a significant part in emphasizing and reinforcing her fear, its initiation was not based on her paranoia. We were all aware of the dreadful reality around us; we were, however, somehow able to manage to distinguish between the reality and the monsters to which our imaginations gave birth. But her fantastic monsters overwhelmed Marjan's reality. She was no longer able to distinguish between the threat that was emerging from within her and that which came from outside. This led her to surrender to constant fear. It was this enslavement to fear that characterized her being. She became a prisoner of horror; she stood at the door all day long, with her ear attached to it, and anxiously awaited her turn to be taken as the next prey of the lashes. Full from drinking and eating this perpetual fear, she no longer felt thirsty or hungry. Her despair was not, like Kobra's, for a particular way of being in the world but rather of being in the world.

In those weeks and months of summer and fall of 1988, we breathed the air of suspension between worlds. Our screams, moans, and fragmented sentences disrupted our sleeping hours. During daytime, however, we made jokes, sang loudly, and as if we were magicians, spoke loudly to scare off the ghosts. We convinced ourselves that as long as we were not physically under the lash or in the face of guns, we would prevent our imaginations from traveling there, however difficult. Many of the prisoners were unsuccessful in this effort and either submitted to the regime's conditions or slipped into the worlds of madness or death.

Eventually, we began to take turns watching out for those who tried to take their lives, as we did for Marjan. Every night, for two hours, each of us was in charge of looking after her. We would sleep opposite her bed in order to observe her every move while pretending we were asleep. How ironic it was that the very same surveillance we resented so much from the collaborators, we were imposing upon her. Yet at that moment all we thought about was saving her from death. We thwarted her desire to end her life, not knowing how else to care for her. We felt obliged to prevent her death, despite the pain that this effort inevitably brought about. We saved her many times, but she finally won, and we failed in our seemingly heroic effort to rescue her from herself.

She would hide safety pins, broken glass, and needles and would try to cut herself under her blanket. But our careful eyes, like hunters', would look through the darkness and trace her hands' movement even beneath the blanket. We would chase her to the bathroom stall where we would climb up the wall of the next stall to watch her, so committed we were to our job of rescue. Finally, one day she acted more intelligently than we did. She had cut herself in the bathroom. I was the first to run to her. She was on the floor of the toilet, pale and still with her eyes colored by fright. We dragged her to the floor of the bathroom and began to undress her. Her wrists and her neck were cut, though not deep enough to kill her, seriously enough to become infected.

For years she came to my dreams with that amazingly beautiful, pale face and her naked delicate body, with a bitterness that astonished me. Was she upset that I dragged her onto the floor and undressed her so hastily that it perhaps hurt her? Does she still remember my hands so carelessly touching her injuries? My heart was in enormous pain, but my hands could not help hurting her while undressing her. I was, however, more concerned about her life than her injuries and her pain. In my dreams, I wonder if she is upset that we did not try harder to convince her that the torture was not going to last forever, that we had to hold on to hope in order to survive? Is she angry that we were ourselves caught up in such fear that we were unable to get closer to her? Were we afraid of becoming obsessed with the fear as much as she was? Would she forgive us for spying on her and depriving her of her right to decide whether to live or die? I wish there were a way to communicate with her. Should we have tried harder to save her, or let her be the one who chooses to live or die as she wishes? But since when have our lives and deaths been only our own? What kind of subject was she really, when she was so lost in and controlled by fear?

I wonder, what were we saving her from? What was our task: to prolong her misery, to let her exercise her freedom, or to try to integrate her into our normalized yet extreme order? I am still baffled by these questions; however, I feel the primary challenge is to face these questions directly without seeking easy answers and without pursuing survival at any cost. Probably the challenge is not necessarily to inquire into ways to live longer but to seek answers to these impossible questions life offers, knowing no perfect or complete answer is available.

Innocent Cruelty

YOUSUF

The government of men by men—whether they form small or large groups, whether it is power exerted by men over women, or by adults over children, or by one class over another, or by a bureaucracy over a population—involves a certain type of rationality. . . . Consequently, those who resist or rebel against a form of power cannot merely be content to denounce violence or criticize an institution. Nor is it enough to cast the blame on reason in general. What has to be questioned is the form of rationality at stake. . . . The question is: how are such relations rationalized.

—Michel Foucault, *Religion and Culture*

Yousuf, my paternal cousin, was born in a poor peasant family in a village in eastern Azarbaijan, a large and densely populated province in the northwest of Iran. The ethnicity of the majority of the population in Azarbaijan is Azarian, and the language they speak is called Turkey in Iran, but Azari outside Iran to avoid confusing it with Turkish. Most of the children of my uncle and his wife were slightly challenged, either physically or mentally, or both. This was apparently due to the familial relationship between my uncle and his wife, who was his maternal cousin. They had also lost two of their children at birth. Among the five surviving children, Yousuf was the second youngest. He was only about five feet tall with a limp from the polio with which apparently he was infected when he was two years old. Although now that I think back, perhaps his problem was not really polio but the same genetic problem that later caught up with a couple of other siblings, only in a later stage of their lives.

With his beautiful blue eyes, his rosy cheeks, and his blond hair, he resembled, and thus reminded me of, my paternal grandfather whom I loved so much but lost when I was only nine years old. Yet their resemblance perhaps remained limited to their appearance and kindness. My grandfather was a dynamic, strong, and sharp man, while Yousuf spoke softly and slowly, mostly due to the weakness of his jaw and his facial muscles. His fair face and the innocence that seeped into his blue eyes made him appear as tame as a sheep. As a shepherd, he was so close to the sheep that one could somehow imagine a kinship between them. But Yousuf was not lifeless. He was very much in love with life and sang passionately, even in Farsi, a language he did not understand well. With their rural lifestyle, his impoverished family was not much concerned about his lack of success in school. He was needed for taking care of the chores on the farm, in the garden, and at home. In the village, his physical and mental slowness, though ridiculed, was less noticeable than it would be in his later years in the fast-paced life of the city.

When he was thirteen years old, his life shifted from that of a shepherd who watched over his father's sheep in the village to working for my other uncle (my father's youngest brother) in his small construction firm in Tehran. Yousuf's older brother was already working there. Yousuf was thus sent to Tehran to join his brother and be a construction worker. All the workers, who were mostly relatives, were from the same village and lived together in a big room in a very poor neighborhood. Yousuf became the source of entertainment and the subject of their ordinary cruelty. In the Qur'anic narratives, Satan often seeks out the most pure and honest person to trick; these young men, too, discovered the Satans in themselves by playing with Yousuf's innocence. His presence animated the evil inside them. Those nasty little savages who so often had chased a limping dog with their sticks, beating the poor creature until it was torn into pieces, had now found a new target to torment, the lame Yousuf. Reenacting their early training, now as young men, they were engaging in atrocious acts, perhaps as a way of releasing their anger from the miserable years of their childhood when they felt small and defenseless. Not merely an outlet for the frustration that was accumulated in them from the past, Yousuf also presented them with the temptation to exercise the power they were lacking in so many respects in their current lives. In exaggerating Yousuf's weakness, they took pride in their own comparatively manly power. More often than not, I have witnessed this pathological yet often normalized behavior from those whose sense of inferiority seeks remedy in overpowering those in a lower position than themselves. It is thus not too far fetched to imagine that for these men, too, Yousuf became the embodiment of the inner weakness they felt in relationship to those above them—the very weakness they so strongly resented that they had to project it onto an exterior target.

These men, who had all migrated from the same village as Yousuf's, were construction workers, building luxurious houses in the rich neighborhoods in the north of Tehran where pretty, half-naked women were playing around in their swimming pools. After work, the men went back to their room where the rotten smell would have given them headaches, if their sensitivity had remained intact. They watched the lavish world of extravagant food, fanciful love, and excessive fun on their television set or in movie theaters. They spent their meager savings in the closest brothel. Here, on the prostitutes' bodies, they first practiced their manhood. Their money had bought them the prostitutes, and for those couple of hours they owned these women. Hence, bragging about these activities was an attempt to establish their masculinity. To ridicule the impotence of others was to recollect this sense of shattered and belittled identity—in the rich houses, women seemed to be entirely oblivious to their presence as humans, let alone as desiring men.

Yousuf, on the other hand, was the embodiment of all the victims in the history of humanity. He was the victim of genetics, disease, and human cruelty, all linked to, and feeding, one another. At work, he was the subject of other workers' mockery for his slowness, his limp, and his gentleness that were so inconvenient for the proper masculinity required of his gender and his class. Despite the fact that he worked hard and undertook all the low-status tasks, his deviance defined him as insufficient. He was to believe that his job had been offered to him as charity. His coworkers would send him back and forth to one another, one ordering him to do the chores that the other would have him undo. Imitating his walk and his speech would fill their break hours with laughter.

Beyond work, his leisure time allowed even more opportunities for the everyday viciousness of these men, who compensated for the many deprivations in their lives by making fun of Yousuf and gratifying themselves through his humiliation. His erratic victimization was intensified in Tehran. His abnormality, both physical and mental, was quite mild when he was in the village, where his deviance from the norm was nearly unnoticed or ignored. However, in the crowded, alienating city of Tehran, where everything moved and changed so rapidly and where people's integration into its gigantic yet extremely constricted urban boundaries was so complex, Yousuf's "tame" character made his exclusion from this community almost inevitable.

The paradox lay in the particulars of where and when he was raised, and ironically in the mildness of his abnormality. Yousuf felt torn between two worlds, the world of the rural and that of modern urbanity. Since the Shah's regime's White Revolution, which had resulted in the migration of a great many villagers to the large cities, the foundation of the former lifestyle was shaken to its core. The distribution of land under the pretext of freeing the peasants from the chains of the landlords shackled them to small plots with no real resources to compete with the products imported from foreign countries. Destitute, they had to leave their villages behind and migrate to the cities with the dream of a better life, often only to find themselves at the margins of urban life and random or no employment. The attitudes and the lifestyle that originated in these rural worlds had, however, not entirely perished. Modern urbanity had conquered and often destroyed the economic, social, and cultural landscapes of the rural forms of life, rendering them utterly marginal. Yet their vestiges were alive and well in the villages as well as in the large cities, which were turning into discordant fragments of various cultural, religious, and linguistic identities compressed in the ghettos, which occupied different corners of the cities, some constituted of shanties.

The older ways of life were losing ground to the emergent ones in many arenas; the new ones, however, had not yet manifested in ways in which Yousuf's life could be positively affected, or at least sufficiently adjusted. He was required to be tested in a new system of education at the age of seven, in Farsi rather than Azarian, his native language, and on courses of study for which his lifestyle did not provide any tangible ground for comprehension. If for other children these unfamiliar challenges offered a way to fulfill their curiosity, for Yousuf they became a mirror upon which his seeming incompetence was reflected.

In the city, everyone seemed to be rushing to achieve something, which Yousuf with his slower pace could never reach. His familiar world was disappearing in front of his blue eyes as if fading away into the clouds. With his lame leg, he was neither strong enough to stop the vanishing of the familiar world nor fast enough to acquire the skill to live in accordance with the rules of the strange one. For years, he had heard the old songs from his parents and grandparents, and he learned to sing them in Azarian. They were, however, losing their echoes since the radio, which had just entered the village, was offering the swift production of a variety of songs in a strange yet fascinating language, Farsi, the official national language. Before Yousuf could repeat the first song, even partially, it had lost its popularity and was no longer played. Several others had already been produced and were on their way to becoming passé.

In the village, rice from Thailand and the United States cost less than their own local rice, and the farmers lost the means and motivation for competition. Before long, many farms were acquired by larger companies at low prices or were abandoned. The cities were overcrowded with villagers coming in waves to become part of this new urbanity. Yousuf's mind and body were aching from running all the time and never reaching any destination. Things came and went at such a speed that he no longer knew what was there and what had already disappeared. The entire world appeared ghostly, at once alive and yet already dead, at once present yet passed away. At nights when the room was as dark as the bottom of a well amid the mysterious shadows on the roof, Yousuf took journeys back in time and space. He was lying down in the large meadow in his village watching the white clouds building their beautiful castles. Some distance away, the sheep were feeding while the birds were singing their lovely songs.

In his dream, his brother screamed at him and asked him to walk faster and bring them something, but he did not hear what. All of the others were exhausted and asleep, dreaming of the luxuries they lacked. Yousuf was awakened and pulled back to this world of speed and complexity where he was struggling to establish his footing. His efforts to create a world of his own appeared unsuccessful. He, nevertheless, neither wanted nor could return to his previous life. But this life in between worlds, into which he was born, was rupturing everything familiar without offering him any place of his own. In addition to physical and mental challenges, he was on the bottom of the social and economic system and belonged to an ethnic group that was the subject of common jokes by other ethnic groups in Tehran. His class status automatically deprived him of access to any possibilities of special education or other services that the modern world could provide for a child of his condition born into an urban middle-class family. Every aspect of city life, however attractive, appeared to him as a threat, harshly challenging his limitations.

Perhaps if he had been more severely challenged, his more radical otherness would have isolated him or would not have forced him to even try to compete on the same grounds as other people. But as it was, he was obliged to work. Physical, especially sexual, potency was perhaps a compensation for all the lacks experienced by these young men whose dreams and desires had expanded beyond their wildest imagination of what they could have had in the village. Yousuf was dragged into a competition for which he was neither prepared nor interested. Being younger than the others, with a slower process of sexual maturity, he was incessantly taunted as being impotent and less than a man. In fact, Yousuf's greatest inadequacy lay in his inability to enact the masculine role required of him.

The River, Nightmares, and Madness

Early in the morning my father awakened and, while making tea, told my mother that he had had a dreadful dream. "Please don't tell me about it. You know you shouldn't talk about bad dreams. Go and say it to the river. Let the river wash its evil power away," my mother had advised. My father, however, refused to believe in such "nonsensical, nonmodern, superstitious beliefs."

He described his dream in a matter-of-fact manner, pretending that he did not care. "I was drowning in Ganly Goul [Bloody Pond], a natural pond in my parents' village. The pond was full of blood, and soon I realized that it was my own blood. However, it was very strange since I was unable to feel my own body; neither my hands nor my body felt like my own. I was swimming in my own blood, but it felt very bizarre that I could not feel it."

This was how my father had narrated his dream to my mother against her will. Somewhat relieved, my mother had reassured him that he did not have to be worried since blood invalidates the dream, hence nothing bad was going to happen. She nevertheless had tried to convince my father not to go to work, but he teased her and left to do his job at the railroad where he attached the train cars to one another.

I had not been born yet, but I later heard this story many times and in different versions. My mother suggested that my father was very upset. He could sense that something was about to happen. He, however, denied it, for in his view, dreams did not have the power to foretell one's future. Only a couple of hours later, my father was swimming in his blood, unconscious and unable to feel himself. He was securing the train cars when the driver of the train, having forgotten about him, drove backward and pressed my father in between two cars. Did my father shout? He did not remember. The driver, unaware of what had happened, left while my father lay bleeding on the railroad, with his ribs severely smashed and his arm nearly amputated. "Half consciously, as if dreaming, I felt that I was drowning in my blood. But it was strange that I could not feel myself, as if neither my hands nor my body were mine," my father would tell us, always with amazement in his voice, as if implicitly confessing to a premonition, the reason or source of which he could not explain rationally.

In the telling and retelling of this story, my mother always complained that if my father had listened to her and, instead of telling her, had given his dream away to the river, the accident might not have happened. My father, on the other hand, would teasingly say, "But you were the Imam, and you said that blood would invalidate my dream." To which Mother would respond, "That's right. Don't you realize that if there had been no blood in your dream, the miracle that saved your life and your arm would not have happened?"

The miracle that my mother was referring to concerned the fact that my father was the first person in Iran on whom an operation to reattach a detached extremity was performed. This procedure was, ironically, performed in a public hospital in a poor neighborhood, the only place my father could afford to have his operation. All the doctors in the hospital believed that there was no hope of saving his arm. However, a team of doctors from the former Soviet Union was visiting that particular hospital. They were experimenting with this kind of operation and offered to operate on my father. The experimental surgery was successful, and his life and his arm were saved. My father, of course, perceived this event as one of the advantages of modern medical advancements and the creativity and superiority of socialism that had trained such skillful doctors who cared about him as a human being, despite his low social class. For my mother, the fact that this accident coincided with this Soviet team's visit to the hospital and their work on this project was all God's will to save my father, and hence, a true miracle.

They would earnestly pursue this conversation-debate for years afterward, while we, the children, vacillated between these two ways of perceiving the event. As a child, I could not decide which perspective was valid. The conflict between these two views from two different worlds confused me. Later, however, I came to realize that, while they both were partially true, the story was not complete without the interplay between the two. My early bewilderment from living in the midst of an ongoing battle-negotiation between science and faith taught me invaluable lessons about the complexities of our lives and the absurdity of simplified dichotomies and categories. It introduced to me a new horizon, a vast space in which I could create a world of my own that was neither of those but had the advantage of accessing them both.

I did not feel obliged to limit myself to the peculiar boundaries of these seemingly incommensurate worlds. I looked at my father's arm and saw the positive mark of advanced technology, science, and medicine on it. Every time he held me in his arms, I remembered with gratitude the gift they had offered my family. Yet I could not simply dismiss my mother's belief in the miracle of coincidence that had brought the doctors to operate on my father. Neither could any of the doctors who had performed the operation explain the miracle of the new thin veins that began to grow in his arm. On the smashed surface of his recovered arm and its new veins, the two worlds coexisted, as well as the possibility of something beyond.

SINCE MY CHILDHOOD, the connection between dreaming, the river, and blood has permeated my experiences in the realms of both dreams and waking consciousness and was repeated over and over in my later encounters with these two territories. Ganly Goul was where two rivers in our village branched off. The water supply for the farms and gardens of the entire village came from this pond. There is an Azarian legend about this pond that explains its being called Bloody Pond: A young peasant couple fall madly in love, but the feudal lord of the village wants the woman. Secretly, the couple get married and attempt to escape the village. But while escaping, they are caught by the feudal lord's agents, who shoot and kill them on the bridge over the pond. Their bodies are thrown into the pond and turn the water into blood.

While the rivers stretch out their arms to bear life, their nefarious mouth swallows young couples. By the rivers, plants and flowers flourish, yet in the conflicts over their life-bearing qualities many lives are ended. I still remember the fight that occurred in our village, during the summers of my childhood, about whose turn it was to use the rivers to water their farms and gardens, and about who had stolen the water by redirecting it toward their farm. The river that opens its heart to embrace everyone's nightmares and to take the evil away from them becomes the burial place for love and loved ones. Violence, death, and love spurt through them and into the whole village so that whatever people eat has the flavors of love, creation, and destruction. As in the rivers, and in the villagers' bodies, life and death, love and hatred, and creation and desolation cohabit.

AMONG THE MOST POPULAR CELEBRATIONS by children and adults in Iran is Chahar Shanbeh Suri, the last Tuesday of the old year—before the Iranian New Year that begins on March 20, the first day of spring. On the evening of this day, we build a fire and jump over it while repeating these verses: "Zardi man az tou, surkhi tou az man," which means "My yellowness (paleness) becomes yours, and your redness comes to me." These verses address the fire and implore it to take our paleness, which indicates sickness and unhappiness, and give its redness, health and joy, to us. People believe that all the problems of the old year are thrown into the fire through reciting these verses. The morning after, we gather the ashes and give them away to the river. Is it the power of all these disastrous qualities offered to the rivers that provokes their evil powers? The villagers believe that the jinns and mad people would wander along the rivers and that madness resulted from sitting in the hot sun and staring at the river. As a child, I always wondered how two completely different and contradictory legends could exist around this one object.

Almost seventy-two hours after my arrest, I finally fall asleep while my feet and my body are in unbearable pain. My back is seriously damaged so that I am unable to move. The doctor has told my interrogator that I might become permanently paralyzed. Despite the fact that I am unable to move, my feet hurt so much that I barely think about my back.

They have finally brought a wheelchair to take me to the interrogation, but in the cell I have to manage to move without it. Despite the pain, I finally sleep, totally exhausted. I dream that I am being chased by my torturers and several dogs—why dogs? I am not sure, for in Iranian prisons (unlike Abu Ghraib or Guantanomo) dogs were not included among the torture techniques. In our childhood memories, however, dogs were sometimes a source of anxiety and threat. But I am now in jail, and in the world of dreams, where everything is possible.

In my dream, chased by dogs and interrogators, I am running in a thick wood; my face and body are constantly cut by the bushes and the branches of the trees. They are getting closer. I am running even faster. We proceed to an open space that seems like a desert. I feel extremely thirsty. The dogs have gotten closer and are biting me. I notice that they look more like wolves than dogs. I feel extremely tired, but I can't stop. I know that if I can just get to the river and jump into it, I will be free. I run and run and at the last minute, right when they are about to catch me, there, I see the river. Squeezing every bit of might and energy left in me, I release myself from their grip and jump into the river. I am free! The sky is amazingly blue and beautiful. Under the sun, the river shines like a gorgeous pearl. And my body feels as if in heaven.

The illusion of a dream, I realize as soon as I wake up. Despite the promise of the fire of Chahar Shanbeh Suri, the burning pain in my body convinces me that I have been tricked and offered only suffering rather than healing. I am burning with pain and have no ashes to throw into the river for my pain to be washed away. Such perplexing notions we human beings convince ourselves to believe in, I think to myself. As a child, I often wondered why fire should put itself into such an obviously unfair position, to present health and joy in exchange for sickness and misery. However, I do not recall asking myself why we did not recognize that the ashes of destruction and disaster would be coming back to us through the river that ran through our land, and therefore into whatever we saw, ate, and drank. It ran into and became the substance of our bodies and souls. These metaphorical images mirror our lives, condensing our fears and hopes into these contradictory and complicated symbolic elements, which are so vividly illustrated in this ritualized theatricality. This condensation, however, reveals all of the perplexities in the very act of simplifying, in the act that expresses our nostalgia or our longing for a utopian world of clarity and lucidity.

It is hot, and the light in the small cell is hurting my eyes. Where is the sun of my dream? I wonder. The only trace of it, besides that bitterness of feeling betrayed by my own dream, is my heartbeat and the sweating, as if after a long run. Yet it is this betrayal that banishes the horror, even though temporarily. Escape from prison, which in reality is so incredibly unlikely, constantly emanates in prisoners' dreams, especially while under torture. Dreams and imagination create a state of being and experiencing that makes the impossible the subject of everyday occurrence. With the wounded feet that are chained within the multiple boundaries of prison, one runs up hills, climbs mountains and swims in the ocean, and breaks the thick walls and doors wherever the wings of dreams fly. They are essential elements that help prisoners survive the dread of torture. But when the fall comes, dreams and imagination fall, too. Which happens first, I do not know. What seems clear to me, however, is that when hope vanishes, for a prisoner left with a ravished body and soul, it vanishes both from her dreams and reality. With the vanishing of hope, the soul shrinks; it evaporates.

YOUSUF WAS AFRAID of rivers and swimming—did he know what his life had in store for him in relation to the river? He was only sixteen years old when my uncle took all of his construction workers to Khouzestan Province, in the south of Iran, for a project. In Khouzestan, both its extreme climate and language, a particular dialect of Farsi spoken by its non-Arabic-speaking population, differed from the climate and language of Yousuf's and the other workers' homeland. The scorching sun, under which they had to work the whole day, was driving them crazy. In the eve-

nings, exhausted and sweaty, they would run to the river in the town of
Dezful to cool themselves off. The very strong, rapid current made swimming in the river dangerous, especially for those who were not familiar
with it. Tempted to jump into it and let the heat and exhaustion be washed
away, they limited themselves to playing on its banks. Yet frustrated by
their fear, they sought an outlet, someone on whom they could play out
their temptations and let go of their fear. Yousuf was within reach, his
limitations inviting.

He was dragging himself toward the bridge over the river, trying not
to fall behind. The workers, his relatives, were pouring out their frustration from this hot, long day through their loud voices, dirty jokes, and
hysterical laughter. One of them noticed Yousuf's limping and his effort to catch up with them. An evil idea ran through his mind and soon
spread to the rest in whispers. In no time it had become a collective plan,
as though everybody had been contemplating the same idea for quite a
while. Yousuf had finally caught up with the others, or so he thought,
while in fact they had slowed down for him to catch up. It was in fact the
evil idea in their mind that had slowed them down in order to entrap him.
Thinking he had caught up with them, he probably experienced a few
moments of joy before his fall.

He was suddenly up off the ground, grabbed by all those familiar
hands. Could he comprehend the meaning of this generosity, being up
off the ground and carried by his coworkers? But in a few seconds, his
arms were swimming through the air trying to reach someone or something to grasp while his feet were still gripped by those hands. His aching body was desperately looking for somewhere to rest itself, but being
upside down, he had lost his limited sense of orientation. His blue eyes
were blazing with fear and confusion, as he kept trying harder not to
plunge into the river. The loud laughter stopped only at the moment they
dropped him into the river from far above on the bridge; they were silenced as if their own fear were being tested.

Gulping the water, frozen and paralyzed, he stared at death spreading over him. His last look at the world he knew till then was at the

devilish expressions in his friends' eyes and their grinning faces enjoying themselves at his expense. This time of eternity for Yousuf was also
the moment of exceeding pleasure for his coworkers—an instant during
which Yousuf crossed the line to the world of the absolute other.

When they took him out, forced him to throw up in order to be able
to breathe, and helped him to walk home, Yousuf walked mechanically and mindlessly and in the absolute silence of death. His brother,
a bit ashamed after all, changed his clothes and put him to bed. Everybody went to sleep. Silence took over the place. Something in Yousuf
had changed in ways that disturbed his brother and made him anxious,
though he could not say what. Later he related the events of that night:
"Yousuf stared at the darkness for the rest of that night. I usually sleep
through the entire night. But that night I was somewhat anxious and thus
woke up several times. Every time I woke up, I noticed Yousuf's blue
eyes were wide open, gazing at the ceiling." For several days, he neither
moved nor spoke. Without eating or sleeping, his frozen body and still
eyes looked like those of a lifeless statue. But he had in fact turned into a
volcano, which sleeps quietly only to suddenly go wild and burn everything on its way by vomiting its fiery lava onto its surrounding world.
Yousuf, too, suddenly exploded. With no warning, he began screaming
at the top of his lungs so loudly and so persistently that everyone around
him became agitated. They came close to calm him down, but it was like
trying to prevent an explosion.

He was no longer that lame sheep who could be beaten up by anyone.
He now possessed the powers of death and madness. The evils of the
river had taken him over, enacting themselves through him. Yousuf tore
things apart, broke the objects of the world to which he had never actually belonged, and acted like a wounded tiger ready to attack and destroy
anything that moved toward him. He screamed for all those years he had
been silenced and for that eternity during which the river had revealed
and transmitted all the evils and miseries hidden in its heart. He, however, did not attack anyone, except his father and his brother, and only
when they tried to talk to him or stop him. While still a source of humili-

ation to his family, instead of tempting others to play tricks on him, now Yousuf scared them off. This could not go on. He had to be disciplined; his new powers had to be controlled and limited, if not drawn out of him. First, the psychiatrists only drove him more toward madness. But they finally found the correct medication to subdue or tame him. I was arrested during this phase of his enforced calmness in which he remained for a while, but he never resumed that sense of normalcy that his family desired to see in him.

During those nearly two years of my imprisonment, my family's remarks were limited to some general comments about his situation: "He is calm and back in the village. . . . He has gone totally mad again. . . . He broke your uncle's TV," and so on. He was no longer able to work and had become a burden on his family or anyone else with whom he stayed. I remembered how excited he was when his family bought a small radio. He would hold it to his ear and repeat the words of popular songs in Farsi. There was one particular song he loved the most and often tried to sing. I always wondered why he chose specific songs as his favorites despite their rapid rhythm, which was so difficult for him to follow. Was it the very speed that attracted him? Was it the simplicity of the lyrics that, though he could not understand them, was easier to imitate, or was it the folk style of the music that felt closer to his heart? Who knows, perhaps all these, or even none of them, and something entirely different that my mind did not grasp.

As everything else in his life, Yousuf's crisis coincided with the country's rapidly increasing tensions that eventually led to the Revolution of 1979. His detachment from the world around him and the loss of his senses about what was going on did not render him immune from the conflicts, gunfire, and killings that had now become daily scenes on the streets. Fear and confusion had suffused every moment of his life, and nobody was there to help him make sense of these realities. People were so involved trying to change their future that they did not have time to look back to see him trying to find his way through these convoluted labyrinths of social transformations. Every day was another push for him to feel even more lost than the day before. His final disappearance was waiting for my participation.

The way that everyone seems to have played a part in drawing Yousuf to his final destination reminds me of the massacre of political prisoners in the summer of 1988. The prison officials pursued a policy of having everyone's hands in the system covered with prisoners' blood. This collective involvement of all the prison personnel in the process of torture, execution, and getting rid of their dead bodies was rationalized as a safety valve for those who were the main agents of this crime. It was to keep everyone silent about the massacre, for if they spoke, the secret of their own role in the crime would be revealed. Learning from their experience when the Shah's regime reached the point of sacrificing some to save the bigger fish, they wanted to make sure that no one could claim innocence. From doctors to guards, they made sure that everyone would participate in these dreadful acts of violence. We overheard this from the guards, who were talking about a time when one of them had tried to get out of the task of shooting prisoners or carrying their corpses, and the response from the higher-ranking officers had been that nobody's hands were to remain clean.

The people's uprising had reached a critical point so that its strong tides were shaking the prison walls. With censorship lifted from the newspapers, we learned that the release of political prisoners was a central slogan of the demonstrations. Then came that evening in 1978, only three months before the revolution, when my name was announced along with those of a majority of other prisoners, on the list of those to be released. The story of this release and my going to the demonstration rather than home, the reader already knows.

The waves of the revolutionary movement were too strong and influential to allow my parents to question my decision to join the demonstration. Their hesitance to inquire about my whereabouts since the day of my release did not change the fact that they were extremely worried for and concerned about me. Yet they hid their anxieties by keeping busy with the guests who were coming to congratulate me on my homecoming.

They feigned acceptance of my involvement in the movement, which they realized was inevitable considering the sociopolitical climate of that historical period in Iran. Nevertheless, they strived to eliminate those extraneous factors over which they had control. This included Yousuf.

Since his madness, Yousuf had moved from one place to another, like a wandering dervish. But contrary to dervishes' voluntary relocation, Yousuf was taken to these places without his consent. People were reluctant to put themselves at risk by residing with a mad person, even though a close relative. His parents were under pressure both financially and emotionally since in a small village where everyone knew one another, his madness was well known and spoken about by all the villagers. They preferred not to have him in the village, so he stayed mostly with my family. My parents were anxious about his sexual desire because of my young sisters. Yousuf himself, as my parents explained to me, was restless. In the village, he no longer found the peace of his childhood; instead, he felt frustrated that none of those fascinating aspects of city life existed there. In the city, on the other hand, he became more anxious and angry. He could not find any place for himself in this huge world.

When I returned home, our house was crowded with many of our relatives. I overheard my sister whispering to my mother, complaining that Yousuf had torn her notebook apart. I went downstairs to see him. He was sitting in the room with tiny pieces of paper piled in front of him while he was still tearing the remaining pages. Had he tried to read, and the words had not spoken to him? Was he annoyed that they gazed at him without communicating anything to him but coldness, silence, and death? Yousuf must have read in their seemingly noncommunicative silence that he did not belong even to this world, to the realm of words, which was claimed by educated people. Yousuf was tearing those papers into pieces in such rage, as if they were his worst enemies.

For a few seconds I stood there in silence under the pressure of his gaze. I did not know how to gaze back. Then I said hello and walked toward him. Something like a forgotten smile ran through his face. Did he recognize me? I was eager to know. His blue eyes were red, and I remembered that Mother had told me that he drank a lot. He lit a cigarette and smoked with the gestures of most young workers from villages who imitate the smoking style of film actors. There was, however, a childish manner in him that reminded me of him before he had taken this journey to the other territory. I remembered him sitting in the garden holding his radio by his ear and singing his favorite song. His mispronunciation of these intimate lyrics, because of both his Azarian accent and his effort to repeat them as fast as the singer, sounded so sweet that I never tired of hearing them.

I recalled the stories he had learned from his great-aunt that he would so excitedly tell my sisters and me during our afternoon naps, when we tricked our parents by pretending we were asleep and stayed up to listen to him. He asked us if we would like to hear "Ādi and Boudi" or "Shangoul and Mangoul," the only two stories he had memorized and familiar to every child in the village. I usually asked for "Ādi and Boudi," perhaps because of a similarity between the characters of the story and him. With his soft, low, and endearing voice he told us in detail about Ādi and Boudi, a poor couple whose only child was married to a rich man and lived in a town far from their village. The parents could not afford to regularly travel to visit her. Their daughter was embarrassed to bring her husband and child to her parents' modest place. Finally, they missed her so much that they decided to walk all the way to the town. They baked some bread and took some butter and oil for their daughter and her family. On their way, they noticed how the ground on which they were walking was split. Yousuf explained, "Boudi told Ādi, Ādi Jan, see how the hands of the ground have scars on them because they are working hard to give us all we have. Let's put some oil on them to cure their scars." Ādi agreed, blissfully.

This softhearted, simpleminded, kind couple offered their bread to the birds, gave their water to the fox, covered the shivering leaves with their jackets, and finally, when they arrived at their daughter's house empty handed, embarrassed her even more. While there, their kindness caused even greater and more serious trouble for their daughter. Being left alone in the house for a short period, they went to the basement, where they noticed that several pigeons in their cages were scratching themselves, or so the parents believed. They felt pity for the pigeons and thought that their daughter had been too busy to bathe them. They therefore warmed up some water and washed the pigeons. The daughter's family came back only to find all the pigeons dead, while the parents were happily convinced that the pigeons were merely relaxing calmly after the bathing. The story continued with more of their mistakes and the consequences, all of which resulted from their kindness and generosity, but also their simplemindedness.

The manner in which Yousuf told the story fascinated me more than the story itself. In his version, although as if from the perspective of an intelligent person, he did not mock the couple but somewhat identified with them. He seemed to feel a deep sympathy for them that engendered the same effect in us, at least in me. It was as though he could relate to all their misunderstanding, miscommunication, and especially inadequacy in responding to the world around them. Perhaps in Ādi and Boudi's extreme otherness, Yousuf saw a normalcy for himself, a hope for his inclusion in society. Yet his identification with their perception of the world communicated his problems and the reality of his exclusion. Ādi and Boudi saw everything around them as alive and sensitive and communicated with one and all as equals. Was not this what Yousuf was longing for so much? His gentle voice reshaped the story and gave it a new and different tone. In Yousuf's version, one felt a need to find a way to relate to the perception of the world of silly people.

Yet this Yousuf who was now standing in front of me with red spots spread throughout his blue eyes was an entirely different person. I searched for a sign of that Yousuf who could tell me the story of Ādi and Boudi again. But I could barely recognize him. He smelled of alcohol. I felt sad and embarrassed at the same time: ashamed of myself for being afraid of him, and sad that he had been a victim of such meaningless, aimless cruelty, and for being so helpless to do anything for him. But he began to talk to me, and I was trembling with fear and pleasure, fear of not knowing how to converse with him and pleasure that the ice was broken. I have an acute memory of the events that followed this particular moment when I had just begun thinking I might in fact find a way into his world. As he and I began to talk, my parents kept taking turns to come downstairs and repeatedly check up on us, pretending to have come for something that they needed from downstairs. We spent a couple of hours together, during which he asked me where I had been. I asked him if something was bothering him. "They are driving me crazy. My father, my brother. They tell me not to smoke or drink. They think I am unable to take it like other adults do," Yousuf told me.

"Why do you tear these papers? They are Zari's [my sister] and she needs them. She hasn't hurt you. Has she? Are you angry at her? But she likes you. We all like you." I was trying to find a way to hear about his feelings. He had stopped tearing the papers, but he began again, while whispering to me, "These are very destructive. They let others think we are idiots." We sat for a few more minutes, but he had already begun to act more anxious, and when my younger sister, a fourteen-year-old then, came into the room, his gestures were clearly sexual. I gently held his hands and asked him to continue our conversation. He sat down briefly but looked restless. Chewing his cigarette, which I found very unusual, he said that he needed to go out. It was, however, forbidden for him to go anywhere by himself. He stood at the door and smoked, and I imagined him sitting, walking, and lying down in the open meadow with clouds freely dancing in front of his eyes and the sun playing hide and seek with him. I asked my brother if he could take him for a walk. He could not refuse doing what I had asked him since I had come from prison—how much this annoyed me! Yet I could see the frustration in his eyes.

I went upstairs to the guests who were waiting to see me and hear the horrible stories about those monstrous torturers, asking themselves how people could become so inhuman. I imagined Yousuf falling into the river, screaming, begging for help, and struggling desperately and helplessly. Yousuf's brother was sitting there asking me about prison, and I was imagining his hands among others holding Yousuf over the bridge for that indefinite time. I envisioned him shaking inside but afraid of being considered less of a man if he refused to join others to mock and humiliate him. And I saw Yousuf, the Qur'anic prophet and the biblical Joseph, screaming as his brothers dropped him down the well, so deep that he could no longer be heard. Poor Yousufs, who learn about brutality through their loved ones, their brothers. Poor Yousufs who experience absolute helplessness while feeling so profoundly betrayed!

Tears washed my face. I could not stop them. I had left my friends behind in prison, witnessed people exposing their chests to the Shah's armed soldiers, and had come home to be asked about my heroism while I felt so helpless in understanding Yousuf. Everyone was telling me that I should not upset myself with his problems, that nobody could do much for him. I heard the voice of my interrogator under the Shah ringing in my ears: "You live your life and be successful. You are a smart person. Why should you ruin your chances of achieving your goals for such pathetic, poor people whose miserable lives are beyond help?" Yet these were my relatives whom I loved, who also loved me and were kind to me. I felt ashamed for even comparing their innocent games to torture. I could not, however, deny that while intentions may differ as days and nights do, acts of violence leave irreversible traces and marks on souls and bodies that change forever those subjected to them, and those who have inflicted them. How frightening and disheartening it is to be able to trace torture in such ordinary contexts and situations. And that is what makes it both so prevalent and horrifying.

It was frightening for me to admit how Yousuf's experience in being dropped from the bridge and his loss of sanity in the face of death resembled the experiences of many prisoners who were taken for faked executions. You would stay there waiting to be shot, and they would take as long as they wanted to extend the period of anticipation so that you would wish they would just shoot you and get it over with. Even when they actually fired, it would only be a shot to the side or over the top of your head. Your chador, or even your hair under it, could be burned by the bullet, you could even get a shallow scar, but it would be only a game for them, a game of power to break you down under such intense pressure. While blindfolded, you would never know where, when, or if they were shooting.

بس

When we were in elementary school in a very small town in Azarbaijan and were punished for being late in the morning, we knew when and where our principal would hit. We were, however, rarely able to resist pulling our hands away. He never bothered to question why we were late. It did not matter either how brief our delay was; with his metallic ruler in his hands, he would be waiting. No escape was possible. We never got the chance to tell him about being chased by "Crazy Naser," who was an exhibitionist and of whom we were terribly afraid, or "Wild Ghanbar," who would beat us, or any girl, in his way. My younger sister and I had to take different directions to school to free ourselves from these harassments. But nobody ever asked why we were late, though if they had, we could have said nothing. It would cause a disastrous fight between my brother and Naser and a great humiliation for us, or Ghanbar would be even angrier and beat us harder. But for the principal all that mattered was our lack of discipline to be at school on time—a discipline he was to reinforce by his ruler's pain in the palms of our hands.

We would stand in a line among others who had come late or had not worn their white collar, part of our school uniform, awaiting our turn to be beaten, while watching others' hands turning red and swollen. The rule was that we had to put one hand over the other and keep them open during the beating. Every time we closed them or pulled our hands away, the number of blows would progressively increase. Despite this rule, most students were unable to control their reflexive reaction to the pain and would pull their hands away or close them. I was able to use some techniques of concentration that enabled me to keep my hands open and unmoved during the beatings.

One day, my sister, who was only in the first grade, could not hold her hands still, and her punishment began increasing. She was two years younger than I, and I could not stand watching her suffer. I begged our principal to beat me for her share. Laughing and taunting me for my "stupid heroism," he agreed. In the middle of the beating, however, when my hands were nearly bleeding, my teacher came out and saw me, and as usual I was saved for a trivial reason: my teacher liked me, for I was the top student. My little sister's frightened eyes, and her hands that pulled away any time the ruler moved toward them, were replicated in Roya's effort to escape her ceaseless fear of torture. I feel nauseated when I imagine all those tiny hearts everywhere in the world that pound so rapidly like trapped little birds. Picturing all these scenes of "innocent" cruelty and institutionalized, systematic punishment and torture testifies to how deeply rooted violence is embedded in our societies and in the history of humanity.

～

Ordinary cruelty speaks in different languages, plays itself out in different times and spaces. Yousuf could be called Joseph or even Josephine, but all these particularities would not have changed the fear, humiliation, and degradation that people like my cousin Yousuf experience. My twelve-year-old nephew and his American friends probably have as much fun with their "retarded," "idiot" classmate as my cousin's friends had with Yousuf.

As in the case of ordinary violence, the language of torture might differ from one context to another, but its prevalence is astonishing. Torture and its technologies are shared and exchanged on a global scale. The uniqueness of torture, however, can be traced and examined in the cultural, social, and political settings in which it is deployed.

I WAS A FIRST-YEAR UNIVERSITY STUDENT when I was arrested by SAVAK during the Shah's regime. In their fine suits and ties, the members of SAVAK presented a middle-class professional appearance. Protecting the well-being and the rights of its citizens was a goal trumpeted by the state, and torture was perceived as a means to accomplish this end. I had read banned books and discussed forbidden ideas among a close circle of friends. I was reported as a potential dissident and was therefore arrested. I watched my interrogators addressing one another as "Doctor" and talking about torture as a necessary surgery that removes the infected parts from the body.

Getting information from a prisoner was likened to the procedure of removing a tumor from a person's body. One of my friends was expected to "give birth" to information, so her interrogators spoke of obtaining information from her. According to their metaphor, interrogators were the obstetricians who helped her give birth to the baby. She was, however, not a human who would go through labor to give birth to one baby. She was seen as an animal, forced to bear multiple offspring, in short intervals. These torturers were experts, trained in the best schools of torture to perform a precise, calculated, and spiritless implementation of their tasks. In the torture rooms, or as they called them, "laboratories," advanced technologies of torture were tested.

The psychological factors were as important as the physical aspect of the pressure. Sharing the same cultural ground and aware of my enormous respect for my father, my interrogator would use every opportunity to embarrass me in front of my father. I still sweat, recalling the look on my father's face when my interrogator told him that he had been watching me sleep half naked in my cell. How delighted this interrogator appeared when he caught me so shocked and ashamed. I was totally oblivious to the possibility of his watching me on those long, hot afternoons of that summer. For him, the whole game revolved around this sense of shame and shock that was supposed to shatter my gender identity by shaking my moral foundations and my values. This was the paradox of torture

and interrogation; it interfered with and penetrated into the most intimate and personal aspects of a person's life while remaining extremely
impersonal in its nature.

Under the Shah, the tortured were the torturers' subjects in their laboratories. When I was arrested for the second time, it was under the regime
of the Islamic Republic, which claimed a radical shift from the westernized regime of the Shah to the early Islamic governance where the rul-
ing class was supposed to be also a religious guide for people, who were
called *ommat*, the community of Muslims. As agents of the secret police,
our captors who drove Hamid and me to Evin Prison addressed one another as brothers. Under this new regime, people were to see themselves
as members of a single family of Islam, all belonging to a single community of Muslims. Those who rebelled against this community were either
infidels, thus outside the community, or disobedient children whose required punishment was to return them to the right path or to eliminate
them to preserve the unity of the family of Islam.

Sometimes, the practice of referring to everyone as sisters or brothers
would lead to amusing confusions. I recall that about a year or so after
the 1979 revolution, a young man where I worked expressed his romantic
feelings for me and asked me to marry him, while calling me sister. I joked
and said, "But would not our marriage be incestuous if we married?" But
funny stories were not always the outcome of this notion of a single family. The voices of those prisoners who, while under torture, would beg the
brothers to stop the beatings cried out the paradox of this strange, superfi-
cial relation between the torture and the language used by the torturer. It
alluded to two even more provocative issues. On the one hand, it offered
a commentary on the violent nature of some familial relationships. On
the other hand, it covered up the impersonal and brutal nature of torture
under the guise of mere punishment by the parent or older siblings to
discipline disobedient children.

Indescribable agony seized me as I sat in the wheelchair right after torture, facing a written form on which I was asked if I believed that torture

existed under the Islamic Republic. The question made me so furious that any response to it seemed humiliating. The experience of answering yes to this nonsensical question and being beaten again did little to reduce the bitterness I felt at being forced into such an ironic position. From the first day, a battle began between those prisoners who resisted addressing the prison officials and the interrogators as their sisters and brothers and the prison officials who fought to force them to utter these words, while they called prisoners names and dirty words, making their reference to them in familial terms even more bizarre.

The irony of this fictive kinship, of course, emerged in the light of the antagonism these interrogators felt toward us and their necessity of portraying us as monstrous to justify their brutality. For them we were not sisters or brothers; they never addressed us this way, as we were forced to refer to them. This constant conflict over the way things and people were to be named overshadowed every aspect of life in prison and illustrated the significance of how relationships were articulated and represented. The prison under the Islamic Republic was *daneshgah*, or a university, and the wards were called *Āmouzeshgah*, the Place for Education, or *Āsāyeshgāh*, the Place to Rest. The pain inflicted on prisoners was not torture, but *Tazir* or *Hadd*, Islamic terms for regulatory punishment. The fight extended even to our everyday language where the prison officials would insist on referring to our daily chores in prison as "housekeeping" in opposition to our term, "labor." None of these contradictions, despite their intentions, could obscure the power struggle that lay beneath them. On the contrary, they highlighted this struggle.

Under the Shah, our female bodies were the objects of the lustful eyes of our interrogators, who forceably undressed us using every opportunity to touch us. Under the Islamic Republic, however, guards avoided even touching our hands, as a principle, though during torture, all these rules were thrown out the window. In regard to dealing with the leftists, both regimes claimed that we were communists who lacked any family morals and that we were promiscuous and shared sexual partners; women, especially, were accused of being shared by several men. That men could be with several women did not stir up their blood as much as the idea of women being involved with more than one man. Yet under both regimes, whenever it was required, women were unveiled, undressed, and even raped. This was the common language and practice with which the torture spoke itself and was performed, a language of power, humiliation, and domination. The labyrinths of these power struggles, which were so systematically manifested in relation to prison, also wove their webs through every stitch of the social fabric.

YOUSUF'S EXPERIENCE was one illustration of these interwoven power games. I had come downstairs now that most of our relatives had left. I was standing at the door when Yousuf returned from his walk with my brother. His anxiety had grown now to the point of aggressiveness. I watched my own fear magnified in the mirror of others' eyes. I urged myself to have the courage to approach him and talk to him. We spent the whole night talking, and sharing the silence, and still I was not sure if I had understood anything about his experience. Yet I felt the ice was once again broken, at least on the surface, and we were communicating despite our distance.

Everybody was surprised that Yousuf would talk to me and act as if he accepted me as his friend in such a short span of time. Perhaps this relationship could be explained by my own experiences. I, too, had journeyed through the realms of violence, despair, fear, and pain where I had come so close to madness and death that my blood was frozen in my veins. Was it this similar experience of seeing friends betraying friends that made him feel close to me? Was it these unspeakable feelings that allowed us to speak through silence?

For whatever reason, Yousuf began to trust me, but I apparently betrayed him, as everyone else had. Unable to avoid my sentimentality, I let my parents see through me, and they became concerned about my sadness in sensing his suffering. I was upset that I could not devote all my time and energy to being with him. Still, I tried to convince myself that my participation in the revolutionary movement would be more productive in changing everyone's life in a more profound way than my individual effort to help him. Despite my high spirits at the time, this was a tiresome conflict that consumed a great deal of my energy, of which I was short because of our recent hunger strike in prison.

My parents, however, were worried that I was exhausting myself by the demonstrations, where I faced gunfire and death, and by trying to understand Yousuf beyond or through his world of madness. By unconsciously revealing my emotions, I gave everyone enough excuses to send Yousuf back to his parents to protect me from feeling for him. Later, my parents insisted that they were convinced he would be much better off going back to his hometown and to the refuge of his parents' love. They believed that the social crisis in Tehran was too much for him to deal with, and they were perhaps right. They were also concerned about the safety of my sisters, even though I believed that their act spoke more of their fear of the other than the reality of Yousuf's behavior. Like Yousuf the prophet, our Yousuf, too, disappeared. But since 1978, there has so far been no return.

Everybody was convinced that he would benefit from being sent back to his home where he could be relatively free, since in Tehran he was nearly imprisoned. He could not go anywhere by himself, for he could be lost or killed. My parents would also be relieved of this heavy responsibility and free themselves so that they could concentrate on my return and my readjustment. So, my father asked one of my cousins to take Yousuf to the village. Later my father insisted that he asked this cousin, again and again, to make sure he would himself deliver Yousuf to his parents. But instead, my cousin paid a bus driver and asked him to watch after Yousuf and was assured that he would be delivered to his family. He never reached the village.

Two days later, his parents came to welcome me and asked for their son. They did not even know Yousuf had left. This was a time when there was no phone in the village; even my family in Tehran did not have a phone, so we had not let the family know that Yousuf had been sent to the village. And now the family, his father and mother, were asking for their son. What could we say? There were no bloody clothes to show them to suggest he had been killed by wolves, even though he might have been; who knows? The driver claimed that halfway to the closest town to our village, in the town of Zanjan, he made a stop at a restaurant on the normal bus route to let the passengers eat and perform their prayers. He saw Yousuf getting off the bus but did not recall if he came back. While being questioned about his responsibility to deliver him to his family, he harshly responded that he had fifty passengers and could not follow everyone at every moment. Some passengers who could remember Yousuf by his appearance had contradictory memories. Some had seen him after that stop, while others believed that he had never come back.

His parents were upset at my parents for sending him back by himself. My parents felt it was unfair, for "why should they always take the responsibility for every member of the family?" My father complained that when I was imprisoned, he was not even able to share with his family his horrifying experiences of having his young daughter in such an awful place. He blamed my cousin for his irresponsibility in breaking his promise to take Yousuf to the village, while my cousin was convinced that in fact the guilty one was the bus driver who had promised to watch him but had failed to do so. I was angry with everyone, but more at myself for being such a sentimental brat, for letting my family know about my sympathy for him and for being the center of their attention.

Yousuf, however, had vanished with no trace. After a few months of having his face broadcast on TV, he was almost forsaken. For his parents, despite their grief and their memories of him, his absence ended the humiliation they felt for having a crazy son, though after his disappearance, his father and mother aged very fast. His mother died of cancer a few years ago. His sisters' physical condition worsened, and other concerns occupied the family. At the time, however, while grieving, their worries seemed to have come to an end along with their debt to their relatives for the care they had given him. Did they ever unconsciously wish for his death to relieve them of their guilt over him and his travails? Gradually, his memory seemed to have faded, at least for the more distant relatives. His name came up less and less often in family conversations. But his blue eyes still follow me and stare at me through the sky, through the sea. In 1999, when I initially began to write about jail, with no intention to write about him, or without having even thought about him, his seemingly forgotten story struck me in a dream, in one as invisible and as insignificant as his place in my life seemed to be.

In my dream, it seemed that my relatives were holding a meeting about Yousuf's problems, as if he had not yet disappeared. Except for the faces of my father, my brother, and my cousin, I do not recall recognizing any other persons' faces. I was watching them, hearing them, but somehow I was not there. It appeared as though I was seeing them from a distance, a different time period. My cousin was suggesting raising money for Yousuf; my brother was very enthusiastically supporting this idea. I was annoyed and confused at my cousin's suggestion and suspicious of my brother's enthusiasm about it. When I woke up, I was unaware of the relevance of this dream to my recent experiences, and especially to my writing. Its continuing presence in my mind during the day was, however, at once annoying and intriguing. I often have two different kinds of disturbing dreams: the ones that may bother me at night but can be put out of my mind as mere dreams when I wake up; and the others that stay with me and have such an impact on my day that I have to face them and engage them to recognize their meaning and significance in my life.

This dream, too, seemed to cling in my memory and urged me to speak of it. While recounting it to a friend, I was struck by the way in which it began, suddenly and unexpectedly, to unveil its importance to me in ways I had not fathomed earlier. The figures and names became animated and took on lives of their own. As soon as I said his name, I realized that I had been writing and thinking about Yousuf the prophet. Only then I noticed that my persistence in using "Yousuf" instead of "Joseph," a name that I knew would be more familiar to Western readers, had to do with my attachment to him, to my cousin Yousuf. I described Yousuf's clothing as being covered by sheep's blood—another reminder of my cousin Yousuf as a shepherd and of his sheeplike face and character.

Joseph-Yousuf was favored by his father and thus banished by his brothers. Our Yousuf, however, was banished because he stood alone and was loved but not favored by his parents, and he was banished through the participation, albeit unwitting, of almost everyone. In one way or another, each of us had something to do with his vanishing. My cousin paid the driver to deliver Yousuf, for he did not want to waste time and his peace of mind to go all the way to the village with an insane person. He was still trying to evade responsibility, instead trusting his money to take care of him, just as before. I was also annoyed at my brother, who had not had a specific role in the real story.

Remembering Yousuf was a way of reminiscing about my life in its shreds and pieces, recollecting those incidents of ordinary cruelty and irresponsibility in a mix of different experiences and events. I now realized why among all those stories in the Qur'an, those of Ismail and Yousuf stood out for me. We have been repeatedly reminded of the possibility of the reappearance of the one whose disappearance we had planned. Like Yousuf's return as the treasury minister of Egypt, those we hurt might come back to us in a stronger position than our own. If your love for God is expressed through your willingness to kill the most precious gift of your life, your own son, our stories have assured us, God will spare him and reward you for your devotion. However, beyond these moral lessons, many Yousufs have been disappeared or really offered to wolves by their loved ones and have never returned, at least not to the world we know.

The Islamic narration of the story of Ibrahim (biblical Abraham) who was willing to kill his beloved son to prove his love for God was reenacted under the Islamic Republic. Yet here it was no longer the father who offered the sacrifice, but a woman from the city of Isfahan. It was a mother now who, against her motherly love, offered her leftist son to the Islamic Republic, assuming it to be the representative of God on Earth, whose commands she believed to be coming from Khomeini. Like my cousin, this Yousuf, too, is considered as other to the society, for his leftist views that the mother finds at odds with the ideas of the authorities and the majority of Iranians at the time. Night after night, the government-run television and radio asked mothers, fathers, brothers, and sisters to turn in the deviant members of their families to government agents, for the love of God, Islam, Khomeini, and the Islamic Republic, all collapsing into one another to mean the new regime in power. The mother complied with the command by reporting on her own son. For a couple of nights, the story of her devotion was shown on national television. But in contrast to Ibrahim's story, her son's life was not spared. He was killed as if a sheep. The rumor was spread that she had been promised that her son would only be punished, not killed; hence after learning of his execution, she lost the capacity to live with her guilt of betraying her own son and with the grief. She went mad.

In the case of my cousin, nobody learned what happened to him. Did he walk toward soldiers in a demonstration without realizing it was toward death that he was walking, for he had already been captured by death through madness? Was he shot, and if so, was he aware that he was dying? Or was he just lost in the wilderness and, in fact, eaten by a wolf? Did he starve to death or die from lack of water, as had Imam Hussein, the third imam of Shi'i Muslims who in 681 was killed by Yazid, the caliph, along with seventy-two of his companions because the enemy had deprived them of water, for whose thirst and death Yousuf used to cry so sincerely? Did he become a wandering dervish who just traveled on foot with his lame leg, supported by ordinary villagers?

I used to ask myself similar questions about Hamid: Was he really executed? What did he do in his last moments? Did he recite the poem I had written to him in my last letter, which he said he loved so much? What if he were alive and was just sent to a remote area from which he may one day emerge? This reemergence has been the recurring theme of many dreams I have had, especially in the last couple of years. I will perhaps never know the answers to any of these questions concerning Yousuf and Hamid. About Yousuf, all we know is that his story was never described in any book. Is that why I am writing about him here, to somehow include him in a world, at least in the world of the dead, after a life of exclusion?

6

Maryam
A GOD WHO CRIED

Listen to the song of the reed,
How it wails with the pain of separation:

"Ever since I was taken from my reed bed
My woeful song has caused men and women to weep."

—Rumi, *In the Arms of the Beloved*

It was one of those hot summer afternoons in Ghezel Hesar in 1985, when even the air seemed imprisoned. Any movement of the wind was suppressed, so it appeared. The prisoners lacked the energy even to wipe away their sweat. Conversation, which in a normal situation might shorten the day, was abandoned. In the humid cells, as we lay motionless, in a state between sleep and unconsciousness, time and space escaped their normal frame of existence and reference. In my mind, images and objects were slowly floating on a sea of hazy steam, so obscure and blurry that I could perceive them in infinitely varying shapes or in no familiar fashion. I could not grasp my memories, as if they were melting away, yet like atoms under heat, they became activated, mixing together, running and escaping from one another. In these misty memories, all my life was condensed, yet nothing really existed, as if life were departing from me through the sweat and the heat, which were streaming from my body.

I remembered that, while in Evin Prison in 1983–84, we used to laugh at one of the regime's ideologues who insisted on proving that being a devout Muslim does not necessarily eliminate the possibility of believing in a scientific explanation of the cosmos, assuming his opponents suggested it did. To illustrate, he explained that the reason the people in the south of Iran sleep in large beds is that the weather is hot there, so they need to stretch out. In the northwest of Iran, where he was from, people used smaller mattresses since it was cold and they automatically cpmpressed themselves to stay warm; hence, they do not need large beds. We used to make fun of this curious logic, but on this extremely hot day, the smile was escaping me. A wish vaguely crossed my mind, only on the surface, as light passes through thick fog: how wonderful it would have been if we in fact had more space to really be able to stretch out. But there we were, lying down so close to one another that the heat of the person beside us was indistinguishable from our own. Melancholy had overtaken us.

In the midst of this lethargy, Maryam, looking straight ahead with her dark, burning eyes in her gaunt, bony face, was marching across the hall, taking long steps while rhythmically moving her arms back and forth. In that hallucinatory state, this tall, thin young woman with her short, dark hair, in her white shirt and black pants, looked more like a young man than a woman. When she began to speak in a changed masculine voice, my foggy mind sought to find out who that man was, as if I were dreaming. The man was Moses, preaching to his traitorous and disloyal people, threatening that if they refused to return to God and stop betraying their promises, God's curse would destroy all of them. As she was preaching, she began to look at us as if we were those corrupted people who had betrayed Moses. Her voice was increasingly angrier, as she was roaring more loudly and more coarsely, but all we did was move our heads to watch her, probably less attentive and responsive than Moses' unfaithful followers.

Although it appeared that time was not moving at its ordinary pace, shrunken and swollen as it seemed, I could still estimate that, for about half an hour, this young woman was, so astonishingly, transformed into Moses, the prophet. With a deep, coarse voice delivering a biblical oratory, so poetic and erudite, and with an elegant mixture of Arabic and Persian, she was no longer speaking herself. It was as if she were possessed by Moses who uttered his rhetoric through her. This was Moses returned into a Persian context.

Her performance was so incredibly magnificent that we were torn from our illusory state. A form of possession, an artistic act, or just sheer madness—whatever it was totally baffled us. This twenty-one-year-old woman was transformed into a middle-aged man with no makeup or change of clothes. Her facial expressions, her body movements, and her voice all created a portrayal of Moses as we had imagined him. Still fascinated with this extreme alteration, we felt stunned, realizing that Moses had departed, and we were now encountering a new man, an older one, with a totally different voice and articulation.

This bent old man, with his working-class accent, enacted an episode of his life for us. A hardworking but poor man with a sick wife and eight children, he was struggling for his family's survival and worried about his oldest daughter, Maryam, who was imprisoned. We learned about Maryam's family through her father's words and voice. She walked, spoke, cursed, and cried like an old man. I wondered why she was taking on these other roles. I do not recall how many other voices expressed themselves through her, but I vividly remember that she took all afternoon to go from one metamorphosis to another. At her personification of a woman, who was forced into prostitution under miserable, unfortunate circumstances, many of us cried with her. It was not until the next bewildering scene she created that I could somehow connect all of these roles through a woven thread to her own life.

It had cooled off slightly as the afternoon moved toward the evening. For the first time during the whole afternoon, Maryam returned to herself, even though it seemed that, except for her voice, nothing else was yet completely like her. She was still in a different time frame, in her past, but exactly when and where were not yet clear. In her own voice, she seemed indecisive, as if unfamiliar with herself. She began with fragmented episodes of her life in her high school, in an art class where she was a stage actor. Then she was on the street, distributing flyers against the Islamic Republic, and all of a sudden we recognized her in prison. She was taken to the interrogation and . . .

For a few minutes, we were frozen by her deafening, frantic screams, unable to comprehend what she was experiencing at the moment. It seemed, however, that she was wrestling with a person, or persons, much stronger than herself. Lying down on the floor, as if her hands and her legs were tied, she was barely able to move. Still in a deadly struggle to free herself from this trap, she was screaming for help, crying loudly, cursing and begging all at once. Then her voice was disrupted, as though someone was covering her mouth with his hands. In the brief intervals of biting her hands, she freed her scream, which was growing harsher and lower. But all of a sudden, her voice was totally cut off, and all we could see was her body movement and her heavy breathing. She sounded as though she were suffocating. The whole ward was silenced and dismayed. She failed in the struggle and, now we all knew, she was raped by her interrogators.

Speechless and still, she was left on the ground, seemingly unconscious. Waking up, she had found herself naked, covered in her blood, still tied up to the torture bed with an aching body. What had happened to her afterward, she did not remember. Maryam began to tell her story as if it were someone else's. Although she spoke in her own voice, and sometimes even used the pronoun *I*, the way in which she was telling her story after the rape and her crying seemed as though it had happened to another person, or to the person who had died within her that day, after the rape. We found out that Maryam was left in the room for three days, which was something she had later learned through a woman guard who came to take her to her cell. As soon as the guard had touched her body, she had begun to remember everything, but the guard had slapped her on the face and ordered her to stay silent about it.

Maryam's intense pain filled our hearts. One of my fellow inmates remembered hearing her after these events, screaming for days and nights and finally speaking nonsense. She had now recognized the woman beside her cell, who in her frenzied speeches had talked about her interrogator raping her. The guards had chained her in her cell, covering her mouth except at mealtime. Now almost into the evening, Maryam became herself for a few minutes before she was turned into God, an angry, powerful God who was to bring thunder and floods to destroy these monsters.

God was speaking directly to his creatures, threatening and warning them. In fact, it was too late for warning. He had sent his prophets to guide them, but they ignored all these attempts at their own salvation, so they had to pay for their sins. With a mysterious voice, as if from another world, Maryam embodied God. She went to the bathroom and stood under the cold shower with her clothes on. While water was dripping from her clothes, she returned to the hall and jumped up to reach the huge, hollow aluminum ducts that were close to the ceiling. Clinging to them, she was jumping up and down, making a thunderous sound, which she claimed was thunder. The whole ward was disrupted by the noise of this thunder that the angry God was provoking. So, when the head of the ward, a collaborator, Homa Kalhor, came in and tried to forceably take God down, we were still astounded by Maryam's fascinating talent and creativity in generating such powerful scenes one after another. We had all forgotten about the heat and the trivialities of the ward.

Like Moses' disloyal people, we sat and watched a deadly struggle between God and a traitor. But this God was embedded in the body of an earthly human who was exhausted after several hours of personifying different people. She lost the fight. Wet and shivering, God fell on the floor while the traitor and the guards beat her up. She (he?) was still preaching and cursing, but it seemed the pain destroyed her sense of orientation. We watched this beaten, defeated God, who finally cried and escaped to the corner of the cell, where she was followed and beaten again. While dragged on the floor outside the ward, her bleeding head and leg left a trace of blood behind, the only sign of that crazy God who cried on that hellish day. She remained in our memory the way we saw her for the last time, with her head down. We washed away the trace of her blood on the floor and never heard anything about her again.

We learned from one of our fellow inmates, who used to live in the same neighborhood with her, that Maryam was a very intelligent person and a good student. Her talent as a stage player was known by the whole school district and throughout her crowded, poor neighborhood. She used to write and recite poetry, and write and direct plays, from the time she was a teenager. Knowing that, we debated her performance on that disastrous day, trying to comprehend its meaning. For those of us who had seen

Maryam as merely an insane person and did not have any interaction with her prior to that day, the evening of this theatrical madness raised a lot of questions. Was the whole event an enactment of her artistic talent through which she expressed her intense emotions, or was she really transformed into other characters' personalities? Why would she take on those specific roles? For instance, I wondered why she would let Moses instead of Mohammad speak through her, when she was a Muslim (she was arrested for her affiliation with Mojahedin). Could it be that she thought of Mohammad as an ally of those who had hurt and crushed her whole existence? How would the boundaries between art and insanity be delineated? Is there a specific space where the realm of art ends and we enter the world of madness? Where does one draw the line between imagination and phantasm?

Living in prison, in the world of deprivation and absences, necessitates that one live beyond the images and objects, or rather in the world enriched by one's imagination where desirable objects are created in their recognized absence. It requires an ability to consume images, reshape them, destroy them, and live without them, with the power to create a world without any material grounding. The art of living in prison becomes possible through imagining life in the very presence of death and observing death in the very existence of life. It is living life so vitally and so fully that you are willing, if necessary, to let that very life go, as one would shed chains on the legs. It is embracing and flying on the wings of death as though it is the bird of freedom.

Art in Prison

> When you lose all sense of self,
>> the bonds of a thousand chains will vanish.
> Lose yourself completely,
> Return to the root of the root
>> of your own soul.
>
> —Rumi, *In the Arms of the Beloved*

After months of living furtively, since the beginning of a wave of crackdowns on all dissidents in the summer of 1981, bleeding in our hearts from the news of our close friends' executions, saying good-bye to our beloved ones every morning as if for the last time, and awaiting our turn, finally one evening in the spring of 1983, there came a knock on our door, and Hamid and I were arrested in a small rental apartment in a poor neighborhood of Tehran and were driven to Evin, a notorious prison. It was a long drive from the south to the northwest of Tehran. As soon as my eyes were blindfolded by two big hands, I felt as though they had begun to squeeze my heart. I entered into the darkness of the night while behind my blindfolded eyes the shining sun generously poured its golden rays on everything around me. Still only around five o'clock on a spring evening, the sun had a long way to go before hiding behind the beautiful mountains of Tehran. My mind was still unable to grasp the irony of the eclipse that so suddenly happened. A moment ago, the beautiful spring clouds were gliding in the blue sky inviting the migrant birds. With my whole body, I smelled the buds and blossoms. Was it going to be my last time to smell them? That fragrance would stay in my memory through all the coming years when the rotten smell of infected wounds and the sweat of our own and our friends' bodies were the most familiar odors around us.

The huge metal gates swallowed us. Covered by a chador, I felt like a feather while two strong hands were taking me into a long, narrow hall in which the putrefied smell made me feel nauseated. Those two hands were going to be among others that would tie me to a metallic bed and administer the lashes, which would sweep all over my body and then focus on my feet. Yet before I was taken to the torture room, in between the slaps on my face and the kicks on my legs, in between those breaths of fright and uncertainty during which my heart experienced extreme sensations from pounding as fast as African drums to total breathlessness, I had time to think (did I really think?). And I thought about those whom I loved and things that were precious to me, though I would later learn how fragile some of them could be. The interrogators made me bear witness to the lashes that cut my beloved one's body, an image that would remain in my mind forever.

And now I was tied to the bed and trying to find a way to bear the pain. While the lashes were constantly ripping my feet and the pain had reached an apex, I was no longer able to think or do anything to reduce my sensation of the pain. All I knew was that I did not want to, nor could I, break down. Next came the phase in which I saw the colorful circles, curvy lines, and finally those red stars, and I knew I was going to lose consciousness. Time stopped, and I felt death's ghost flying over my head.

What is it that keeps us from surrendering? Of course, each individual has unique reasons; however, I consider it an element of inner strength, or weakness, a will and a need to protect our souls from banishment, from abandoning the possibility of our humanity, of caring for ourselves and for others, and from giving ourselves away. Our resistance, in refusing to submit to the torturers' desire to break us, overturns, or at least restrains, torture's absolute destruction. Through our resistance, we enliven the struggle against the normalization of injustice, humiliation, and the attack on dignity and the enslavement of our minds and bodies.

I opened my eyes in a small cell. The tiny window, covered by metal bars, was too high to be reached. A toilet and a sink in a corner bound me to that place, and I wondered for how long. It was only a small opening in the metal door that connected me to a narrow hall and to the guards; the door was never opened to me unless I was called for interrogation. Although separated from other prisoners, I knew that many others were locked in their cells trying to fathom the meaning of what had happened to them and ways to cope with it, as I was. I told myself that I should always remind myself of this reality, that no matter how isolated, I was never alone in this world. That I should never forget that none of my actions or decisions were only mine or would affect only my life. On the wall, the prisoners before me had carved their names and inscribed some dates long past. This place had hosted many who had come before me and would hold those who would come after. One thing would, however, remain intact: the challenge to remain connected and committed to our own and others' humanity, regardless of weaknesses.

Blowing Your Soul into Your Fingers

Forced to live in a place where only four steps take you to the other side of the cell, your eyes hungrily swallow the faint light that passes through the bars and plays hide and seek with you on the wall. You let your imagination fly as far and as high as it can go. Your imagination is what you possess and cannot be easily imprisoned; it is your territory of freedom and an essential element that keeps you from drowning in an impossible situation. Lying on imagined clouds, you take off from your small, bizarre cell to the heart of the sky, where you are able to see children still playing, laughing, and growing. You blow your soul into your fingers, which turn into thin rays of sunlight and enable you to go beyond the bars. You pass through your lover's bars, to smoothly and gently touch his aching body to heal him. Having gone through that deathlike trance and returned to life, are you not empowered by supernatural forces? After all, what is supernatural power if not the ability to live and love, surpassing the horror of death, hatred, and despair?

Like the prisoners in Plato's allegorical cave, you are compelled to live in your cavelike cell where the outside world seems so removed and illusory. Your humanity is being questioned. Your body is no longer under your control while it is constantly and violently destroyed. Ironically, your body and your mind are your only belongings and the only means by which you can challenge your perilous circumstances. You use them in both destructive and productive ways. You announce a hunger strike for which you go under another phase of torture, and you become a creator by using your hands and your fingers as vehicles by which your mind takes the imagined journey to the outside world. You create yourself, new selves out of yourself, through your art. You let your mind speak to your fingers, who like goddesses blow the breath of life into the bones in your food, or to the pebbles you find on the yard. These seemingly worthless objects become your precious means of linking you to life while they themselves become alive and initiate a communication of their own. Through them, you learn about your capacities in spite of the limitations of your situation. You become alive by giving birth to these inanimate objects, while the language and the voice that torture aims to eliminate continue in them. This is how prisoners become artists and the art in prison comes into existence, not so much for its aesthetic quality but for its existential purpose.

ﻙ

After four days of torture, finally Hamid was taken to his cell. One of his shoulders and a couple of his ribs were broken. His feet were ripped apart and his legs so swollen that he had to tear the legs of his pants to fit into them. Sleep evaded him; the pain was too intolerable to allow any rest. It was the first night out of the torture room. The evening before his arrest, we had gone to our favorite park, where after a long hike, holding hands, we sat by the river and listened to its music. We watched children play- ing and joyously running after butterflies. Despite that beautiful, relaxing evening, that night I woke up with a nightmare.

It was the spring of 1983: At 3 a.m., sweaty and shaky, I woke up screaming. Hamid tried to calm me down and asked me what I had been dreaming about. Barely able to speak, breathing heavily, I said, "The wolves, the wolves broke into our room. They had come in a pack, broken down the door and the windows, and were all over this place, smelling everything, tearing everything apart and snarling at us." He said nothing; there was nothing to be said, or there was no need for words. We both knew what my dream was about. Holding me tightly, Hamid gently whispered into my ear: "Go back to sleep, honey. Go to sleep." I closed my eyes only to open them a moment later and realize that he was doing the same, watching me while I was seemingly asleep, as if for the last time. Holding each other the rest of that night, we tried to savor our moments together. We did not realize that the wolves were just behind the door. The day after, even before dark, we were in the torture room.

ﻙ

The sound of the reed comes from fire, not wind—
What use is one's life without this fire?
It is the fire of love that brings music to the reed.
It is the ferment of love that gives taste to the wine.
The song of the reed soothes the pain of lost love.

—Rumi, *In the Arms of the Beloved*

Alone in his cell, Hamid had announced a dry hunger strike that deprived him of prisoners' usual pleasure of spending time eating or even drinking tea and water. With his broken body and his torn clothes, his memories and his socks, which had remained untouched since his arrest, for he could not put them on those injured, swollen feet, were the only possessions left for him from the outside world. "What do I need these socks for? By the time they could fit my feet again, I'll be long dead. My feet might not walk again, but I make these socks walk for me where my heart wants to be." In our first meeting, after a year, when Hamid sneaked in the wallet he had sewn for me out of his socks, he explained to me how he had taken them apart with his injured hands, twisted the threads together, and knitted a wallet for me with no access to any tool.

For most prisoners, the period under intense torture is rarely the time for creation. They basically strive to imagine freedom and life beyond their solitary confinement. An enormous power is required to concentrate on making something while pain is so intense. However, a person who achieves this state of living beyond pain gains a remarkable capacity to alter extreme suffering. Instead of being overwhelmed by rage, disappointment, or loss, one challenges destructive forces in the process of creation. Through this creation, one not only communicates with others but also articulates phenomena that are essentially in negation of all that torture seeks to destroy: love, resilience, passion for life, and creativity. Through making, the uncontrollable world becomes tangible. The same body that under torture seems one's enemy, in the process of creating, returns to us and helps us feel ourselves again.

The Art of Living and Becoming in Prison

They smell your mouth to assure

that you have not said you loved [someone].

They smell your heart

It is a strange era, my sweetheart.

And they whip love on the obstructed road.

Love must be hidden in the house's closet

—Shamlu, "They Smell Your Mouth"

What strikes me is the fact that, in our society, art has become something that is related only to objects and not to individuals or to life. That art is something which is specialized or done by experts who are artists. But couldn't everyone's life become a work of art? Why should the lamp or the house be an art object, but not our life?

—Foucault, "On the Genealogy of Ethics"

It is the art of living and the power of resistance in an inhumane situation that gives birth to the delicate handicrafts produced by prisoners. Locked up in their small cells, unable to move their injured feet, prisoners preserve their soul through nourishing their creativity, against the ravages of time and death. In the world of isolation and forbidden love, loved ones become the source of imaginative power for prisoners. Prisoners engrave their names on such things as pebbles, coins, or woven wallets. The work of art in prison signifies the prisoner's refusal to become a totalized, faceless cipher among others. In their struggle against submission, prisoners employ and reshape objects that cry out their resistance to becoming imprisoned souls and slaves of imposed identities. The possibility of a departure is embedded in the labor, desire, and imagination invested in producing this art, which creates life in the midst of the prisoners' deadly situation. For all these reasons, art in prison is not a luxury but an essential element to keep the spirit moving, which might make survival possible.

It is also for this very reason that some of the most intense battles between prison officials and prisoners were over the making of artwork. Endless rules were announced to forbid the production of anything that expressed prisoners' creativity and artistic experiences. It was not merely the content of the art, but far more important perhaps, the very basic desire of the prisoner for making the art that these rules targeted. The argument was that by occupying themselves with these trivial things, prisoners were avoiding reflection on their past and therefore continued their enmity toward the regime. Guards' and collaborators' scrutinizing eyes were present in every corner of the wards to catch prisoners while working on a little pebble, a bone, or a seed found in the meal, or other objects through which their creativity could materialize itself. Even letters to the families, which appeared to prison inspectors as too poetic, too aesthetically literary, or too symbolic and metaphoric did not pass inspection because the officials could either read something more into an ordinary conversation or could not understand the implications contained in symbolic words. Their rules and regulations imposed on us a limited vocabulary, one that had already been worn out by extensive overuse.

We were supposed to follow a highly formalized style of writing letters in a restricted seven-line space that had to start by greeting and telling the family that we were doing fine, hoping they were healthy and happy, and finally saying good-bye. In response to our constant complaints about not delivering our letters to our families, the prison's director responded, "You are prisoners, supposed to be isolated from your normal life. The coming of spring or the leaving of winter should be none of your business, so don't write about them as though we don't understand what you really mean by the imminent arrival of spring and departure of the winter." The paper provided for writing our letters was embossed with a printed statement at the top: "In the name of God, the compassionate and the merciful."

Yet all these restrictions only urged us to create our own unique style of writing. We had to condense our thoughts in that limited space in a metaphoric way that did not arouse the inspectors' suspicions. A poetic concision characterized these letters. New symbols and metaphors were created. The words were crafted prudently and in such a fashion that each word conveyed multiple meanings. Certain prisoners were distinguished for their highly stylized and skilled letters, developing aesthetic forms while achieving the main goal of crossing the barriers of communication. Despite the constant instructions by the prison officials that we could not write about spring's triumph over winter, or about spring's blossoms, we would usually find ways to express ourselves to pass through their inquisition. The letter that was sent by my husband to my mother on the occasion of my birthday, which falls on the winter solstice, the longest night of the year, exemplifies how other deeper messages were simultaneously conveyed. Even though the poetic language, the rhyme, and the harmony are mostly lost because of the translation, the symbolic political message is still readable.

> Each year on this night, I try to imagine the long cold night of autumn in which the cold winter wind lashes madly at nature's body and the darkness of night tries in despair to forestall the dawn, but in spite of all this, there are mothers who burn in the fever of labor and heroically bear a night of hardship. Finally, the dawn in its full beauty prevails, and the night fades away, the wind subsides, the mothers calm down in triumph, and children come to the forefront of existence.

Only through living the same experience of being whipped on a long, endless night during which you have been able to victoriously keep silent and not lose your integrity, when the morning greets your injured body and the faint stream of the sun's rays strokes your aching face and warms your bloody feet, only then, you might understand what this letter speaks of.

On the Ashes: Words That Replace Tears

> To say that the pain has no music is to know that those who suffer are in a hell without song. Broken speech and scars are metaphors that cannot be laced with romantic meaning. Yet, in the very hell of grief, a rope is flung or created.
>
> —Vera Schwarcz, "The Pane of Sorrow"

The trees were upside down as I stared at the mirrorlike glass window of the meeting room when my father said, "They gave us a number, number fifteen, and told us to come back tomorrow to get news about your husband." This meant that they were announcing his execution and delivering his meager possessions. The thought immediately passed through my mind: they finally did it; they killed him. I could shed no tears, not only because I knew my parents, especially my father, could not bear seeing my tears—my mother was already crying hard and beating her chest—but I also did not want to give the guards the pleasure of watching me crying. Today when I think about it, though, I feel that maybe I was also, and perhaps even more so, afraid of letting my grief out without being able to contain it, for how many tears could have brought me relief from the enormity of my loss?

Silently therefore, I walked toward the ward as snow was washing my fiery face. For three nights, I stayed awake and thought of writing a letter to my brother-in-law. I wondered if I could condense all those complex and intense emotions in seven lines, pondering how I was going to escape the inspectors' watchful eyes. Those seven lines wept my experience while I was able to walk in the ward without tears in my eyes. They lived me when I felt dead in my heart, made me alive by going beyond my loss of existence, and helped me climb out of my despair by giving me the language of departure. They spoke me while I was unable to mourn in any other way. They pulled me out from the well of despair by forcing me to give them acknowledgment. To do so, I had to depart from myself, to think about my brother-in-law and his pain. In convincing him of the meaningfulness of Hamid's death, I was also convincing myself. That was how I gave birth to a new self and survived the most horrifying death, dying inside.

Living in prison is an art for which you have to train yourself. Prisoners who accomplish the goal of living through this hell and surviving with their integrity not radically damaged are creators of the art that is simply their lives. It is so easy to be tempted to stop living. Committing suicide can be—not only physically but spiritually—the most inviting drive for prisoners. One of the most terrifying experiences in prison is to constantly encounter inmates who are seemingly alive yet utterly detached from life. These are prisoners who never attempt to bend the bars in order to have a glimpse of the sky, stars, or anything that belongs to the outside world. It is the absolute loss of the ability for love that defines this kind of existence. It is the horror of realizing the danger of dying inside that urges resistant prisoners to hold on to whatever protects them from such a death. Being capable of laughter is one of those ropes that link these prisoners to life.

The Art of Creating Laughter

Laughter was an essential element in prisoners' lives. It gained such an important place that amateurs worked hard to become more experienced in initiating genuine laughter. "It was the victory of laughter over fear" that impressed these resisting political prisoners the most. Prisoners would talk about their fear of torture in such a comic way that it would put them at ease to laugh about it. This laughter would curtail the horror and the fear to such a level that one could now speak through ridiculing. As we focused on the irrationality of torture and the torturer, ridiculing our own fear and their worries, the boundaries of the rational and irrational collapsed. Our jokes would target both the authorities and ourselves. We mocked the ways in which we failed to go beyond our limitations, our narrow-mindedness, and also our fears. Through these humorous comments, both in our daily conversations and in satiric plays, we criticized ourselves and, though briefly, stepped out of our situation. Laughter, the ability to laugh, was in and of itself a victory we could recognize. Laughter also provided a different level of interior and interpersonal communication and sometimes was more effective in making changes in our perceptions than a serious conversation.

Prisoners had to confront the alienation and the estrangement toward one another that the authorities were so vigorously trying to generate and reinforce by different tactics. The prison's officials and the guards reported any close relationship between prisoners, separating them from one another or employing methods that used one against the other. Religious rules and cultural norms served to disguise the crushing of strong bonding among members of the same sex, labeling such closeness as unhealthy and disgusting, as homosexual relationships. Prisoners could not share their belongings with one another since sharing was considered a symptom of communist sympathies. They were not supposed to care for one another during illnesses or after being beaten. On many occasions, prisoners' refusal to watch their friends being tortured led to their collective resistance and, consequently, collective punishment and torture. Our ordinary life therefore was suffused with constant innovation to make a truly social and caring life possible. The essential element of the art of living in prison was to be able to preserve compassion, care for one's self and others in the world in which, in the words of Shamlu, my favorite Iranian poet, "they whip love on the obstructed road."

Bahar's Birthday

In 1981, Bahar was fifteen days old when she was arrested with her mother. On her second birthday, more than eighty prisoners in her room decided to celebrate the occasion. We got together and talked about our plans and offered what we had. Some of us unraveled our new clothing to make dresses for her. Some prisoners made the clothes while others did the embroidery. Dozens of suggestions were made. When the day came, we were surprised by the variety and beauty of the things that had been made for her. Farangis, a seventeen-year-old prisoner who was arrested when she was fourteen and is now a painter, had prepared a notebook in which she had painted pictures of animals, flowers, and trees that Bahar had never seen in her life. In addition to her aesthetic style, the labor and materials from which this work was constituted were extraordinary.

Under the Islamic Republic, any nonreligious celebration in prison was considered anti-Islamic. However, celebrating special occasions such as New Year, our friends' birthdays, Women's Day, the *Shab-e Yalda*, or Solstice Night, were very significant to us, and we vigorously fought to preserve such celebrations. At night, regardless of the consequences of being caught and punished, we practiced our plays on our makeshift stage. Some of the prisoners excelled in decorating the stage by using simple materials. This was the case both in this regime and under the Shah. I still joyously recall a time in the New Year of 1978 when the chief of Qasr Prison came to visit our ward and was astounded by our stage decoration. He could not believe that the furnished living room created by prisoners for our play about the life of an urban middle-class couple was made entirely from newspapers, plastic, and fabrics, dyed with pills or skillfully embroidered. The flowers on the table were molded from kneaded wheat flour that we fashioned by saving our bread; they had been colored with dyes from various pills we dissolved. To obtain the desired color, we had to investigate what kinds of pills provided the specific colors that we needed, and what kinds of diseases we had to claim to be suffering from in order to have them prescribed. Unfortunately, during the Islamic Republic, the medications and the health services were so scarce that we were no longer able to use these resources for our art.

In prison, everything from a peach pit to a bone to an empty can was considered precious, since these objects became the means by which the prisoner, the artist, communicated and created a new life. On our few-minute trips to the meeting rooms, on our way to the clinic or to interrogation, we highly cherished every chance we could get to grab some soil or anything that might be useful for our artwork. We would conceal these under our chadors until we got to the ward. Empty cans were turned into vases or small pots by using a sharp tool also made out of empty cans. We planted our stolen flower seeds and waited for them to rebelliously throw the soil away and raise their heads toward the sun while we were joyfully celebrating their/our victory.

Mouloud was one of the prisoners who planted the morning glories in the yard in such designs that they could convey her feelings and ideas. In order to make them grow in the desired way, she would carefully study the direction of the sun's rays toward which the flowers would predictably grow. She used thin, nearly invisible threads to make the flowers lean in the direction she wished. One morning she called us to the yard to demonstrate her art of gardening, though she never considered it an art but simply a language that, as she claimed, gave her the opportunity to express herself. Her morning glories looked like children held by their mother with her multiple arms stretched around them. Mouloud, an older woman whose only son was growing up without her, always felt upset that she was unable to protect us from the violence and brutality of prison. Her flowers represented the dream of this mother with a huge bosom and many long arms by which she could safeguard her children from cruelty. "It is also my passion," she commented. She loved designing flowers, since through their silence she could say much. With their beauty, vitality, and color they were full of the force of life and even death.

Niko, another prisoner and a painter, would use the flowers and leaves to make color for her paintings. She would put the flowers into small eye-drop bottles and wait until they decayed and turned into specific colors. Sometimes, she would add several different flowers or leaves to obtain her favored color. She then would cut someone's hair to make a paintbrush, using a broomstick for its handle. Her amazingly beautiful paintings with their fresh natural colors would bring life into our wards and our lives.

The extraordinarily beautiful jewelry—necklaces, bracelets, or hair clips made out of date seeds—likewise shows that in prison anything can be the ground on which creativity blossoms. Dates were almost the only supplemental source of energy, and prisoners treasured them whenever they were given the chance to buy them. The dates were eaten, yet their contribution was not over. The prisoners would wash the seeds, put them in some kind of container, and add hot water. The water would soften the hard seeds, making it easier to reshape them. After a few days, the prisoners would take the seeds out and rub them on any hard surface, such as the asphalt ground in the yard or a stone found either in the yard or in one of those trips out of the ward. After reshaping the dates, they would polish them by using a piece of broken glass and color them by soaking them in black tea, olive oil, or a flower solution. Simple tools such as safety pins, hairpins, and broken glass were used to reshape the hard surfaces of coins, pebbles, dates, and seeds.

IN THE WINTER OF 1978, just a few days before the Iranian New Year, in Qasr Prison in Tehran we were attacked by a death squad, the special prison guards of the Shah's regime. Injured and angry, we declared a hunger strike. We informed our families by sending two of our fellow inmates to family visit while the rest of us also announced a strike on family visits. That same day we were taken, though temporarily, to a different ward where through its window we could see the sky. At dawn the next day, while my hungry stomach was denying me sleep, I got up and sat by the window to watch the sky. Watching the sky, the sun, and the clouds and talking to the stars have been some of my greatest pleasures since childhood. However, the sunrise that I watched that morning was, and still is, one of the most memorable ones I have ever seen. When the sun rose, it was truly like a huge, fiery red ball, with an intense palpitation as of a heart. I kept observing it as though it were a living heart or a fetus.

This incredible scene so allured and fascinated me that I woke my friends up to watch it. We sat there until it had risen completely and the color of the mountains turned into a variety of shades, far more beautiful than any masterpiece. Singing together, we treasured this rare opportunity of observing and sharing such an extraordinary moment together. That dawn remained in my memory, awash in gorgeous shades—a memory that allowed me to face death, promise to myself that no matter when, where, or how I die, I would live every day of my life "as if it were the last." Whenever my heart ached with loneliness, I remembered Hamid and my other loved ones, like that sunrise, and I felt alive again. Being able to cherish those beautiful experiences with my friends gave me the courage and the hope to confront the horror of prison. It expanded the possibility of daring to know, to care, and to live life, no matter how long or how short, but as responsibly and joyously as possible. Having known how to live joyously by flying on the wings of my imagination, and enamored with the beauty of a sunrise, I understood that living beautifully depended not on possessing luxurious objects but on knowing how to love and care under conditions that seem to render loving impossible.

EXPERIENCING HORRIBLE TRAUMAS in life and surviving them do not automatically make us invulnerable or triumphant for the rest of our lives. Lessons of life can be forgotten, as can many other acquired gifts. In this constant process of learning, forgetting, and relearning, our memories betray us by being prey to our current moods and predilections. The possibility for change occurs through a type of dynamic relationship to the present that necessitates constant reflection and reexamination of our thoughts and lives. The destructive impact of an experience as traumatic as imprisonment, especially under such conditions as the prisons of the regimes of the Shah and the Islamic Republic, extends beyond the thick walls surrounding prison. The incessant pressure that prisoners experience, the ceaseless fright of impending torture and execution, drains the energy necessary to face the changes. The result is lethargy, exhaustion, lack of desire for change, and the tendency not to make decisions.

These qualities, in turn, induce an attitude of conformity toward the very social norms against which a former political prisoner has been fighting. Reliving the experience repeatedly manifests itself in being bound to a frozen self, a subject that relies on known feelings and fears. Learning how to refuse the tendency to remain imprisoned within the boundaries of an immutable self is as imperative for the resistant prisoner as the refusal to submit to authorities. The loss of motivation to challenge oneself out of entrapment within oneself and failing to seek new ways of thinking and being are potent dangers that prisoners face even, or in fact more, after they leave prison.

When I initially began to write this text in 1999, I realized that my memories of my imprisonment were particularly triggered by my experiences in a new country, the United States, where I had simultaneously found myself a stranger yet at home, for it was here that I had once again fallen in love and lost my love. The failure had pushed me into a state of despair. I had begun to forget that I had lived, regardless of all its pain and suffering, a joyous and lively life, full of love and beauty. I had nearly forsaken the very basic principle of a creative life, to make the remaking of myself the task and the goal of my life in the face of death, and to be present to death and remember the dead. This remaking of oneself is an art of living and hence dying, eventually possible in the very act of reconnecting with, thus re-creating, others and the world within which one lives.

I told our story.

I was unfaithful to you tonight with this stranger.

I told our story.

It was, you see, a story that could be told.

—*Hiroshima mon amour*

O seeker,

Listen to your heart's true yearning—

Don't sleep!

—Rumi, *In the Arms of the Beloved*

1999

In the summer of 1988, while we were cut off from the outside world, the gaps between our nightmares were filled by the sound of gunshots and the guards' malicious chants calling for our deaths. Every morning began with our anticipation of another group's being called for execution or for whipping. Meanwhile, madness and suicide linked these days and nights with their omnipresent shadows. It was a period during which we gulped down fear and horror and swallowed sorrow, waiting for our own executions or breakdowns, or those of our loved ones. The anxiety of these losses was so overwhelming for me that I clung to my oldest friend, my writing, to survive this lethal, imminent experience. While the lashes were probably ripping the skin from our friends' bodies, I stole some moments from breathing sorrow to write. I addressed Hamid in my writing, even though I was no longer sure if he was alive. Dripping my feelings drop by drop onto the paper, as though my blood, I gave myself to the words that depleted my worries and sadness. These words enabled me to wake up in the mornings and face the challenges of my life and feel an inner strength to be there for my friends with their losses and fear.

I was, however, caught by a strange power that I had attributed to these words. Like talisman writings that villagers hang on their children to keep them safe from the evil eye and terrible events, I carried that piece of writing with me, as if it would keep my Hamid alive. Not that I had thought about it that way; how could I have? I assumed that I did not believe in ideas I considered superstitious. I had even mentioned in my writing that he might never get the chance to read it, but scared of the power of the words, I avoided using words such as *dead* or *executed*. It was as though I had bargained with my writing over Hamid's destiny. After I learned about his execution, I felt that the horizon of my imagination was diminished. Mesmerized by the image, I had missed the possibility of remembering, which occurs only when one leaves the experience and looks back through imagining it.

And now I had begun writing, years afterward, about prison, but why was I writing? Was I writing to give voice to those whose voices were violently silenced? Was I trying to address a moral dilemma of human nature or give people moral lessons? Was this supposed to heal my wounds and help me move on with my life, as though such moving on was ever possible? Was I writing to put those nightmarish experiences behind and forget all about them, again as though such forgetting could happen? And what about all those beautiful experiences I lived in jail, those joyous moments of the victory of love, resilience, and friendship over the dark forces of torture, violence, and hatred? I tried to explain to my friends this urge to write about my life and the difficulty of writing about it, yet each time, I think, I made them as confused as I was.

With any fragments of memory that appeared to me, I felt as if a lost, sunken soul were coming back to the surface. Remembering the injuries hurt, but life was rekindled through the open mouth of the wounds, like the faint flames under the ashes. I was yet unable to fathom the uncanny manner in which I was expressing myself. It seemed as if I were still writing behind a curtain. Afraid to face those horrifying memories in my loneliness, I took refuge in the illusion of a safe space in the presence of those strangers on my television screen. Evading the events, I was moving in between the spaces. As though to protect myself from being burned by the flame of those gushing memories, my fingers typed the words after the blaze died down. Furthermore, writing in English, I had even more difficulty pouring my emotions instantly from my heart into words. Hence, they were digested, examined, and finally consumed cautiously. It enabled me to think over what I was writing while cooling the blaze of my emotions.

English, however, was not "the language of forgetting" for me; instead, it offered me a distance from which I was able to reflect on my past. I returned to my story, also in a different site, as Marguerite Duras has the protagonist of her movie *Hiroshima mon amour*, a Frenchwoman, tell the story of her traumatic loss of her German lover during World War II in Hiroshima, the site of another trauma. I came to tell my story in the United States, a place with its own history of violence and suffering, from the earlier genocide of Native Americans, to the enslavement of African Americans, racism, its wars on other countries, and an increasing divide between its haves and have-nots. It, too, had its inspiring stories of resistance and incredible achievements in creating new possibilities for a better world.

Here, in the United States, which has now become my second home, I came to relive my trauma through another kind of loss and a new sense of estrangement and humiliation, which I experienced in a different place, time, and language. This new wound, however, opened the old, hidden ones, slowly and painstakingly, as if with a dull knife. I had left the country in which my voice was violently silenced, where many of my beloved ones' lives were taken from them simply over one word, *no*. While in prison, where I could sacrifice my life and body over the words I consumed, I had fought against this silence. Emerging from prison, however, I needed a different space from which I could tell my story. I left the country in which nearly one-third of my life had been spent behind bars, yet it was in this country that I had fallen in love for the first time. It was there I had learned how to see and feel the spirit of the change in the air so that I could join and swim with others on the tide toward the ocean of freedom, even though it turned out to be so extremely short lived and fleeting.

Nevertheless, it was from the very same country that I needed to exit in order to return to it, from a distance, with a deeper understanding. It was probably this very gap, this very heartache, that I felt in this new land that evoked my memory, renewed my sensitivities, and made me realize the acuteness of my pain. I felt mute where so much conversation was going on. Paradoxically, it was through this language that I was finally able to tell my story. Perhaps the loss of my language was the slap I needed to be able to recognize my silence and to distinguish between myself and my life, on the one hand, and those who were dead and their deaths, on the other.

I struggled with myself, falling and rising as I relived these experiences. However, when I reached the last chapter, where I had decided that I wanted to convey hope instead of despair, I felt mentally paralyzed. Something like an intense magnetic force was pulling me away, as though whatever I wrote would take over my life, that I would become doomed to live according to what I wrote. It terrified me. I could neither sleep nor rest. What if I wrote something that was either trivial and meaningless or impossible to live up to? What if I could not face my new challenges? Fear captured me, and I was desperately seeking a way out.

Suddenly it was revealed to me. I was in the light. It was the fear of being trapped by my own words that was so incapacitating—the horror that unveiled the dread of imprisonment, as if the words were going to define me, control my life, or I were going to be possessed by them. Was that not what had occurred to me with my secret missive to Hamid, which I felt so attached to as if a part of myself, like the child that I never had? Yet it had failed to make Hamid invisible to the regime or to protect him from being killed, just as these words here will not protect me from falling down and rising again.

I was hoping to achieve a new relationship between myself and my writing, one that could be liberating rather than imprisoning, one that was able to illuminate my experience in its various dimensions. I needed to establish a relation to my own writing that could open passageways to re-creating myself and envisioning new possibilities and new horizons of the imagination. Being alive, I was subjected to constant changes, not willing to be chained by the objectified words, even my own. This means to seek a way of living that redefines oneself on a daily basis yet is never unfaithful to one's humanity, to one's dignity.

In the light of this disclosure, I reconsidered the space from which I was writing. I was not writing because I felt the obligation to give voice to those who had been silenced. In fact, I could never have been able to do justice to those voices. If my writing has shed some light on their experiences, it is mostly due to the fact that we do not live in isolation, and others' voices and experiences are always intertwined with our own.

Moreover, I was not writing to be healed or to forget, for how is it even possible to forget if one is trapped so that one cannot move beyond it? When one is haunted by an infinite moment, the possibility of having memory vanishes, since memory belongs to the past as history. There will be no past when one is frozen in an illusory present. But if one is no longer caught, why would one be willing to forget? How can one be willing to forget about history when history is what makes us who we are?

Thus, I am writing not to forget but to remember and to understand; though in order to remember in this new way, one has to also learn how to forget. This forgetting somehow recalls the essence of the experience. It is this kind of remembering my experience as a history that allows me to step back in order to look at it and think critically about it. I want to remember the moments of resistance to discover those sides of myself I have forgotten. I want to remember the humiliation, the pain, and the suffering to be able to live every joyous moment of my life as a moment to treasure, as if it were the last moment before death knocks on my door.

I am writing to release myself into the world beyond boundaries where the imagination expands horizons for creating new selves, the selves that have their roots in the past but are not chained to it. I am writing to refuse being caught in the past, in an imposed image of the future, or even in this writing. Free agency is an illusive modern liberal concept, true. But rethinking it in a context of the other and within a collective notion of human existence concerned with an ethics of living responsibly and responsively in relation to others is the ideal that, no matter how utopian it may be, is worth pursuing. As long as one is alive, confrontations will continue. Being kissed by death so closely, I remind myself that life is not a given, nor is freedom, so that tasting life in all its flavors is my desire and mission. I am, of course, well aware that the wolves are waiting behind the door. I am, however, still ready to take up the challenge of fighting the chains that may bind me to the totalizing regimes and to myself. Free from these chains, I want to fly.

2010

The world has seen enormous changes since this text initially came into being in 1999. At the time, I had already been out of Iran for five years. My return appeared more like a dream than a real possibility. Yet in the summer of 2002, I had taken the risk of visiting my family and my home country, ironically also after more than eight years, nearly the same length of time I had spent in prison before returning to my family and Iranian society in 1991. The transformations I encountered during my visit, which I repeated in a longer stay from 2003 to 2004 and later again for three months in the spring of 2005, were as drastic as the ones during the period of my imprisonment, if not more so. With Mohammad Khatami in his second term of presidency, the Iran to which I returned was entirely different from the one I had left behind in late 1993. Discussions about many sensitive issues were prevailing in public. The idea and the culture of clandestine activism seemed to have become a thing of the past. Surprisingly, I attended seminars in which even previously taboo topics such as Marxism were openly debated, or so it appeared. Arrests and imprisonments occurred, but neither in scale nor in the treatment and persecution of prisoners could one compare this period to that of 1980s.

Many individuals of the generation who had participated in the Revolution of 1979 expressed dismay at what they believed was the loss of all the values for which so many sacrifices had been made prior to and during the revolution. In this particular case of loss of values, both religious and nonreligious parents seemed to agree, though each pointed the finger at the other side. When faced by their children's blame for having brought this regime to power, those who were not supporters of the regime, which now included a large majority of the population, especially in Tehran, often distanced themselves by putting the blame on others. Yet they were also quick to express discontent about their youngsters' lack of ideals and beliefs, suggesting that the youth of today were very individualistic and had little or no concern for their communities.

The younger generation, in turn, complained about the mistakes of their parents and ridiculed them for believing, at least in 1979, that revolutions could create a better world. These young people seemed to adamantly adhere to the idea that changes should be forced on the system from within and through small, open fights and subversive actions. They sought this in everyday activities, more at a sociocultural than political level. They illustrated their transgressions in their language, artistic productions, jokes, clothing, and social manners, through which they were in fact able to stretch the boundaries of the norms and regulations a great deal. What these youth, many of them urban middle class, did not perhaps take into serious consideration was that the more they succeeded in opening up new spaces for themselves and their social interactions, the greater the hostility grew within those sectors of society and the government who believed in far more rigid boundaries, particularly for gender relations.

Among these, the ones with stronger positions of power felt great animosity, for they perceived these transgressions, the bending of their fixed rules and regulations, as threats to their totalizing power and an undermining of their authority. They were, therefore, the main forces behind organizing the backlash against a wide array of social groups gathered under the umbrella of the "reform movement." The participants of this movement were as diverse and complex as Iranian society. Popular support, to the extent to which we may speak of popular support here in the conventional sense of the term, relied on the years of a widening economic, and consequently sociocultural and eventually political, gap within society. More than anything else, they benefited from radically unequal access to different media and cybernet communication technologies. Even more important was dealing with the political ramifications of these apparently apolitical acts and forms of speech for the society and the state.

The more the regime lost its legitimacy and popularity among its citizens, the greater its need became to depend on dogmatic interpretations of Islamic law and fixed social codes. Every seemingly simple act of transgression undermined the monopoly of the state over both violence and the life and death of its citizens. The state-run media and the Internet access that was made possible through mosques or other religious institutions, often supervised by government agents, offered a particular lens through which the less privileged population saw the world. Within this closed circuit, and through the constant portrayal of the revival of Islamic movements, while obscuring their entirely different contexts and diverse sociopolitical conditions from those in Iran, the regime unleashed a crusade along with its small but strong group of supporters against a wide range of enemies it grouped together as the forces of imperialism, secularism, and corruption. Any movement to question its authority was portrayed and stigmatized as the embodiment of the wealthy, corrupt, westernized group of nonbelievers fighting the government, which is paving the way for Imam Mahdi, the last absent imam of Shi'i.

Under Khatami, however, the penal system, despite all its cruelties, did not seem tough enough for those in the government who sought to eradicate their enemies, the people who simply read, wrote, or produced artistic forms of expression that did not fit within the limits of their views. They thus killed people on the street, later referred to as *ghatlha-ye zanjirayee*, or chained killings. Writers, journalists, and artists were secretly blacklisted and kidnapped, only for their bodies to be found in front of their own houses, in a corner of an alley, or in a remote area, without hiding the fact that they had been killed, almost always in a most brutal manner. While in Iran in 2004, I attended the wedding of a young woman whose father was killed in this manner, dropped in front of their house, and found by the family one morning, weeks after his disappearance.

Nothing could have given this government better grounds for reigning supreme than the disjointed politics of the Western countries, especially the United States since September 11, 2001. What better opportunity to gain momentum than the U.S. involvement in two wars in the Middle East and its constant threats at the time to bring Ahmadinezhad and his allies to power? His shaky ground among the clergy and the people, combined with his desire to hold on to power until his last breath, drove the Supreme Religious Leader Khomeini to draw closer to the most conservative clergy and rely on the power of the Revolutionary Guard and an increasingly dominant and dominating penal system. The louder the Bush administration threatened Iran, the worse conditions became for the voices of dissent in Iran. The more scandalous the treatment of terrorist suspects by the United States, the less shame on the Iranian side in the face of the revelation of the Iranian citizens' subjection to the cruelty of the state and its paramilitary or non-uniformed agents.

The confrontation within society had reached the boiling point and had to be somehow contained. The threats of the outside world did the trick to help the so-called hard-liners mobilize enough people to elect Mahmoud Ahmadinezhad, a relatively unknown figure, to the presidency, though by a combination of fraud and the lowest percentage of voter turnout since the inception of the Islamic Republic in 1979. A new reign of power began that immediately bore a terrifyingly uncanny resemblance to those dark years following the Iran-Iraq War, the reign of an incredible brutality toward any voice of dissent. The worse was yet to come. It came.

Mohsen, my nephew, was one and a half years old when my sister and my parents brought him to prison for my first meeting with the family in 1977. He was the first nephew, and the first child born since my youngest brother had been born nine years earlier. He was thus absolutely loved and adored by many aunts and uncles on both sides of his family. His beautiful facial features—large eyes, long thick eyelashes, and thick long straight hair (my sister had wanted to have a daughter but gave birth to a son, hence his long hair)—made him appear even more adorable and innocent looking. That day in the meeting room, which in the United Anti-sabotage Committee was supervised by the interrogators themselves, Mohsen sat in his mother's lap and began singing a childish song for me, the first he had learned, in which a thief is advised not to shoot the person who is advising him, for it would lead to his incarceration.

All of a sudden, in the middle of his singing and my affectionate words, Rahmani, my interrogator, who was a large man, grabbed Mohsen by his shirt collar and raised him to the level of his eyes, while his feet were hanging in the air and his tightened collar was preventing him from breathing, so his face was turning blue. With his words emerging through his teeth, in an angry tone, and with eyes that even terrified me, Rahmani told Mohsen, "Motherfucker, you little ant are threatening me with your gun." In the song, ironically, it is the thief who uses the gun, not the child, but somehow Rahmani had read Mohsen's song as a preplanned threat on himself. "I will show you what incarceration means. You will be here before you know it," he went on to say and kept him in the air until my sister began begging him to leave Mohsen alone, explaining that he was only a child and had just learned this song for his aunt. I will never forget the terror in Mohsen's eyes that day; nor can I ever lose sight of my parents' shock and my sister's shivering body and sobbing to save her child.

And now he is really in jail, arrested in relation to the events following the disputed presidential election in Iran in June 2009. He is no longer a child; he is now married and imprisoned along with his wife. He no longer sings; who knows, perhaps the terror he experienced that day silenced his desire for singing. But he loves music and frees himself in the bosom of imaginary meadows, oceans, and skies and flies on the wings of its harmonious rhythm to leave the world of terror, cruelty, and violence.

When I was released from my second term of imprisonment in 1991, he was already sixteen years old and no longer a child so attached to his maternal aunts and uncles, almost all of whom, including me, left him at about the same time in the early 1980s because of the crackdown on the opposition. They were either imprisoned, had fled the country for exile in Europe or the United States, or lived as fugitives. I tried hard to reconnect with him after I returned from prison, but one day in the middle of a frank conversation, he told me that during all those years while growing up, when he had needed us the most, none of us were there for him. Now he told me, "Now that I am a grown-up and have learned how to handle my life on my own, what do I need you for?" This was, of course, more than painful to hear, but what I could hear was the fear of being attached once again, as he had been after I returned from imprisonment under the Shah only to leave for an even longer period. I could see how his bitter words were both words of pain and a way for him to protect himself from reattachment and, in his mind and perhaps rightly so, yet another emotional hurt. Frankness was one of Mohsen's main characteristics and perhaps why he never wanted to be involved in any dissident activism, for he knew his frankness could cost him dearly.

Mohsen hated to get involved in politics, so he kept telling everyone. Yet, like so many young people who used to blame their parents for sacrificing their lives without thinking about those who loved them, whose blood is now shed on the streets, who have now crowded the jails once again, Mohsen, too, is imprisoned and tortured simply for daring to think and to speak up. A couple of nights ago, I woke up, once again screaming at the top of my lungs and sweaty, but this time my dream was about Mohsen. It was the night of the same day I was working on the section of this text where I had a vision of Hamid's execution and his attempt to communicate with me, striving to reach out to me beyond prison walls. I had later read the vision as his coming to me to make sure I would be all right in his absence and to bid me farewell. I had, however, refused to speak to him (to him as a ghost?). I tried to convince myself that my dream about Mohsen was influenced by this writing, but I could not calm myself down.

I called my mother, hoping she would say, "No darling, it was just a dream." But my mother was crying the way I had only seen her cry when she heard of Hamid's execution. Blood froze in my veins. Fearfully, I asked her what had happened. They had brought Mohsen for his first visit with his family, but right after severe torture and three days of sleep deprivation with no food or water. My sister, like my mother then, had tried to stay strong for him but had come back home and passed out. Oh, my poor sister, how could you go through this once again? She was the only one of my siblings who was old enough to come to visit me in jail, and now she had to visit her own son in jail. My mother kept crying: "But Mohsen is innocent. He has never been involved in politics. He does not know how to be in jail. He is not made for this." I wanted to ask her, "Mom, were we not also innocent? Were we made for the brutality we lived through?" But I did not ask. I knew what she meant.

We were the children of a time when we had known the price of saying "I love you" was being murdered or being chained in a torture chamber, when the idea of political reform in the system seemed entirely impossible. The Shah's regime did not even pretend to govern according to the people's vote. He was the monarch who knew better than the people what was good for them. Under the Islamic Republic, especially since the late 1990s, on the other hand, it appeared as though votes could mean something, even though limited and always involving some level of fraud, and always under the supervision and veto of the Supreme Religious Leader. Not only did many people seem to believe that reform was a possible means of bringing about some desirable changes but they in fact did not see any other way out of the situation. They did not necessarily support the system, but their disillusionment with the Revolution of 1979 prevented them from seeking a revolutionary solution. Mohsen was less hopeful, for he had seen what happened in the early 1980s; but his most recent memory was of the Khatami era, when dissidents did not seem to be treated as harshly as in the 1980s or at the present time. Yet, no matter the child of what era one may be, the desire to be free, to care to know, and to love seems to never cease, nor does the will of the totalitarian regimes and technologies of power to silence dissident voices.

I wrote the first epilogue in 1999, from the space of memory, hoping that through my voice, a survivor of many brutal events, other voices could be heard. In 2010, however, my writing is immersed in the pain of all those bodies and souls, including my beloved nephew and his wife, undergoing torture. If this writing can reveal something of our resilience and determination to withstand injustice and the destructive force of torture and violence through re-creating our love and remaking our life, I will have achieved more than I could have imagined.

Acknowledgments

In March 1978, we were temporarily transferred to a new ward, also located in Ghasr Prison, supposedly because the well in the yard of our ward was clogged. Here, in this temporary ward, I would have the strangest visit ever with my family in more than a decade of my imprisonment under the regimes of Shah and the Islamic Republic. On the day of our meeting, at nine in the morning, a guard called my name, but I looked at him with confusion because I did not know where I was to meet my family. There seemed to be no meeting room attached to this ward, like the one in the permanent ward. The guard told me to go to the room across the hall and climb up to the third story of the only metal bed in the room and look out the window. As I looked through the window, I saw, on a wide dirt road, my father nearly running while looking around in confusion, evidently not knowing where to go, and my mother trying to keep up with him, perhaps both waiting to see an entrance to a meeting hall. Suddenly my father saw me and I heard his sigh—I am not sure whether this was a sigh of relief, exhaustion, a mixture of joy and grief, or all of these. They stopped, looking bewildered yet happy to see me alive and well. My joy was, however, tarnished by the awkwardness of this meeting. I was sitting on the bed and looking down at them while they stood on the ground with their necks bent backward so they could see me. From above, they both appeared smaller. I felt ashamed both for putting them through all the torments that having a loved one in prison entailed and for making them look smaller. My father was exemplary in his resistance to living an undignified life but, since my arrest, how often he had endured humiliation for my sake.

This was the first time I was spending the New Year away from my family. It would be many more years, but each time I would remember my father's voice reciting, "Ya Moghallebal Gholobo Val Absar . . . Havval halena ela ahsanol hal," meaning "You who are the transformer of our hearts and visions . . . change our mode to the best of the modes." Years would pass without my mother's loving eyes looking at me while trying to hide the tears they had shed for me. I have lived most of my life in separation from and in longing for my family. Yet, without my parents' love, their incredible humanity, and their trust in me, I could have neither overcome the torture and imprisonment of those many years nor been able to write about my experience.

When I lost my father in 2004, I literally felt that the ground began to shake under my feet. It was as though I had lost my anchor in life. I no longer knew how to go on or how to make sense of my life. Then one night my father came to me in a dream, along with Hamid. This dream awakened all my memories of the joy they both felt at my accomplishments. I remembered my father's many "escapes" from the hospital, despite his poor health and against the doctors' advice, and his returning home so we did not feel depressed or our education did not suffer because of his absence. I recalled his confrontation with his own family members to make sure his daughters received treatment equal to that of his sons, if not better, and that they grew up to become independent, strong individuals. From my late father and my husband, Hamid, I have learned so much about love and integrity, and it is to their memory and their dedication to live and die with dignity that I dedicate this book. My mother's loving and beautiful spirit has kept me from turning bitter then and now. My life is enriched by the potency of her love that reaches me across the oceans and soothes my heart so softly and pleasantly as if the morning breeze.

When in 1999 I initially wrote these fragmented stories of lives in Iranian prisons—lives that had been ruptured, cut short, or lived in insidious proximity to, and at the verge of, madness and death—my narrating voice vibrated with hesitation and burden that stemmed from the loneliness of the voices, of my own and of those whose stories I was trying to tell. The stories of these sufferings had been forced into silence and hence did not enter into the pages of recent Iranian history or the Iranians' collective consciousness. The families of those imprisoned, tortured, driven to insanity, or killed by the state were stigmatized and lived under constant scrutiny in a state of near terror. They were not allowed to hold public mourning, nor were they given the bodies of their loved ones to bury in a proper funeral ceremony.

Even those families who were told of the whereabouts of their loved ones' graves were not allowed to mark them or put a tombstone on them. Communicating about their sufferings could lead to persecution. More often than not, they hid their predicament even from their own children to protect them from pain. But they also feared that these children could unwittingly reveal the "family's secrets," which could bring further harassment and greater suffering to them. Thus, the younger generation lived without any real knowledge of the history through which their parents, uncles, and aunts had lived.

Many, including myself, who had been subjects of imprisonment and torture, left our home country, family, and the mass graves of our loved ones to face the challenges of a new life in an unfamiliar place and with a language that we had to learn as adults. Those who stayed were often pushed to the margins of sociopolitical life in Iran. Most of these survivors and their families never ceased to fight to keep the memories of resistance and the dead alive, yet their voices were either too far away or too low to be heard amid the state propaganda and everyday noises. The pain of denying the fact of the mass killings by the regime, which covered up their deaths as well as undermining the very existence of their loved ones, was excruciating for these families. For me, what was even more unbearable was the fear that these atrocities would be repeated in the future.

In light of this danger, the manuscript was haunted by the enormity of the burden of responsibility to make these voices audible. I hesitated, however, for fear of failing to do so and instead ending up offering the kind of self-pitying "victim" account that I so adamantly opposed. Lacking confidence in my ability to convey the complexities of the voices and uneasy about the manuscript's possible political use, I avoided pursuing its publication and left the very ghosts I had awakened to return to their slumber. A few years later, during my several returns to Iran between 2002 and 2005, however, I became privy to the deep scars left by the state-imposed silence on the souls of the families whose lives were torn apart not simply by the violence but by its subsequent lies and secrets. I was also struck by the resilience and creativity with which they sustained, and created new communities in which, as in prison, the living and the dead continued to live in love and as witnesses to the injustices of the past and present and those that might occur in the future. This book owes its existence to all these unnamed people whose lives and continuous struggles have touched my soul in everlastingly profound ways.

It is with dismay, however, that I realize, as I am bringing this text to an end with the hope of a new beginning, that the generation born and raised after the revolution, or even after the Iran-Iraq War, has now populated prisons their parents once occupied. They, too, experience the undignified and cruel treatment of torture chambers. Yet the secrets of the massacres of the 1980s, especially that of the summer of 1988, which the regime had so persistently tried to conceal, have finally begun to be revealed. This is due to the unwavering struggles of the families of the executed dissidents. These families created novel ways of mourning and commemoration, despite all the pressure, through which they kept the memory of their loved ones alive. Gradually, they were able to relate their own sufferings to those of the other marginalized groups. To these families I am hugely indebted. However, the new dissident movement that has resurfaced since the mid- to late 1990s has been critical in summoning the ghosts of the revolutionary period and in exposing the suppression of the early 1980s.

The significance of this new movement is that some of its constituencies are former supporters of the regime, which allowed them more access to the classified information within the regime. If some of these people had previously convinced themselves that the government's harsh treatment of dissidents in the early years was justified because those dissidents were seeking a radical change in the system, they have found that this justification no longer works for the present moment. Here they were themselves tortured, imprisoned, raped, and killed for speaking their minds, asking for their vote, or freedom of expression. The stories of the 1980s were now seen more sympathetically. The news of the massacre of 1988 has also now been leaked, albeit in bits and pieces, mainly by government officials who are currently lined up on different sides, as *eslah 'talab*, or reformists, and *osolgara*, or those who follow principles. Those supporting this group are often referred to as "hardliners."

There are also the memoirs of the high-ranking government officials, such as Rafsanjani, Ray Shahri, and others, all of whom, while writing from an official point of view and thus always leaving many secrets still veiled, point out the mass killings of the 1980s. Montazari's memoir reveals more than the others do about this massacre. While the regime officials have strived to keep the veil as tight as possible, the ghosts of justice, those whose lives were so unjustly annihilated, have nonetheless haunted the Islamic Republic and kept it restless, alert to their haunting presence and to the questions of justice that they raise.

Former political prisoners have also published a growing number of memoirs outside Iran about the experience of imprisonment, each opening up a window to the dark, secretive maze of this monstrous system. Writing about prison, I know firsthand, is a daunting task, and I am extremely grateful to those who have taken the steps to give voice to these silenced stories. To these everpresent ghosts and witnesses I will always remain indebted. Most particularly, I am grateful to those generous souls who move beyond their own pain to listen to the sufferings of others and are capable of opening their embrace to whoever joins the fight for justice.

The recent uprising that followed the disputed presidential election of 2009 has made considerable use of new cybermedia technology that has enabled many unheard voices to become audible. Here, a new dialogue was created, mostly by the younger generation, but now put to use by the generation of the 1980s who tell the stories of their suffering to the younger Iranians and listen, with agony, to those of the youth. This has thus generated a novel mode of conversation between and within generations, with history, and between the living and the dead, along different political spectrums. Particularly intriguing is the way some individuals, especially young people, have begun to hear from and converse with the ghosts, in contrast to the way the state and those with older attitudes often impose their words on the dead or summon selective voices at the cost of silencing others. It is to these refreshing voices that I owe the strength to finally let go of this book, hoping that, in light of this new attitude, it may be read, despite its flaws and shortcomings, for its efforts to tell a more complex story of violence and resilience to survive it, even at the cost of letting go of life when it may bring death to others.

When I began revisiting the original manuscript in late 2009, the uprising in Iran was still at its peak. Even though my analysis of its dynamics led me to the horrifying prediction of yet another, at least momentary, defeat for the voices of freedom, I allowed myself to hope otherwise. This was not the result of a naïve optimism. I was cognizant of the ruthless determination and the experience of this regime in eradicating its dissidents, as well as the fractures and gaps within the opposition movement and the global politics that could allow the Iranian government to succeed in cracking down on uprisings. While I was very much aware of the regime's incredibly high stakes in suppressing this movement by any means possible, the monster that this violence unleashed, as it always does, went beyond my wildest imagination. I had seen more than my share of the brutality and lies of the regime, but to witness the vicious crimes that it committed in the last year was even beyond my darkest prediction. What was even more shocking was the fact that some of the subjects of these brutalities were the children of those killed in the Iran-Iraq War, recognized by the regime as martyrs, or former war veterans, the former supporters of the regime. Even if the government had justified its harsh measures against the dissidents of the 1980s by portraying them as the absolute other of its own revolution, many of these new dissidents were part of the system and did not pursue revolution as a remedy to the evils of the system but simply sought some changes within it.

This ruthless suppression illustrates how deeply violence permeates the fabric of the society and seems indispensable to masculine power, be it that of the state, political parties, or individuals. It also shows how fluid the line delineating those belonging to the other and the us can be. It teaches us that what happens to the others of today should terrify us, for it can easily happen to us, the others of tomorrow. The history of state violence in the world has many such examples to offer us. I am thus humbled by those spirits, living or dead, who have dared to take responsibility for their complicity toward the injustices of the recent past, be it those of the pre-revolution, the 1980s, or after. In spite of this severe crackdown on the opposition, which has led to a temporary quietness in Iran, I still believe both in its dynamic rooted quality and in the humanity that has grown to become its unique characteristic. This humanity, I like to hope, will over-come the malevolence of those who defend the status quo at any cost. To all those young spirits whose fight seems to have been in vain, I wish to echo the lessons of history, reflected in the stories of the subjects of this book.

Behind every word in this book shimmers the resilient hope to which we hold on in desperate times and in the midst of our deepest despair. Every page offers testimony to the power of love that makes endurance of torture possible and heals the wounds of the soul and the body. Each of its chapters becomes entangled with the others while making a life of its own by the creative force of imagination and fantasy that enables us to fly beyond the boundaries of prison and the cages erected by despotic regimes. The book in its entirety is a witness to the desire for freedom that outlives the desire for self-preservation or conformism, as are the lives and/or deaths of the subjects of this book, and the spirits whose struggles have been currently adding new pages of human dignity to our recent history. To the young people of yesterday and today I owe my never-ceasing certainty and unwavering belief that no matter how silenced and crushed the people's spirits may become, from their ashes, new resistance will always emerge.

My debt to Iranian and world literature, especially to the poetry of Hafiz and Rumi, Ahmad Shamlu, Shafiyee Kadkani, and Forough Farrokhzad, extends beyond this book. Their poems, a great many of which we knew by heart, not only brought color to the gray life of prison and even the larger prison of Iran but also enabled us to converse with one another under the censorship. Shamlu's verse "A butcher was crying for he had fallen in love with a canary" reminded us of the complexity of the human spirit in a language that was reminiscent of and sought beauty in the human soul.

If seemingly dead poetry could enliven our sometimes fatally injured souls, those who, in Shamlu's words, "made their death a revolutionary song" render our entire existence luminous. I am so profoundly indebted to these dead, whose absence compels me to remain present to the injustices of our time and to the calls of responsibility for human dignity. If choosing to die rather than submit to an undignified life takes courage, coming to terms with one's survival and continuing to live meaningfully, in connection with the community, requires a never-ceasing resilience and acceptance of one's vulnerability that seems nearly impossible. Yet many of the survivors of the violence of the 1980s demonstrate such an exemplary dynamic life that only affirms the potency of the human spirit in the ugly face of violence. I observed with delight these caring souls extending themselves to the survivors of the 2003 catastrophic earthquake in the Iranian city of Bam. I also watched these resilient souls in 2009 during a hunger strike in Berlin in the rain and cold, in protest of imprisonment, torture, and execution in Iran. But even in their everyday lives, these survivors and their families have shown me the meaning of resistance by their ability to love, to laugh, to tell stories, to make friendships, and to become active members of their societies. I owe an enormous debt to those surviving fellow men and women through their exemplary lives who have denied the regime its claim to victory for eliminating the spirit of resistance.

Acknowledging my debts to others in relation to this book is intertwined with the recognition of my life as a survivor. The gift of life is not simply given or received in the conventional sense of these terms, nor is this giving and receiving, if it may even be possible to use these words, a one-time occurrence. In Derrida's notion of the gift, to learn and to teach someone how to live, or rather survive—for is it not true that living is in fact always already a survival?—is a lifelong process. One learns only by receiving, yet the reception of the gift, which is confined to no particular time and no specific recognition of its reception, is rendered possible through one's learning how to live as a survivor, which means, in turn, to become the recipient and the giver of the gift. This real gift is thus received in the very act of giving and given by the way of receiving, while the boundaries between them and the time of their happening may never be clearly delineated. Thus, if I give the names of people to whom I am greatly indebted, I should note that there are many others whose lives and deaths have touched the core of my existence, either without my recognition or that I herein do not or cannot name. The order with which the names of people appear in the following passages does not imply the quality or the quantity of my debt to them. They are randomly and somewhat chronologically noted.

I could not have written this text in its initial form, as an undergraduate honors' thesis, without the support and critical insights of Stefania Pandolfo and Paul Rabinow, who were the best advisers I could have imagined. The voice of wisdom and a passionate energy were combined in the personas of these two great scholars, along with their shared willingness to encourage my unconventional style of writing. Beyond her advising role, Stefania has offered me the gift of her friendship along with the depth and breadth of her intellect, to both of which I will remain indebted as long as I live. I am deeply grateful to Diana Blank, whose generous soul was a precious gift in the difficult period of my life in 1998 and 1999. I am forever indebted to her for showing me that deep friendship can also be found in the United States. I thank Carmen, Daniel, Jacki, and Renate, my friends at the University of California, Berkeley, whose energy and laughter were a driving force for me. The recognition I received from the Department of Anthropology at UC, Berkeley, where my text was selected as the best honors' thesis of the year in 1999, boosted my confidence in communicating this unusual story to a Western audience.

I extend deepest thanks to Cynthia Kaufman, my community college instructor, who provided me an example of a great teacher and mentor.

Richard Wood's sensitive questions about my past life compelled me to tell these stories in my then poor English, which he generously corrected. To Lila Abu-Lughod I owe more than any words of gratitude can convey. Her generous soul in friendship and her trust in me and her unwavering support of my work have enriched my life in ways that my words cannot express. Hamid Dabashi's great voice of conscience, scholarship, and incredible energy continues to inspire me. Despite establishing himself as a public intellectual, I am amazed at how he still finds time to be an incredible friend. This is a gift that I have yet to learn how to reciprocate as well as how to receive it for its richness. Hossein Kamaly has been a wonderful friend and interlocutor to whom I am enormously indebted, for many hours of wonderfully fruitful conversation, for his deep knowledge of Rumi, whom I so love and cherish, and for his constant encouragement.

Brinkley Messick may not have read this work, but his words of confidence in me when I myself lost it have echoed in my ear during reworking this manuscript. Similarly, although this text was originally written even before I knew Rosalind Morris, in my return to it she has been an absent presence, speaking to me like many other absent voices whose presence pulsates on every page. There are many people to whom I am indebted whose names do not appear here. But I should mention Ofra Block for her wisdom that keeps me sane and Lauren Meeker for her friendship. I am so grateful to Susan and Robert Meeker, Lauren's parents, for offering me their beautiful place in the best location on Riverside Drive in New York City, away from Arizona's summer heat, to work on the final stages of this manuscript.

My colleagues in religious studies at the School of Historical, Philosophical, and Religious Studies have been incredibly generous to me since my arrival in 2007. I could not have survived the distressing events that were happening to my family both in Iran and abroad in the last couple of years had it not been for the friendship I found among some of my colleagues. I am more than thankful for the beautiful friendship, and gorgeous desert hikes, with Alexander Henn and his wife, Gabrielle, whose kindness shines like sunrays; Ann Feldhaus and Stephen Mackinnon, whose house generated new friendships; and Juliane Schober, whose generosity knows no limit; along with the radiant spirits of Françoise Mirguet and Sunil Kumar Bhatt. The trace of Françoise's beautiful soul can also be found in her fine arrangement of the table of contents of this manuscript. I will never forget how she came through for me with so much kindness when she called the night when I was panicking because my computer was playing tricks on me. Diana Coleman offered her gracious assistance in reading through and editing the text when I was so exhausted that I could not catch my own typos. But I am thankful to her also for offering me her encouraging comments about the importance of this work when I was losing confidence.

I should extend my gratitude to Mark Von-Hagen for his incredibly sensitive reading of my manuscript and his encouraging words. I am grateful to Joel Gereboff for never failing to extend his words of support for my work. I should thank Ann Feldhaus again for going out of her way to offer her generously positive comments about this manuscript at critical moments. My thanks also go to Tracy Fessenden, Tisa Wenger, Linell Cady, Sally Kitch, Margaret Walker, and others with whom I have had stimulating conversations that, even though not about this book, proved extremely helpful to me. Again, I am grateful to all my colleagues and many others whose names I have not mentioned here, but their presence has made me feel at home in my new job and situation.

I also owe a great deal to my students. It is in the everyday challenge of teaching and sometimes even failing to teach that I am reminded of the responsibility I have for living a meaningful life in relation to others. Semiha Topal's pursuit of her intellectual journey, which is so often challenged by her personal convictions, keeps me keener to the realities of my own life and urges me to never sit comfortably in the same place or call any place unproblematically my home. It pushes me to revisit my own dilemmas in finding new homes and languages while recognizing and accepting a relative out-of-placeness that could keep me sensitive to the problems of others. Sadia Mahmood's courage to pursue a project that goes beyond her zone of comfort, and her attempts to remake herself in each step while falling here and rising there, teach me, once again, about the complexities of our humanities, cultures, and subjectivities. From each and every student whose name I cannot mention here, I have learned enormous lessons.

My words will not be sufficient to express my deepest gratitude to my wonderful friend of more than three decades, Ida Mirzayee, whom I found, once again, in the United States. She is a sister I did not have in this country. I cannot thank her sufficiently for her help. When I had lost the electronic copy of this text and had only a PDF copy, she suggested and took time to convert the entire original text to a Word document so I could work on it. Her encouragement throughout this work has been a persistent force to keep me going. Jeremy Soh, on the other hand, is a new friend whose soul feels so familiar that it is as if we have known each other forever. He also speaks through this text, not only because he read the first thirty pages, and later one of its chapters, but his reading of its original form gave birth to our friendship, which I so greatly cherish. To his encouraging words, to his trust to share his tears with me, and to his sensitive insights I owe a great deal. My many thanks to Milad Odabaei for his beautiful reading of the original version of this text and to his kind and insightful comments. I owe special thanks to Stefania Pandolfo for the gift of the friendship of Jeremy, Milad, and Khashayar Beigi. The friend I have found in Gabriele Schwab goes beyond my expectations. In her I find a friend that I feel I have known forever. To Shahrzad Mojab and her wonderful family I will always remain indebted.

I am so incredibly grateful to Stanford University Press for making the publication of this book possible and to Kate Wahl for her absolutely sensitive and constructive reading of this manuscript. My thanks go to the two generous readers whose comments were essential to making the revisions that I believe improved the text. Thanks also to Carolyn Brown at the Press and to copyeditor Cynthia Lindlof and proofreader Christine Gever.

Finally, how can I ever repay my debt to my father and my mother, whose struggles and desire to raise their children as socially sensitive individuals who would never waver against injustices have shaped so much of who I am today? My father was a present voice when I began this work in 1999, but now he is the specter demanding me to remember the injustices that he endured. And what of my mother, of whose voice I have now become deprived because of the new wave of fear and silence to which, yet again, my family along with many others in Iran have been subjected? Not even once during all those years of my imprisonment did she pressure me to do anything against my will, even though this meant more suffering for her. Although she was illiterate, what she taught me about love and resilience, and even her beautiful version of faith, which so radically differs from that of the state, has allowed me to see the complexity and beauty of our humanity in the face of all the monstrosity of our world. I can never drink enough of the ocean of her unconditional love, her capacity to endure hardship, and her incredible desire for joy and friendship.

To all my siblings, and my brothers-in-law and sisters-in-law, whose names I cannot mention here, I owe every minute of living this rich life of love and compassion. To my nieces and nephews, whose days have now become saturated with violence and terror, I owe my rekindled belief in the spirit of youth. Their love and energy brought bright light back to my life, and I hope that this book offers them some hope that this horrific period will not last. To one of my uncles and his beautiful family, especially to his son, I am particularly indebted for trying to keep me somewhat connected with my family now that I am temporarily cut off from them. To my husband's family, who are as much my own family, I owe many heartfelt thanks. Without their love, the world would have been a sad place to live after Hamid. I go to sleep wishing that one day I can hold my mother-in-law in my arms and thank her for being such a gracious soul, and her children and grandchildren who still relate to me as if I am involved in their everyday lives. I could not have survived reliving these experiences without Hamid's constant presence, despite his physical absence. He has never left me; he has in fact become the conscience inside me at those moments when my own seems to collapse. His never-ceasing presence keeps me connected to both communities, which I see as inseparable from one another, the community of the living and the dead.

Notes

Prologue

Page 4 *Cheshmhayash* It is true that sometimes inmates did not tell the entire story of the activities for which they were arrested, but persecution over trivial issues such as Goli's were not rare occurrences.

Page 6 *tabootha or dastgahha* In Farsi, the plural is formed by adding *ha*, but colloquially the plural is formed by adding only *a*. So prisoners themselves referred to *taboota* or *dastgaha*, the plural terms used in this book.

Page 6 *enhanced interrogation techniques* This term has been used by the government of the United States to legalize and exercise torture without naming it so. Following September 11, 2001, the United States performed enhanced interrogation techniques and exceeded them in ways that shocked even those for whom the brutalities of torture were too familiar. As I think back, it occurs to me that since the training and technology for the techniques of interrogation and torture previously utilized by the Shah's regime were imported from the United States, so were the new ones, perhaps in accordance with the advice of the U.S. agents.

Page 6 *waterboarding* In the best scenario, when moral values are mentioned, they are discussed in relation to the benefits that these measures may or may not entail. See, for instance, David Corn's essay "This Is What Waterboarding Looks Like," posted September 28, 2006, on huffingtonpost.com. He writes: "Bottom line: Not only do waterboarding and the other types of torture currently being debated put us in company with the most vile regimes of the past half-century; they're also designed specifically to generate a (usually false) confession, not to obtain genuinely actionable intel. This isn't a matter of sacrificing moral values to keep us safe; it's sacrificing moral values for no purpose whatsoever."

Page 7 *banned books and pamphlets* Hamaseh-ye moghavemat-e Ashraf Dehghani (Epics of Ahraf Dehghani's resistance) and Sirus Nahavandi's *Farar-e man az zendadn* (My escape from prison) were the most important of these books. Ironically, later I learned that the story of the second book, the escape of Sirus Nahavandi, was nothing but a lie. The escape was in fact planned by the regime to create a fake heroic figure that allowed Nahavandi to then create a fake organization, Sazman-e Azadibakhsh-e Khalghha-ye Iran (Iranian People's Liberating Organization), which recruited potential young dissidents and thus prevented them from joining the real opposition organizations. Run by SAVAK, the Shah's secret police, it reported on these dissidents, who wasted their energy thinking they were fighting the regime while they were in fact entrapped in the SAVAK net. It also infiltrated other organizations and finally caused a serious crackdown on the dissident movements.

Page 9   *bare life*   I am alluding to Giorgio Agamben and his notion of a bare life as one stripped of its political sociality and reduced to a mere organic, vegetative existence. Agamben, *Homo Sacer: Sovereign Power and Bare Life*, trans. Daniel Heller-Roazen (Stanford: Stanford University Press, 1998).

Chapter 1

Page 13   *Rahmani*   Rahmani is not his real name. All the interrogators had pseudonyms by which they were known, at least to prisoners.

Page 16   *balance of power*   See the BBC documentary *The Fall of the Shah*. Also, there are numerous authors who have attempted to explain the reasons for the fall of the Shah's regime, including Said Amir Arjomand, *The Turban for the Crown: The Islamic Revolution in Iran* (New York: Oxford University Press, 1989); Charles Kurzman, *Unthinkable Revolution in Iran* (Cambridge, Mass.: Harvard University Press, 2004); and Marvin Zonis, *Majestic Failure: The Fall of the Shah* (Chicago: University of Chicago Press, 1998), which offers a psychoanalytical study of the Shah's character, tracing what he assumes to be his change of character from dependence to a tendency to dominate. See also Ervand Abrahamian, *Iran Between Two Revolutions* (Princeton, N.J.: Princeton University Press, 1982); Nikki Keddi and Yann Richard, *Modern Iran: Roots and Results of Revolution* (New Haven, Conn.: Yale University Press, 2006); Hamid Dabashi, *Iran: A People Interrupted* (New York: New Press, 2007); and Roy Mottahedeh, *Mantle of the Prophet* (Oxford: Oneworld Publications, 2008). Many other scholars have written about the Iranian revolution, and some authors, such as Abrahamian and Dabashi, have written several books on the subject.

Page 22   *silence their opponents*   In *Mimesis and Alterity* (New York: Routledge, 1993) Michael Taussig elaborates on this technique of creating fear through exaggeration. He uses the example of a rumor in a small village in Spain under Franco's dictatorship about a truth-telling machine that was supposedly used by interrogators to obtain information from prisoners. He argues that spreading the rumor was a technique used by the regime to create fear and thus silence people. People also convinced themselves of its truth in order to justify their fear and silence.

Page 31   *one-year-old niece*   Only a little over a year old then, my niece is now a college freshman. In light of the recent events in Iran, I fear that someday she may end up spending years of her life in jail and return, if lucky, to a new family member whose birth she too will have missed.

Page 33   *uncovered these mass graves*   See the Amnesty International report about these families and their predicaments in *Report on Human Rights Violations in Iran, 1987 to 1990*, at www.iranrights.org/english/document-349.ph.

Page 39 *Soudabeh Ardavan* Soudabeh Ardavan's book of illustrations about torture in Iranian prisons, *Yaadnegaarehaaye zendaan* (Reminiscences of prison years), was published in Sweden in 2003. She was herself a prisoner for eight years, and we shared years in similar wards. Soudabeh currently lives in Sweden.

Page 39 *Vahed-e 1* To learn more about Vahed-e 1, see two documentaries made by Pantea Bahrami, *From Scream to Scream* (2004) and *And in Love I Live* (2008). There are also several prison memoirs that deal with this particular ward and the experiences lived within it, but all are published in Farsi and are works in progress. One is the Ph.D. dissertation by a former political prisoner, Shokoufeh Sakhi, a student at York University in Canada, on her experience of prison.

Page 41 *turned their brain to "mush"* I am alluding here to Georges Bataille's emphasis on pain as that which shapes one's character. He writes: "Pain is the teacher. Without your pain, you're nothing!" But at the same time, intense pain reduces one to nothing—"my brain turns to mush"—and reduces one to a state of abjection—"tears in my eyes at the idea of being waste!" Fred Botting and Scott Wilson, eds., *Bataille: A Critical Reader* (Oxford: Blackwell, 1998).

Page 44 *kinship* In a documentary film by Pantea Bahrami, *And in Love I Live*, a set of interviews with former Iranian women political prisoners, Mina Akhbari speaks of a strong bond that she feels with her former fellow inmates, a bond that she says remains strong even if they do not see one another for years. It is a kind of connection that, she suggests, cannot be created outside prison.

Chapter 2

Page 57 *traumatic experience* Trauma, as Freud reminds us, is the infliction of the wound in the mind that forces itself on the subjects through a repetition of nightmares and the "repetitive actions of the survivor." Cathy Caruth, *Unclaimed Experiences: Trauma, Narrative and History* (Baltimore: Johns Hopkins University Press, 1996), 4.

Page 57 *escape the torture* In her discussion of Freud's reading of trauma in his *Beyond the Pleasure Principle*, Cathy Caruth brings up the interesting point that "the literary resonance of Freud's example [a story told by Tasso in his romantic epic *Gerusalemme liberata*] goes beyond this dramatic illustration of repetition compulsion and exceeds, perhaps, the limits of Freud's conceptual or conscious theory of trauma." As Caruth asserts, what is "striking in the example of Tasso is not just the unconscious act of the infliction of the injury and its inadvertent and unwished-for repetition, but the moving and sorrowful voice that cries out, a voice that is paradoxically released through the wound." Caruth, *Unclaimed Experience: Trauma and the Possibility of History*, Yale French Studies 79 (New Haven: Yale University, 1991), 2.

Page 59 *whipping their own friends* Taifour [Bathayee], *Az ancheh bar ma gozasht: Chahar ravayat bar asas-e chahar goftego ba chahar zan* [Of what happened to us: Four stories based on four conversations with four women] (Göteborg, Sweden, 1998), 52.

Page 65   *counting, cursing*   Taifour, *Az ancheh bar ma gozasht*, 40–41.

Page 66   *impairment in perception*   Elaine Scarry speaks of the "obliteration of the content of consciousness" as one of the elements of torture. Pain, in her words, "annihilates not only the objects of complex thought and emotion but also the objects of the most elemental acts of perception." It goes so far as to impede the tortured person's "ability simply to see." Scarry, *The Body in Pain: The Making and Unmaking of the World* (New York: Oxford University Press, 1987), 54.

Page 69   *source of pain*   Scarry, in *The Body in Pain*, points to this reality when she argues that "the torturers, like pain itself, continually multiply their resources and means of access until the room and everything in it becomes a giant externalized map of the prisoner's feelings" (55).

Page 70   *totalizing and individualizing systems*   Michel Foucault uses the terms "totalization and individualization" and argues that "power is not exercised simply as an obligation or prohibition on those who 'do not have it'; it invests them, is transmitted by them and through them; it exerts pressure upon them, just as they themselves, in their struggle against it, resist the grip it has on them. . . . Lastly, they are not univocal; they define innumerable points of confrontation, focuses of instability, each of which has its own risks of conflicts, of struggles, and of an at least temporary inversion of the power relations." Foucault, *Discipline and Punish: The Birth of the Prison*, trans. Alan Sheridan (New York: Vintage Books, 1979), 27.

Page 72   *soul that was being tortured*   Taifour, *Az ancheh bar ma gozasht*, 52.

Page 73   *energy of our free will*   As Michel Foucault so eloquently contends in *Discipline and Punish*, power is transmitted by its subjects and through them (27).

Page 73   *plants personified growth*   Plants also characterize the existence of a human being who lacks consciousness. In prison a vegetative life, or becoming like a plant, implied a lack of integrity, empathy, and free will, giving up on the social, emotional, and thoughtful aspects of a human life. What is left is breathing and eating, without thinking about and exercising the impact of our thought.

Page 74   *new ways to resist*   The "productive" aspect of power relations, as Foucault refers to it in *Discipline and Punish*, comes into existence through a constant struggle to explore new space in which to resist domination.

Page 76   *refusing to be detached*   For Foucault "in order to establish the right relationship to the present—to things, to oneself—one must stay close to events, experience them, be willing to be affected by them." Paul Rabinow, ed., *Ethics: Subjectivity and Truth*, vol. 1 of *The Essential Works of Michel Foucault 1954–1984* (New York: New Press, 1997), xviii.

Page 76   *world of death*   "The substitution of the theme of madness for that of death does not mark a break, but rather a torsion within the same anxiety." Michel Foucault, *Madness and Civilization: A History of Insanity in the Age of Reason* (New York: Vintage Books, 1988), 13.

Chapter 3

Page 82 *their community* I am alluding to David Morris's term "moral community," in his article "About Suffering: Voice, Genre, and Moral Community," in *Social Suffering*, ed. Arthur Kleinman, Veena Das, and Margaret Lock (Berkeley: University of California Press, 1997).

Page 83 *lost her way* I am reminded of the words that describe the crimes in the wards as contagious: "Do not glory in your state, if you are wise and civilized men; an instant suffices to disturb you and annihilate that supposed wisdom of which you are so proud; an unexpected event, a sharp and sudden emotion of the soul will abruptly change the most reasonable and intelligent man into a raving idiot." Michel Foucault, *Madness and Civilization*, 212, quoting Swiss physician André Matthey.

Page 87 *persecution and torture* Elaine Scarry in *The Body in Pain* suggests that "the presence of pain is the absence of world" and that "the pain, like the interrogation, is a vehicle of self-betrayal" (46–47). While I agree with Scarry's points, my experiences in jail led me to realize that what pains one individual may not pain another in the same way or even with the same effect. What is more important is that for some, the possibility of losing the world may be much more painful and frightening than the pain of torture. Scarry argues that the notion of betrayal does not take into account that what cannot betray is that which is absent and argues that the memory of the world ceases for the person under torture. However, I have seen and believe that sometimes there are other memories much more deeply engraved in one's body and mind, and the pain of their loss, such as the loss of the self and the community, may surpass the pain of torture. There are individuals who would rather endure the pain of torture, even die under it, than drag others into it. The world for these people does not become absent even while they are under the excruciating pain of torture; for them the real torture is to lose themselves and the world.

Page 88 *torture's victory* In her powerful rendition of torture and resistance, Shokufeh Sakhi, a former political prisoner herself and now a Ph.D. candidate at York University in Canada, cites a collaborator: "They [the Islamic torturers] see a metaphysical power in the cable, a supra-human power. For them the cable works miracles. The entire body of the prisoner must be touched by the cable for the miracle to occur: that is, the person is changed from being a filthy, illegitimate creature who would be burned in the fires of hell into a clean, pure and legitimate creature who will go to heaven." Paper presented at the ISIS Conference, "On the Ethical Meaning of Torture and Resistance," Toronto, Canada, summer 2008, http://www.dialogt.org/english/Shokoufeh%20Sakhi2.htm.

Page 89 *resistant prisoners* Again, in her reading of the citation from *We Lived to Tell: Political Prison Memoirs of Iranian Women* (Toronto: McGilligan Books, 2007), Shokoufeh Sakhi emphasizes the sociality of the impact of the tortured person's reaction, including her or his resistance. She writes: "I contend that, beyond and aside from obtaining information, etc., it is the ethical humanity, the socially responsible being, that torture seeks to foul with its rancid touch. This ancient but occluded, most fundamental ethic, the primordial being-for-the-other may be glimpsed in the prison memoirs and wills describing the underlying whys of the prisoners' resistance. Words as simple as a mother's advice to her daughter upon their first visit: 'Just try to keep your dignity. Never do anything to harm people'" (53), or the oath a prisoner makes as she inherits a condemned prisoner's piece of clothing: "I promise I won't turn my back on your owner's pain" (37). "One's dignity is in her relation to the Others. One's humanity is in her response to the pain of the Other. Resistance and capitulation is, therefore, not only an individual endeavor; it is also the responsibility of the human community and the human community's response to all totalizing systems, systems, that is, with the intention of rendering everyone—at their deepest levels—the same as them. It is exactly this social aspect of resistance against and capitulation to the paideia of the totalizing system that urges us to analyze and understand both the success and failure of tavabization, a phenomenon that has not, of course, been limited to prison systems or Iran" (ibid).

Page 91   *crossed into a country*   See Alice Wexler, *Mapping Fate: A Memoir of Family, Risk, and Genetic Research* (Berkeley: University of California Press, 1996), 160.

Page 92   *care for one's self*   I am here taking a cue from Foucault's reading of the ethics of the self while remaining attentive to the emphasis both Jacques Derrida and Emmanuel Levinas put on the inseparable relationship of the self to the other. See Foucault, *The History of Sexuality,* vol. 3, *The Care of the Self,* trans. Robert Hurley (New York: Pantheon Books, 1986). For Derrida, see *Politics of Friendship,* trans. George Collins (London: Verso, 1997), and *Specters of Marx: The State of the Debt, the Work of Mourning, and the New International,* trans. Peggy Kamuf (New York: Routledge, 1994). For Levinas's views on the relationship to others, see *Totality and Infinity: An Essay on Exteriority,* trans. Alphonso Lingis (Pittsburgh: Duquesne University Press, 1969).

Page 93   *sacred word*   Ahmad Shamlu is a prominent Iranian poet whose poetry has been a source of inspiration and a means of emotional expression for resistant prisoners both under the Shah and under the Islamic Republic. The poem in Farsi reads:

Ba ma gofeth boodand ān kalam-e moughaddas ra ba shoma khahim amoukht
Leikan baray-i amoukhtan-e an oughoubati dushvar ra tahammul bayadetan kard
Oughoubat-e doshvar ra chandan tab avardim ari
Keh kalam-e mughaddas az khatereman gorikht.

Shamlu, *Collection of Poetry, 1962–80,* vol. 2 (Tehran: Kanoun-i Intisharati Va Farhangi-i Bamdad, 1989).

Page 95   *O love, O love*   In Farsi the poem reads:
Āy eshq, āy eshq, Rang-e surkh-Chehreat peidā nist.
Āy eshq, āy eshq , Rang-e ābiyat peidā nist.

(Shamlu, "Āy Eshgh," in *Collection of Poetry*)

The particular verses recited by this woman inmate are these:
My hands and my heart trembled of the fear
that love becomes a refuge instead of a flight
that love becomes a place to escape, instead of a flight.
O, love, O love, your blue face is no longer apparent.
For the prisoners, redness in this poem symbolized courage and revolutionary ideals, while blue indicated honesty and purity of the heart, the person, and the cause. For this prisoner, her breaking under lashes and her submission to profess her faith in Islam and pray indicated the failure of her revolutionary spirit and ideals. She saw her submission as a lack of revolutionary courage and the sincerity of her devotion to her ideals.

Page 96   *pain of the defeat*   Nima Parvaresh, "Talkh, Na Hamchon Hameyeh Talkheeha [Bitter, unlike any other bitterness], in *Cheshmandaz*, vol. 14 (Paris: Pakdaman, 1994), 67.

Page 97   *escaped the suffering*   This reaction reminds me of the work of Nancy Scheper-Hughes, *Death Without Weeping: The Violence of Everyday Life in Brazil* (Berkeley: University of California Press, 1993), where she discusses the violence inherent in the everyday life of poverty being of a kind wherein the very possibility of death as a mundane, uneventful occurrence in the everyday—indeed, even a kind of mercy for an otherwise cruel existence—also measures the abjectness of life within that existence.

Page 104   *soul loses touch*   Veena Das, "Language and Body: The Transactions in Construction of Pain," in Kleinman, Das, and Lock, *Social Suffering*, writes of the relationship between the other's pain and its register in one's spirit and body: "Denial of the other's pain is not about the failings of the intellect, but the failings of the spirit. In the register of the imaginary, the pain of the other not only asks for a home in language, but also seeks a home in the body" (88).

Page 111   *distinguished a human from an animal*   Michel Foucault's passage considering the relationship between madness and animality and the threat that it poses to the modern subject is quite relevant here. According to him, "Madness threatens modern man only with the return to the bleak world of beasts and things, to their fettered freedom. It is not on the horizon of *nature* that the seventeenth and eighteenth centuries recognized madness, but against a background of *Unreason*; madness did not disclose a mechanism, but revealed a liberty raging in the monstrous forms of animality." Foucault, *Madness and Civilization*, 25.

Chapter 4

Page 121   *rapture of burning*   Hafiz, *The Green Sea of Heaven: Fifty Ghazals from the Diwan of Hafiz*, trans. Elizabeth T. Gray Jr. (Ashland, Ore.: White Cloud Press, 1995).

Page 123   *conditioned behaviors*   She was dipped into the state that Søren Kierkegaard would refer to as the "sickness of the self," where one "dies the death" rather than lives the experience of death. Kierkegaard, *The Sickness unto Death* (Radford, Va.: A & D Publishing, 2008).

Page 123   *not able to die*   In *The Sickness unto Death*, Kierkegaard defines despair as "the situation of the moribund when he lies and struggles with death, and cannot die" (13). In fact, according to Kierkegaard, "the torment of despair is precisely this, not to be able to die" (13).

Page 125   *grave digger's wage*   Ahmad Shamlu, "The Grave Digger's Wage," in Shamlu, *Collection of Poetry*.

Page 131   *because of a flower*   These verses are from an Azarian folk song that was very popular among political activists, especially leftists, in Iran. These are the verses in Azari:

Azizim baghda dara
Ach zoulfoun baghda dara
Boulbouli gouldan outour
Chakiblar bahgda dara

Page 131   *valleys of the mirror*   Ahmad Shamlu, "Mahi" (Fish), in *Collection of Poetry*. In Farsi the poem reads:

Man Abgir-e safeeam eenak beh sehr-e eshq
Az berkehaaye ayeneh raai beh man bejooy.

Page 133   *every day was my last day*   Michel Foucault, *Ethics: Subjectivity and Truth*, ed. Paul Rabinow, trans. Robert Hurley et al. (New York: New Press, 1997), 105.

Page 133   *space between deaths*   I am borrowing this from Veena Das's insightful reading of Lacan's interpretation of Antigone's story, in which Lacan argues that differentiating between two deaths, the death of a brother and a husband or a child, makes it possible for Antigone to "voice the truth of the uniqueness of being." It is in speaking from this "zone between two deaths," Das suggests, "that the unspeakable truth about the criminal nature of the law" might be exposed. Das, *Life and Words: Violence and the Descent into the Ordinary* (Berkeley: University of California Press, 2007), 61.

Page 135   *chance of bidding farewell*   This reminds me of another phrase, "the moment of his death actually escaped me," a phrase that is an invocation of Cathy Caruth's reading of Freud's meditation of a father's dream about his son's burning while he falls asleep watching over his ill son. The son dies while the father is dreaming about his burning. He thus misses the very moment of his son's death. The moment of Hamid's execution escaped me but not in the same way as it escaped the woman in *Hiroshima mon amour*, who so near her lover's body could not "feel the slightest difference between his dead body and [her own]." Caruth, *Unclaimed Experience: Trauma and the Possibility of History*, 38, 39.

Page 139   *revolutionary phase*   The term *Vazeey'at-e Enghleabi*, or "revolutionary phase," was coined by Lenin to describe a condition in society when the conflict between the state and the nation has reached a level under which neither the government nor the people want to or can any longer go on living. The revolutionary phase or condition implies that a revolution is inevitable and imminent.

Page 141 *subjectivity* In Foucault's definition, "subjectivity" has two different connotations. On the one hand, one may speak of one's subjectivity as in subjection to something or someone "through control and dependence." Subjectivity also implies being the subject of one's own will and action; in this sense, it is a subjection that ties the person to her or his own identity, by "conscience or self-knowledge." It is obvious that this conscience or self-knowledge is itself tied to the knowledge or conscience that is larger than an individual, and that there never exists an isolated individual and thus an utterly individual-based conscience or knowledge. Aside from this fact, the significance of Foucault's point remains that both meanings of subjectivity insinuate "a form of power which subjugates and makes subject to." Foucault, "The Subject and Power," in *Beyond Structuralism and Hermeneutics*, ed. and trans. Hubert L. Dreyfus and Paul Rabinow (Chicago: University of Chicago Press, 1982), 212.

Page 142 *boundaries of these norms* Ludwig Binswanger, "Dream and Existence," in *Selected Papers of Ludwig Binswanger and Michel Foucault*, ed. Keith Hoeller (Atlantic Highlands, N.J.: Humanities Press, 1993), 292.

Page 142 *ultimate fall from existence* As Kierkegaard writes in *Sickness unto Death*, "With every increase in the degree of consciousness, and in proportion to that increase, the intensity of despair increases: the more consciousness, the more intense the despair" (34).

Page 142 *corpse of her ideals* In Kierkegaard's words, "To be the self as he wills to be would be his delight (though in another sense it would be equally in despair), but to be compelled to be the self as he does not will to be is his torment, namely, that he cannot get rid of himself" (ibid., 15).

Page 142 *sense of identity* I am referring to Freud's reading of "Mourning and Melancholia," in *General Psychological Theory: Papers on Metapsychology* (New York: Collier, 1963), which is further developed by Maria Torok and Nicholas Abraham, *The Shell and the Kernel: Renewals of Psychoanalysis*, vol. 1 (Chicago: University of Chicago Press, 1994).

Page 144 *the fall from existence* Binswanger, "Dream and Existence."

Page 146 *political beings* I am using the term "political" here in a general Aristotelian sense, according to which all humans are political animals. Afsaneh Najmabadi discusses this issue of women's propriety as a persistent preoccupation of the modern Iranian states. She elaborates how, despite the shifts in sociopolitical and economic conditions, concern about women's modesty continues from Pahlavi to the Islamic Republic era. She argues that "the shift in the image of the ideal woman from 'modern-yet-modest' at the turn of this century to 'Islamic-thus-modest' within the present [Islamic] paradigm could only take place because a crucial shared social boundary regarding modesty was retained between the two." She, however, suggests a paradigm shift and argues that to understand "the workings of that common boundary, we need to differentiate and investigate the significance of each paradigm." Najmabadi, "Hazards of Modernity and Morality: Women, State and Ideology in Contemporary Iran," in *Women, Islam and the State*, ed. Deniz Kandiyoti (Philadelphia: Temple University Press, 1991), 49.

Page 147   *M. Raha*   M. Raha, *Simple Truth* (Hanover, Germany: Independent Democratic Association of Iranian Women, 1997).

Page 147   *horror of torture*   The term "naked horror" used by Binswanger in "Dream and Existence" best describes what Marjan was captivated by, due not to the "fear of annihilation" (312) but to the horror of sheer violence and the anxiety about the loss of the self that could follow.

Page 147   *no escape was possible*   Marjan's existence had, in Binswanger's words, "totally surrendered to the Uncanny and the Dreadful [and could] no longer be aware of the fact that the Dreadful emerges from itself, out of its very own ground. Hence there is no escape from such fear." Cited in Anthony Vidler, *Warped Space: Art, Architecture, and Anxiety in Modern Culture* (Cambridge, Mass.: MIT Press, 2001), 46.

Page 147   *prisoner of horror*   Binswanger's words in "Dream and Existence" could have been literally written about Marjan when he states that the subject for whom dread is internalized is imprisoned by her dread and thus "desperately beats at the walls of its prison" (314).

Page 147   *being in the world*   Once again Binswanger's phrasing best describes the distinction between Kobra's and Marjan's states of despair. Kobra's despair is "at having to be in the world in a particular way and no other," while that of Marjan is "a despair at being-in-the-world at all!" Binswanger, *Being-in-the-World*, ed. Rollo May (Atlantic Highlands, N.J.: Humanities Press, 1956), 286.

Page 149   *impossible questions*   As Jacques Derrida suggests, we need "even to question the interrogative form itself." Derrida, "Unconditional University," Stanford University, April 15, 1999.

Chapter 5

Page 159   *new horizon*   "Blanqui's description of the present history" is very telling in articulating the false assumption of the eternal present. "The new is always old and the old continuously new," according to Blanqui. "The number of our doubles is infinite in time and space. . . . They are the present eternalized. Here, however is a great flaw: there exists no progress. Alas! No, they are vulgar re-editions." Susan Buck-Morss, *The Dialectics of Seeing: Walter Benjamin and the Arcades Project* (Cambridge, Mass.: MIT Press, 1969), 106, 107.

Page 160   *contradictory legends*   This reminds me of the possibility of "heal or harm" that Stefania Pandolfo describes in the "'scene of Sra'a.' . . . When he utters his incantation, Si Lhassan says, he is afraid of becoming maftun—carried away to the other side, and 'disappearing' in a space of madness." Pandolfo, *Impasse of the Angels*, 26.

Page 166 *collective involvement* There is also another reason for this tendency to act collectively in relation to violence that has to do with the power of mimesis, which allows the role of an agent and individual responsibility to be obscured and renders it easier to act violently. In collective acts of violence, either a single or a few individuals are singled out as the agents of the crime while others simply claim to have followed orders, as in Nazi Germany or South Africa and many other similar situations, or an unaccountable guilty collective is identified without the possibility for any real identification. Yousuf's fate reminds me of this collective responsibility for tragic and inhuman treatment that continues to occur, on a routine and daily basis, without a possibility of holding anyone accountable for it.

Page 168 *Ādi Jan* Jan in both Farsi and Azari is an affectionate word to call people close to someone and is used at the end of a person's first name.

Page 168 *simpleminded* This word in Farsi does not necessarily have a negative connotation. It just refers to people who do not make things complicated and see them in simple, direct terms.

Page 171 *prevalent and horrifying* In his discussion of "pathological forms" of power, or "diseases of power," Michel Foucault argues that the reasons these regimes "are so puzzling for us is that, in spite of their historical uniqueness, they are not quite original. They used and extended mechanisms already present in most other societies." Foucault, "The Subject and Power," 208.

Page 182 *Imam Hussein* Islam's third imam, who was killed in Karbala. It is believed that he and his family were deprived of water for days.

Chapter 6

Page 185 *song of the reed* *Rumi: In the Arms of the Beloved*, trans. Jonathan Star (Los Angeles: Jeremy P. Tarcher / Putnam Penguin, 1997). In Farsi:

Beshnou az nei choun hekayat mikounad
Vaz jodaeyha shekayat mikonad.

"Kaz neistan ta mara bebridahand
az nafiram mard-o zan nalideand."

Page 188 *raped by her interrogators* Veena Das, in "Language and Body," points out the danger that women who were raped during the partition between Pakistan and India felt in remembering those events: "These memories were sometimes compared to poison that makes the inside of the woman dissolve" (84). Was it the effect of this poisonous knowledge that made Maryam become God?

Page 190 *imagination and phantasm* As Foucault asserts, "To imagine is not so much a behavior towards others which intends them as quasi-presences on an essential ground of absence; it is rather to intend oneself as movement of freedom which makes itself world and finally anchors itself in this world as its destiny." Michel Foucault, "Dream, Imagination and Existence," Introduction to Michel Foucault and Ludwig Binswanger, *Dream and Existence*, ed. Keith Hoeller (Atlantic Highlands, N.J.: Humanities Press, 1994), 68. Phantasm, according to Foucault's definition, on the other hand, "emerge[s] when the subject finds the free movements of its existence crushed in the presence of a quasi-perception which envelops and immobilizes it" (72).

Imagination flies freely in the absence of specific objects and fixed images to create an imaginative world, while phantasm loses the possibility of free movement by becoming fixed on the world that has vanished. This differentiation between the imagination and phantasm is what makes the former the embodiment of the possibility of creation and the latter the subject of imprisonment by the power of morbid images. In the creative imagination, images can be manipulated and even destroyed. "The value of a poetic imagination," Foucault believes, "is to be measured by the inner destructive power of the image" (72). While Maryam becomes attached to and fixated by the images she perceives as present, she loses the possibility of differentiating between what is there and what is phantasmagoric.

Page 192 *giving ourselves away* Foucault writes: "The relationship between power and freedom's refusal to submit cannot therefore be separated. The crucial problem of power is not that of voluntary servitude (how could we seek to be slaves?). At the very heart of the power relationship, and constantly provoking it, are the recalcitrance of the will and the intransigence of freedom." Michel Foucault, "The Subject and the Power," in Hubert Dreyfus and Paul Rabinow, *Michel Foucault: Beyond Structuralism and Hermeneutics* (Chicago: University of Chicago Press, 1982), 222.

Page 192 *for how long* Nawal El Saadawi describes her first night in her cell in regard to time as "time is no longer time. Time and the wall have merged into one." Saadawi, *Memories from the Women's Prison*, trans. Marilyn Booth (Berkeley: University of California Press, 1994; originally published in 1986), 31.

Page 192 *challenge to remain connected and committed* Although I use the term "we" or "us" seemingly unproblematically, I am very much aware of the danger of essentializing pain and suffering. As Arthur Kleinman writes, "It is important to avoid essentializing, naturalizing, or sentimentalizing suffering. There is no single way to suffer; there is no timeless or spaceless universal shape to suffering. . . . Pain is perceived and expressed differently, even in the same community." Arthur Kleinman and Joan Kleinman, "The Appeal of Experience; The Dismay of Images: Cultural Appropriations of Sufferings in Our Times," in Kleinman, Das, and Lock, *Social Suffering*, 2. In the same vein but extending this view, in "The Pane of Sorrow," Vera Schwarcz asserts, "Suffering cannot be sought or manufactured. Once encountered, however, it may be used to illuminate corners of human experience too dark to even imagine before" (142).

Page 193   *imagination is what you possess*   By claiming this, I am taking the risk of sentimentalizing the power of individuals' imagination as an ahistorical, nonsociopolitical phenomenon. This is not what I am trying to imply. I am convinced that our imagination can be and is greatly influenced by our surroundings, yet I also believe in its relative freedom that goes beyond our physical surroundings.

Page 195   *through making*   Elaine Scarry, in *The Body in Pain*, distinguishes between "interior" and "exterior making." According to her, "interior making," or as she calls it, "imagining," occurs "when the activity and its objects are interior." It is, however, "'making' or 'creating' when the activity is extended into the external world, and has as its outcome a material or verbal artifact" (177).

Page 196   *they smell your mouth*   Shamlu, *Collection of Poetry*, 1120. In Farsi:

Dahanat ra mibouyand mabada keh gufteh bashi doustat midaram.

Delat ra mibouyand

Rouzgar-i gharibist, nazanin

Va eshq ra kenar-i tirak-i yabbandan

taziyaneh mizanand.

Eshq ra dar pastou-yi khaneh nahan bayad kard.

Page 196   *life become a work of art*   Foucault, "On the Genealogy of Ethics," in *The Continental Ethics Reader*, ed. Matthew Calarco and Peter Atterton (New York: Routledge, 2003), 201.

Page 196   *handicrafts produced by prisoners*   Arguing that art cannot be confined to what appears in an "art gallery," Paul Willis, in studying "ordinary" young people's lives in Western countries, and specifically in Britain, insists that "there is a vibrant symbolic life and symbolic creativity in everyday life, everyday activity and expression" that should be recognized. Willis, *Common Culture: Symbolic Work at Play in the Everyday Cultures of the Young* (Milton Keynes, U.K.: Open University Press, 1990), 1. His argument seems relevant in thinking about the power of art in prison.

Page 196   *ravages of time and death*   Allusion to Aiwa Ong in Walter J. Ong, "Subway Graffiti and the Design of the Self," in *The State of the Language*, ed. Christopher Ricks and Leonard Michaels (Berkeley: University of California Press, 1990), 405.

Page 196   *engrave their names*   Interestingly enough, like the graffiti writers of Paul Willis's study, male prisoners almost always write their own names on everything they make, while females usually put down their loved ones' names, rarely their own. Willis, *Common Culture*.

Page 197   *worn out by extensive overuse*   Edward Said argues that the result of working with worn-out frames of reference is "that the mind is numbed and remains inactive while language that has the effect of background music in a supermarket washes over consciousness, seducing it into passive acceptance of unexamined ideas and sentiments." Said, *Representations of the Intellectual: The 1993 Reith Lectures* (New York: Vintage Books, 1994), 27–28.

Page 199   *pain has no music*   Vera Schwarcz, "The Pane of Sorrow, 142.

Page 200   *victory of laughter over fear*   As, in Mikhail Bakhtin's view, had impressed the medieval populace. Bakhtin, "Rabelais and His World," in *Rabelais and His World*, trans. Hélène Iswolsky (Bloomington: Indiana University Press, 1984), 90.

Page 205   *as if it were the last*   These are Foucault's words in *Ethics*. Foucault also suggests that one needs to learn how to live a "long span of life as if it were as short as a day, and living each day as if one's entire life depended on it" (105). In his reading of this particular ethics of living, one learns how to live one's life in such a manner that "every morning one ought to be in the childhood of his life, but one ought to live the whole day as if the evening would be the moment of death" (105).

Epilogue

Page 210   *power of the words*   Jeanne Favret-Saada in her discussion of the power of speech, deadly words, and witchcraft asserts that "the less one talks, the less one is caught." Favret-Saada, *Deadly Words: Witchcraft in the Bocage*, trans. Catherine Cullen (Cambridge: Cambridge University Press, 1980), 64.

Page 211   *language of forgetting*   Cathy Caruth in her discussion of the film *Hiroshima mon amour*. Caruth, *Unclaimed Experience: Trauma and the Possibility of History*.

Page 211   *left the country*   Freud uses these words in the preface to his book *Moses and Monotheism*, published after he fled to England. "I left with many friends, the city which from early childhood, through seventy-eight years, had been a home to me." Quoted in ibid., 57.

Page 212   *this new land*   As it was for Freud when writing *Moses and Monotheism*, this "leaving home" was "also a kind of freedom" for me, "the freedom to bring forth" my writing in the United States, "the freedom, that is to bring [my] voice to another place." Quoted in ibid.

Page 212   *the slap*   In the film *Hiroshima mon amour*, the Frenchwoman's Japanese lover slaps her on the face to make her distinguish between life and death and her German and Japanese lovers. Ibid., 42.

Page 212   *distinguish between myself and my life*   The ambiguity inherent in this phrase—suggesting both an extrication of self from within self and an untangling of self and other—is intended.

Page 213   *passageways to re-creating myself*   I intend here to echo Michel de Certeau's phrase when he speaks of opening up passageways to constructing new worlds and visions. De Certeau, "Surin's Melancholy," in *Heterologies: Discourse on the Other*, trans. B. Massoumi (Minneapolis: University of Minnesota Press, 1993).

Page 213   *intertwined with our own*   In Cathy Caruth's words in *Unclaimed Experience*, "history, like trauma, is never simply one's own," but rather "history is precisely the way we are implicated in each other's traumas" (24).

Page 213   *not to forget*   "Painful memories are not always disabling, and narratives about them—at least this is true of Holocaust testimony—rarely 'liberate' witnesses from a past they cannot and do not wish to escape." Lawrence L. Langer, "The Alarmed Vision: Social Suffering and Holocaust Atrocity," in Kleinman, Das, and Lock, *Social Suffering*, 54–55.

Page 220   *revolutionary solution*   As part of the world polity, many Iranians were also influenced by the changes and paradigm shifts in the world. The idea of the end of revolution had become a quite popular view when I visited Iran for some length of time between 2002 and 2005. I personally do not believe in such ideas as "the end of history" (see Francis Fukuyama, *The End of History and the Last Man* [New York: Free Press, 1992] and his essay "The End of History?" *National Interest* [1989]) or "the end of revolutions," which tend to perceive the world and its events in a linear manner, according to a particular formula in which certain things occur or stop occurring. I believe that sociohistorical phenomena are rather more complicated and unpredictable. A revolution is not a static reality, nor is it possible to simply stop a movement that may have begun with demands for reform but that goes beyond its initial goal simply because it cannot achieve its goal within the system. Similarly, nobody can guarantee that a movement for progressive change will not take a regressive turn. These are situations that are as unpredictable as the people who "make their own history." Moreover, as Marx would tell us, "they do not make it as they please; they do not make it under self-selected circumstances, but under circumstances existing already, given and transmitted from the past." These circumstances are not determined by the individuals, but, again as Marx suggests, they are confined and influenced by the "tradition of all dead generations" that "weighs like a nightmare on the brains of the living." Marx, *The Eighteenth Brumaire of Louis Bonaparte*, 1952, 1, available online at www .marxists.org.

Glossary

Āmouzeshgāh   Place for Education; ward in Evin Prison

Āsāyeshgāh   Place to Relax or Rest; ward in Evin Prison

ashhad   profession of belief in Islam

barzakh   in-between world where one is in a state of suspension

daneshgah   university

dastgah (plural, *dastgahha* or *dastgaha*, colloquial version)   machine

dastgah-e-ādam sāzi   human-making machine

e'edām   execution

enzejar nameh   letter of repugnance or repudiation; expresses repugnance of one's own ideas and deeds and promises no future contact with anti-revolutionary organizations

Ettehadiyeh-ye komonistha   Communists Union

ettela'at   information obtained and revealed by the secret police; information as knowledge whose purpose is to raise consciousness

Ganly Goul   Bloody Pond

ghabrha or *ghabra* (colloquial version)   graves

gharantineh   quarantine

ghatlha-ye zanjirayee   chained killings

husseiniyeh   a large hall in prison used mainly for prisoners' public recantation

j'abehha   boxes

kārkhāneh-ye-ādam sāzi   human-making factory

kharabkari   sabotage

Komiteh-ye Moshtarak-e Zedd-e Kharabkari   United Anti-sabotage Committee

Komiteh-ye Touhid   Unity Committee

marg bar Shah   down with the Shah

mojahed   literally, a warrior, God, or Islam; refers to those affiliated with the Sazman-e Mojahedin-e Khalgh-e Iran

Monafeghin   hypocrites; a derogatory term used by the regime to refer to Mojahedin, those affiliated with Sazman-e Mojahedin-e Khalgh-e Iran

Moozeh-ye Ettela'at   Museum of Information; a former prison turned into a
museum under the presidency of Mohammad Khatami

morakhasi   temporary release

mosahebeh   literally, interview; public confession or recantation

mosahebeh-ye enzejar   renunciation interview

ney   flutelike instrument

ommat   community of Muslims

piche toubeh   repentance curve

sabzeh   green; refers to a particular kind of green plant, often grown from lentil or
wheat seeds, for putting on the table among seven items whose names all begin
with the letter *s* in celebration of the Iranian New Year.

sar-e mozehyee   refers to prisoners who maintained their stand against the regime

Sazman-e Azadibakhsh-e Khalghha-ye Iran   Iranian People's Liberating
Organization

Sazman-e Cherikha-ye Fadayee-e Khalgh-e Iran   Iranian People's Self-Sacrificing
Guerrilla Organization

Sazman-e Mojahedin-e Khalgh-e Iran   Iranian People's Warriors' Organization, a
militant Islamic organization that fought against both the Shah and the Islamic
Republic and is now based mainly in France and Iraq

shirin   sweet

tabootha or *taboota* (colloquial version)   coffins, graves

takhtha or *takhta* (colloquial version)   beds or wooden beds

Vahed-e 1   Unit 1

zadan   beating; among male prisoners, also refers to execution

zir-e hasht   a small entrance hall in front of each ward that separated the main ward
from the guards' office, often used for punishment, but food was also divided
and distributed there